Fearless Change

Fearless Change

Patterns for Introducing New Ideas

Mary Lynn Manns, Ph.D.

Linda Rising, Ph.D.

❦

♦♦Addison-Wesley

Boston · San Francisco · New York · Toronto · Montreal
London · Munich · Paris · Madrid
Capetown · Sydney · Tokyo · Singapore · Mexico City

The publisher offers discounts on this book when ordered in quantity for bulk purchases and special sales. For more information, please contact:

U.S. Corporate and Government Sales
(800) 382-3419
corpsales@pearsontechgroup.com

For sales outside of the U.S., please contact:
International Sales
international@pearsoned.com

Visit Addison-Wesley on the Web: www.awprofessional.com

Library of Congress Cataloging-in-Publication Data
Manns, Mary Lynn.
Fearless Change: patterns for introducing new ideas / Manns, Mary Lynn,
Linda Rising.
p. cm.
Includes bibliographical references and index.
ISBN 0-201-74157-1 (pbk. : alk. paper)
1. Organizational change. 2. Technological innovations. 3. Industrial management. I. Manns, Mary Lynn, 1955 II. Title.

HD58.8.R57 2005

658.4—dc22   2004013261

Chapter opener illustrations by Rich "Fack" Fackrell.

For information on obtaining permission for use of material from this work, please submit a written request to:

Pearson Education, Inc.
Rights and Contracts Department
75 Arlington Street, Suite 300
Boston, MA 02116
Fax: (617) 848-7047

ISBN 0-201-74157-1
Text printed on recycled paper
1 2 3 4 5 6 7 8 9 10—CRW—0807060504
First printing, September 2004

FOR OUR DAUGHTERS, ALISON MANNS
AND AMY RISING BROWN,

*who gave us our first real lessons in "change," who taught us that patience
is the best practice for dealing with people, and who helped us
see the benefit of celebrating even the smallest success.*

Contents

PART TWO
Experiences

PART THREE
The Patterns

Foreword

There is increasing pressure on all our organizations to succeed in an ever more rapidly changing world. We all need to play our part in creating the new ideas that will enable our organizations to succeed, and in driving success by sharing, adopting, and building on best practices. This is a particular issue for knowledge-intensive companies, particularly those facing the digital economy where technology becomes ever more complex and more deeply woven into the fabric of the business. The ability of these learning organizations to generate and exploit ideas is fundamental and crucial to success.

The nature of learning organizations has been debated for a number of years, throwing into sharp relief the need to develop and manage new ideas as intellectual capital and develop the knowledge that is spread around our companies into best practices. There are many views on how this intellectual capital can be managed, but there is little disagreement that it is critically important to future success. Introducing new ideas into organizations is a challenge that faces us all.

Business value and the productive exploitation of technology have always been important to Microsoft. As a Microsoft business value consultant working with a wide variety of commercial and noncommercial organizations, it is clear that achieving highly beneficial use of new technologies depends on people and how they work, on individuals and their patterns of behavior. In so many cases the best ideas on how to take advantage of technology come from within the organization, often from unexpected quarters where business workers are quietly exploiting the technology in innovative new ways for business benefit. The business value challenge becomes one of helping individuals at all levels in the organization to develop fresh ideas and to introduce their ideas more widely into the organization.

Introducing new ideas into organizations continues to be a challenge. Some of us within Microsoft champion the importance of achieving business value from the productive exploitation of technology. We are passionate about this idea. But at Microsoft, surrounded by so many bright people brimming with new ideas, it is always a challenge to get attention for your own. In this competitive ecosystem, it is even more challenging to get them to stick when the organization is so fast moving. The real passion comes from being expected to have ideas and to champion them, whatever your level at Microsoft. Finding new and sustainable ways of achieving business advantage through technology is one such example.

We do use patterns that Mary Lynn and Linda describe to share our enthusiasm. We regularly use Brown Bag* sessions and take advantage of other opportunities as Evangelists. We use External Validation from respected organizations to bring credibility, and hold significant events offsite (Location, Location, Location) with the support of Local Sponsors to give the best chance of convincing others in the organization (Personal Touch). Having read Mary Lynn and Linda's book, it is evident that we also work to Sustain Momentum.

Your organization will have its own culture and ways of introducing new ideas. It may encourage new ideas, or it may discourage them. Either way, explore whether you can find patterns here to help. Finding a Corporate Angel or engaging in Corridor Politics may work for you. Does your organization recognize new ideas but need help with exploiting them? Creating a Group Identity could help to provide a focus and direction.

The most innovative and competitive organizations are those that make the most of their people's skills and knowledge. Yet describing knowledge in a way that it can be recognized, shared, and used by others has long been a problem. The patterns in this book describe a practical structure for capturing that hard-to-record knowledge. Whether to share "how to do it" gems or to capture the subtleties of a deep subject matter expert's experience, the experience reports demonstrate that the structure and language works.

---

*Names that appear in this special font are references to the patterns that are described in this book.

This is not a step-by-step cookbook, but then change never happens quite as expected. Whether you are introducing change in an organization, creating new networks, finding new levels of empowerment that involve participation at all levels, or just aiming to work together smarter, you could use a Brown Bag, set up an e-Forum, or share your passion as an Evangelist. Whether you decide to Involve Everyone or choose to Just Do It, the first step is to remind yourself that there are many ways to Test the Waters, and you may proceed best Step by Step. Either by dipping straight into the patterns, or by studying them more methodically, let Mary Lynn and Linda guide you toward those techniques that will work for you.

Andy Ellis
Business Value Consultant, Microsoft

Preface

...there is nothing more difficult to carry out, nor more doubtful of success, nor more dangerous to handle, than to initiate a new order of things. For the reformer has enemies in all those who profit by the old order, and only lukewarm defenders in all those who would profit by the new order, this lukewarmness arising partly from fear of their adversaries...and partly from the incredulity of mankind, who do not truly believe in anything new until they have had actual experience of it.

—NICCOLO MACHIAVELLI, the prince

You miss one hundred percent of the shots you never take.

—WAYNE GRETZKY, HALL OF FAME HOCKEY PLAYER

Since you picked up this book, we assume that you've tried to introduce something new into your organization. Maybe you were successful or maybe you were not completely happy with the result. Change is hard. Wouldn't it be wonderful if all the people who have had some success in their attempts to introduce a new idea could sit down with you and share their secrets? This book will provide the next best thing. We've gathered strategies from those successful people so you can take advantage of their experiences.

We've been working on introducing new ideas into the workplace for some time. Mary Lynn Manns is a professor at the University of North Carolina at Asheville whose recent doctoral work concerned this topic. Linda Rising is an independent consultant who has experience introducing new ideas both in academia and industry. Together with all the others who have shared their experiences with us, we have many years of documented successes.

Each technique or strategy we have collected is written as a pattern—a form of knowledge management for capturing a recurring, successful practice. The patterns in this book are the result of years of documenting our observations, hearing from people who have introduced new ideas, reading a variety of views on the topics of change and influence, studying how change agents throughout history have tackled the problems they faced, and sharing our work for comments and feedback. This book does not simply reflect *our* ideas, but includes those of many different people in many different organizations throughout the world. Expert change leaders are likely to say "I do that!" when they read many of these techniques. We will take this comment as a tribute to our work because our goal was to identify tried and true practices, not just a collection of good ideas that may or may not work.

History of These Patterns

The idea of documenting patterns for successful solutions to recurring problems was introduced by a building architect named Christopher Alexander. Even though we are not architects, a number of us in the software development community have adopted Alexander's approach as a way to capture known solutions for software architecture, software design, testing, customer interaction, and other aspects of software development. The introduction of new ideas is, of course, not limited to the software area, but it's where we both began to see a new source for important and useful patterns.

In 1996, Linda was working with a colleague, David DeLano, to introduce patterns into their organization. They were having considerable success, so they began documenting their practices as a collection of patterns. They realized that one instance of a successful solution to a problem is the beginning but not enough to define a pattern. The next step was to validate their experiences with those of change agents in other organizations. They led a workshop at the Object-Oriented Programming, Systems, Languages, and Applications (OOPSLA) conference in 1996 on Introducing Patterns into the Workplace. Workshop participants improved the collection by adding their experiences or Known Uses and by writing new patterns. The resulting collection was shepherded and workshopped at the Pattern Languages of Programs Conference (PLoP) in 1997. In both workshops, participants commented that the patterns could be used for introducing any new idea—not just patterns.

In 1998, Mary Lynn was hired by a large telecommunications company to introduce patterns into that organization. She not only used the patterns David and Linda and others had written (and added Known Uses) but also wrote many new patterns. These were shepherded and workshopped at PLoP '99. Again, participants commented that the patterns had a broader application than simply introducing patterns.

At the ChiliPLoP conference in March 2000, we collaborated for the first time and sponsored a workshop on Introducing Patterns into the Workplace. Participants worked to combine all the patterns into a fledgling language. At this juncture, after a great deal of soul searching, we decided to follow the advice of many reviewers and expand the topic to include any innovation, not just patterns. The focus was narrowed to just introducing an innovation, that is, targeting Innovators, Early Adopters, and the Early Majority to "cross the chasm." The resulting context of applying the patterns would be that the innovation would have taken root in the mainstream of the organization.

The patterns were refined in workshops at other conferences (OOPSLA 2000 and OT 2001) and presented in a tutorial for the first time at OOPSLA 2001. At each of these conferences and workshops, participants improved the patterns by sharing their experiences and suggesting new patterns.

We began to apply these patterns in a variety of domains and to hear from others about similar experiences. It's clear that the techniques can be used to introduce any new idea. The known uses in each pattern and the experience reports describe some of these domains.

How This Book Is Organized

The patterns are listed alphabetically, with a brief summary in the Appendix of this book. Pattern names include a page reference where the complete pattern may be found, for example, Fear Less(151). As we describe pattern uses and experience reports in the first two parts of this book, you will see patterns referenced, and you can turn to the appropriate page and read more about the pattern in Part Three. This book can thus become a reference after you have read the initial chapters. When looking for the solution to a particular problem, you can simply skim the summaries in the Appendix and refer to the complete pattern description for a more detailed explanation.

This work is built on the experiences of many people and on research from Robert Cialdini, Malcolm Gladwell, Geoffrey Moore, E. M. Rogers, Peter Senge, and others. We have included a complete list of citations in the References section if you would like to read further.

Audience

This book will be of interest to anyone who is trying to introduce a new idea of any kind into an organization of any size. We have all those "powerless leaders" in mind because we have seen that everyone, at any level in an organization, feels powerless when trying to change the minds of others.

The pattern collection has evolved over several years thanks to many pattern originators and countless others who have provided comments, pattern uses, and other feedback. Even though the book has now been published, we continue to care for these patterns and would like to hear from all of you, our readers. We are always happy to answer any questions about the specific sources and the patterns. As Christopher Alexander* noted:

> We may then gradually improve these patterns which we share, by testing them against experience: we can determine, very simply, whether these patterns make our surroundings live, or not, by recognizing how they make us feel.

---

*Alexander, C.A., *The Timeless Way of Building*, Oxford University Press, 1979.

Acknowledgments

The creation of a pattern language should be the work of a community. We agree with Christopher Alexander, who states "... many of the people who read, and use this language, will try to improve these patterns—will put their energy to work, in this task of finding more true, more profound invariants—and we hope that gradually these more true patterns, which are slowly discovered, as times goes on, will enter a common language, which all of us can share."*

Many people have contributed, and continue to contribute, to the development of this language. These include the pattern originators, the "shepherds" who helped us improve our work at the Pattern Languages of Programs (PLoP) conferences, those who attended the writers' workshops, and the countless others who have provided feedback and ideas for improving the patterns. This book would not have happened without their contribution, and we'd like to do our best to thank everyone. But since there were so many, we know we are at risk of leaving someone out.

---

*Alexander, C.A. et al., *A Pattern Language*, Oxford University Press, 1977.

First and foremost, the people who originated the patterns (in addition to the book authors):

Jon Collins—Champion Skeptic

Rachel Davies—Shoulder to Cry On

David DeLano—Brown Bag, Do Food, Early Adopter (formerly Grass Roots), Gone to Maui (which became part of Location, Location, Location), and Token (formerly Trinket)

Frances Evans—Gold Mine (which became part of Just Do It)

Daniel Gackle—Trial Run

Jeff Garland—Just Do It

Kevlin Henney—Location, Location, Location

Chuck Hill—Test the Waters

Lise Hvatum—Corridor Politics

Brian Marick—Spotlight on Others (which became part of Involve Everyone)

Jim and Michele McCarthy—Ask for Help

Clive Menhinick—Piggyback

Steven E. Newton—Smell of Success

Peter Sommerlad—External Validation (originally called Bread Upon the Waters)

Carol Stimmel—In Your Space

Tadahiro Uehara—Just Do It

Rob Westgeest—Fear Less

Junichi Yamamoto—Mentor

Rieko Yamamoto—Just Do It

The students in the Systems & Information Management class at the University of North Carolina at Asheville—Adopt a Skeptic (which became part of Bridge-Builder)

The EuroPLoP 2000 Focus Group on Introducing Patterns into Organizations: Gerhard Ackermann, Frances Evans, Peter Gassmann, Jan de Groot, Pavel Hruby, Klaus Marquardt, Amir Raveh, Maks Romih, Didi Schuetz, Alberto Silva, Amy Strucko, and Oliver Vogel, with special thanks to Amir Raveh for capturing the pattern e-Forum.

The authors of the experience reports: John Crupi, Edward Katz, and Jack Watson.

The countless number of people who provided "known uses" for the individual patterns.

The members of the OOPSLA '96 workshop on Introducing Patterns into the Workplace, October 1996: David DeLano, Dan Rawsthorne, Clenio F. Salviano, Peter Sommerlad, Junichi Yamamoto, and Rieko Yamamoto, representing her co-authors: T. Uehara, Y. Nakayama, Y. Yoshida.

Ken Auer, shepherd for PLoP '97, and the members of the PLoP '97 workshop, September 1997: Brad Appleton, Mike Beedle, Charles Crowley, David DeLano, Dave Dikel, David Kane, Don Olson, and Bill Opdyke.

David DeLano, shepherd for PLoP '99, and the members of the PLoP '99 workshop, August 1999: Dwight Duego, Eduardo Fernandez, Martin Fontaine, Nathalie Gaertner, Dorin Sandu, Bernard Thirion, and Xiaohong Yuan.

The participants of the ChiliPLoP 2000 hot topic, March 2000: John Letourneau, Ross McKegney, Don Olson, and Carol Stimmel.

Jim Coplien, shepherd for EuroPLoP 2000, and the members of the Euro-PLoP2000 workshop, July 2000: Joe Bergin, Diethelm Bienhaus, Jane Chandler, Martine Devos, Jutta Eckstein, Julio Garcia-Martin, Christoph Steindl, and Markus Volter.

The members of the OOPSLA 2000 workshop on Introducing Patterns (or any new idea) into Organizations, October 2000: David DeLano, Lucio Dinoto, Frances Evans, Jeff Garland, Neil Harrison, Bill Opdyke, Amy Strucko, and Rieko Yamamoto.

The OT 2001 Conference workshop participants.

Brian Marick, shepherd for PLoP 2001, who encouraged us to add an opening story to each pattern.

David Kane, shepherd for EuroPLoP 2002, and the members of the Euro-PLoP 2002 workshop.

Laurie Williams and Robert Kessler, for providing "external validation" for our patterns by referencing them in their book, *Pair Programming Illuminated*.

Joe Bergin, for providing "external validation" for our patterns by using them in his course at Pace University.

Thanks to Shawn Dagley, whose comment sparked the idea for the pattern Tailor Made. Thanks to Russ Stinehour for the additional inspiration for this pattern.

Jutta Eckstein, for spending a lot of time on the beach studying our patterns, providing valuable feedback, and for referencing our patterns in her book, *Agile Software Development in the Large*.

Lise Hvatum, for teaching us that these patterns could even be applied by an Evangelist who was also a manager!

Torsten Holmer, for being amazingly enthusiastic over an early draft of the patterns.

Alan O'Callaghan, for his unwavering support and his invaluable help with some of our conference sessions and for some editorial help as we got close to the deadline.

Tammy Huffman, for reading and commenting on the almost-final draft of the book.

Cindy Reagan for proofreading the patterns.

Fred Grossman, for suggesting the format for the title of this book.

They say a picture is worth a thousand words but we think the sketches in our book from Rich Fackrell (Fack!) are worth a lot more than that! Thanks, Fack!

John Neidhart and Jennifer Blackwell at Addison-Wesley Professional and Patty Donovan at Pine Tree Composition and Rebecca Greenberg, whose invaluable suggestions helped make this book a finished product we are both proud to have written.

Linda's biggest "local sponsor," her husband, Karl Rehmer.

And last, but certainly not least, for the countless people who kept telling us they couldn't wait until the book came out—here it is!

PART ONE

Overview

So you have an idea you'd like to introduce into your organization. You've come to the right place! In Part I, we look at some of the most important factors that will affect your ability to be a leader of change. We then explain what patterns are and how they can be used to document best practices, such as the ones in this book for introducing new ideas into an organization. Finally we present a framework to help you use these patterns.

CHAPTER ONE

Organizations and Change

In 1993, Eric Saperston graduated from college and bought a 1971 Volkswagen Bus. He set off with his golden retriever, Jack, on a journey. Eric said that he had decided to call some of the most powerful people in the world and ask them out for a cup of coffee. His adventures have been documented in the film *The Journey*. All of us who have been intrigued by a new idea and set off to try to introduce it have felt like this—excited, anticipating a great adventure, ready for a journey! We hope you see these pages as a guidebook when you need help along the way.

You're interested in leading or helping to make a change in your organization and you want to learn more. You'd like to understand why change is so hard for you and your colleagues, and you're concerned about survival in these tough times. The strategies in this book will help you address all these needs. This first chapter introduces the change process and the forces at work that may help or hinder your struggles.

Implementing change takes time. How much time? That depends on many different variables. It may be easy to get a few people interested and, depending upon your goals, that may be enough. For example, if the innovation is a new software tool, your goal may be to persuade your own team to use it. On the other hand, you might eventually hope to encourage the entire company to integrate the software in its processes. This is a substantially more challenging task that may require years of effort with some discouraging slips backward along the way.

Research into the factors that affect change has identified several misconceptions that many of us share. The first is that innovations will be accepted just because they are good ideas. I'm sure you can think of many good ideas that have failed and been replaced by other, sometimes poorer ones. The Sony Beta technology for videocassette recording lost out to the VHS format. The Macintosh operating system clearly had advantages over the DOS operating system for personal computers, but it lost impact in the marketplace, first to DOS and then to Microsoft Windows.

Since those who have discovered an intriguing new possibility clearly see the advantages of the idea, it's easy to be deluded into believing that all you have to do is explain logically why the new idea is better than the one it should replace and voilà, others will sign up. How many times have you made this assumption only to discover that there was much more work to be done?

The second misconception is that once a new idea is introduced, nothing else is required. Adopt this new approach. The end. Drop the seed in the ground. No watering or fertilizing or pruning or tending needed. Unfortunately, the reality is that it takes a lot of persistence. To reach your journey's end, you must be in for the long haul.

You may have heard the argument that the quickest way to introduce a new approach is to mandate its use. While you might get compliance, you probably won't get commitment. An edict from on high may prompt some change in the short term, but there is likely to be resistance in the not-too-distant long term.

A high-level executive cannot simply declare, "Okay, guys, we're going to do <innovation> from now on!" and expect it to happen. With top-down change, the emphasis is on making the changes quickly and dealing with the problems only if necessary. Bottom-up change is more gradual, but it addresses resistance more effectively. The emphasis in bottom-up change is on participation and on keeping people informed about what is going on, so uncertainty and resistance are minimized. Based on our experience, we believe that change is best introduced bottom-up with support at appropriate points from management—both local and at a higher level. Peter Senge, author of *The Fifth Discipline* appears to agree:

> During the last few years, a new understanding of the process of organizational change has emerged. It is not top-down or bottom-up, but participative at all levels—aligned through a common understanding of a system.*

As you can see, we believe in a participatory approach. Otherwise, you may share Carly Fiorina's experience when she became president of Hewlett-Packard and tried to make major changes. Because the workforce had little opportunity to be involved, many were skeptical and resistant. They didn't openly attack her new ideas; they simply appeared to meet her goals while continuing to do things as they always had in the past. The resistance was so subtle and so pervasive that it was difficult to accomplish anything. As an old Chinese proverb states, "There's a lot of noise at the top of the stairs, but no one coming down." Change driven from on high without significant across-the-board participation creates more heat than light and often ends up becoming a recipe for failure.

Our approach in writing this book is to help you introduce new ideas by encouraging others to become intrigued and interested so that they *want* to become involved in the change.

The strategies we recommend take advantage of research by E. M. Rogers and Geoffrey Moore, who observed how individuals become aware of an innovation and make the choice to accept or reject it. They describe change not as an event but a process, the **innovation-decision process**. People move through the stages in this process before adopting or rejecting a new idea. During the first

---

*Senge, P. et al., *The Fifth Discipline Fieldbook: Strategies and Tools for Building a Learning Organization*, Doubleday, 1994.

three stages—knowledge, persuasion, and decision—you gather information and form opinions. If you decide to adopt the innovation, then you proceed through the last two stages—implementation and confirmation—where you are a user but continue to need assurance that your decision was a good one.

This research has identified several factors that speed up or slow down the innovation-decision process and, as a result, the time it will take the change to become part of the environment. We consider three factors: the change agent, the culture, and the people. To begin a successful change effort, you will need to understand all three and how they work together.

The Change Agent

We believe that change can be instigated and led by anyone. Lack of power is no excuse for inactivity or for anticipating failure. In fact, many acts of leadership you see every day are often performed by relatively powerless people—those whose ability to influence others exceeds the extent of their authority. In healthy companies, people not only lead their peers, but also lead their bosses, all without the official sanction to do so.

Back to Eric Saperston's journey. Along the way he met CEOs, authors, and former President Jimmy Carter. When Eric asked what message he had for Eric's generation, President Carter replied, "Remember how powerful you are. Never forget the power of the individual to make a difference. Enroll people in that possibility and change the world, change your community, change your family, change yourself."

We can all take President Carter's message to heart. Appreciate the power you have. If you are a good communicator, genuinely appreciate people, and work well with others, you will have an edge when sharing your ideas. You will have more time to give to the task if the change effort is a part of your job rather than something you are trying to do in your "spare" time. The primary driver, however, is your passion, your deep and continuing belief in the innovation you are trying to introduce. You need three things to successfully share your idea: your belief in it, the drive to bring it into your environment, and some information on how to do it. You supply the first two; the strategies in this book provide the third.

The Culture

It's obvious that culture will have a significant impact on the speed of the innovation-decision process of your colleagues. The process will be easier and faster if the culture supports and nurtures new ideas, allows time for people to learn and do new things, is patient enough to support innovations that have benefits in the long term, accepts that learning curves can be long, and does not consider failure to be a death sentence. A supportive culture helps people to deal with their emotions so that they can focus on the tasks ahead.

There must also be enough flexibility to allow change. In *The 7 Habits of Highly Effective People*, Stephen Covey tells the story of a man in the woods working feverishly to saw down a tree.

> *"What are you doing?"*
> *"Can't you see? I'm sawing down this tree."*
> *"You look exhausted! How long have you been at it?"*
> *"Over five hours, and I'm beat! This is hard work."*
> *"Well, why don't you take a break and sharpen that saw? I'm sure it would go a lot faster."*
> *"I don't have time to sharpen the saw. I'm too busy sawing!"**

Unfortunately, there is usually little or no time to learn something that would increase efficiency and improve quality. Every successful learning initiative requires time for new activities: planning, collaborative work, training, and reflection. But realistically, change cannot occur without an up-front investment, even if there is strong interest. That said, small changes can happen even in the most conservative cultures, but you will need considerable patience because change will be slower.

Culture is also important because you need others who are willing to help with the change effort. Like it or not, you can't do it alone. In *The Dance of Change*, Peter Senge explains that a change effort needs many leaders:

> *It requires seeing how significant change invariably starts locally, and how it grows over time. And it requires recognizing the diverse array of people who play key roles in sustaining change—people who are "leaders." We want to build institutions that,*

---

*Covey, S.R., *The 7 Habits of Highly Effective People*, Simon & Schuster, 1989.

by their very nature, continually adapt and reinvent themselves, with leadership coming from many people in many places, not just from the top.*

The People

In addition to the change agent and the culture, the third influence is the people. As you set off on your journey, you might remind yourself that the entity you want to influence is not a thing but a collection of individuals. To change the thing means changing the individuals in it. Even when a culture is open to new ideas, the people within it will accept the change at different rates. You may think that if the benefits of an innovation are clearly and widely presented, everyone will eventually see the light and adopt it. As rational human beings, we like to think that logic drives most of our decisions, but the reality is, in most persuasive situations, research in influence strategies and social psychology shows that people base their decisions on emotions and then justify them with facts. Nationally syndicated business writer Dale Dauten observed, "Facts are useful; they give the conscious mind something to do while the emotions decide what's true."

Some people may pass through the innovation-decision process quickly, but most will move more slowly, and some may adopt an idea only when they are pressured to do so. Understanding how different people accept—or don't accept—change will help you to appreciate each person's style and adjust your strategies accordingly.

Look for the positive side in each person you are talking to. As Bill O'Brien, former president of Hanover Insurance Company, noted:

> *If you have a deterministic view of people—that they come programmed by their genes, there's only a 10% margin of improvement and 20% of them will screw you if they get a chance—then that belief in itself will severely limit your ability to lead profound change.**

---

*Senge, P., A. Kleiner, C. Roberts, R. Ross, G. Roth, B. Smith, *The Dance of Change: The Challenges to Sustaining Momentum in Learning Organizations*, Doubleday, 1999.

On the other hand, if you genuinely like people and if you believe that in each person contains a vast reservoir just waiting to be tapped, then you will want to help them be all they can be. If you can bring that attitude to your work, along with the courage and compassion to act upon it, then you can be effective.

E. M. Rogers, in his landmark publication *Diffusion of Innovations*, noticed that new ideas tend to originate in a small group he calls the Innovators, then move to a second group, the Early Adopters, and then become accepted by the Early Majority and the Late Majority. Eventually, the Laggards may adopt it. Let's have a closer look at each of these groups.

The **Innovators** make up a very small percentage of a "normal" population—about 2.5%. They accept new ideas quickly. They need little persuasion. They're intrigued with something just because it is new. You know people like this: These are the folks who like something even better if it doesn't work right! Their early interest in new ideas enables them to spark and help test new ideas. But they may not stay interested for long, and because their venturesome nature makes them open to risks, others usually don't accept their opinions. Thus, Innovators are excellent gatekeepers but generally not good opinion leaders.

The **Early Adopters** represent a larger part of a "normal" population—about 13.5%. They are also open to new ideas but will accept them only after serious consideration. They tend to look for the strategic opportunity an innovation can provide and can be persuaded if they see that the new approach provides a fundamental breakthrough. As highly motivated visionaries who are respected by their peers, they can serve as opinion leaders once they have accepted the new idea. However, the Innovators and the Early Adopters are small groups. To have impact, you must convince the majority.

The **Early Majority** is the first significant group (about a third of a "normal" population) to accept a new idea. The Early Majority interact with their peers but are seldom leaders. They tend to follow, and they want to know that others have been successful with a new idea before they consider accepting it themselves. As pragmatists, they are persuaded if the innovation can provide incremental, measurable, and predictable improvement. Once this large group is convinced, a grassroots foundation is established for the innovation. The Early Majority provides a vital link between the Early and the Late Adopters. The Early Majority is your bridge between the old and the new.

The **Late Majority** is the second significant group (about a third of a "normal" population) to accept a new idea. The Late Majority is composed of people who approach new ideas with skepticism and caution. They are conservative in nature and are persuaded only after most of the uncertainty is removed. They need some kind of pressure before they accept a new idea. This pressure can take many forms: seeing people all around them using it, a boss strongly suggesting that they use it, or their team adopting it so they must follow suit in order to work efficiently in the team.

The **Laggards** are the people who are last to adopt new ideas—when they accept ideas at all. Their view is typically "we've always done it this way." Their friends tend to be other Laggards, and because they are suspicious of innovation and change, their acceptance of a new idea usually comes through extreme pressure from others coupled with the certainty that the innovation cannot fail.

Notice that we keep referring to a "normal" population. We've never seen a "normal" organization! Each has its own character. Some very innovative companies have a larger than "normal" population of Innovators, while other companies are more conservative. The numbers that E. M. Rogers and other researchers have observed are only statistical guidelines. You are the best judge of what will work well for you.

Our philosophy is well described by quality management consultant David Hutton in *The Change Agents' Handbook*.

> *You do not have to spend a lot of time and effort on those who strongly resist change. You only have to help and protect those who want to change, so that they are able to succeed. Put another way, your job is not to plant the entire forest, row by row—it is to plant clumps of seedlings in hospitable places and to nurture them. As they mature, these trees will spread their seeds, and the forest will eventually cover the fertile land. The rocks will, of course, remain barren regardless. This is a logical, effective, and responsible way of using your limited resources. This does not mean that you can afford to ignore the existence of committed and influential opponents of change. You may have to find ways to prevent these individuals from sabotaging the process. However, once you have figured out who cannot be converted, you should not waste more time trying to persuade them.**

Because our strategies focus on *introducing* new ideas, they do not target the more skeptical individuals (the Late Majority and Laggards), but we don't ig-

---

*Hutton, D. *The Change Agents' Handbook: A Survival Guide for Quality Improvement Champions*, ASQ Quality Press, 1994.

nore them either. Skeptics may provide valuable opportunities to discover problems with the innovation. Even though many people may consider conflict unpleasant, counter-productive, and time-consuming, we recommend that you see conflict as an opportunity. Conflict doesn't have to be destructive; you can use that energy to help solve problems and make improvements. In some cases, people simply need information about why the change is necessary, about the desired future state, and what needs to happen to get there.

Much of the resistance to change stems from the need for control of our environment and destiny. You've probably enjoyed rearranging your office at times, but it would be a different matter if corporate cubicle police unexpectedly arrived one day to reorganize your office in a style dictated by some authorized master plan—straight out of a Dilbert cartoon! As many students of organizational change have observed, *people do not resist change so much as they resist being changed*. People are better at coping with change if they have a hand in creating it. Therefore, our philosophy in documenting the strategies in this book is to engage people at all levels, so they can participate in planning what should be done and can help to make change happen.

We've outlined one explanation for how individuals accept new ideas. Malcolm Gladwell, author of *The Tipping Point*, describes three roles that are critical for introducing change: Maven, Salesman, and Connector. Mavens are "information specialists." They supply knowledge about the innovation. However, to spread the innovation, you must have Salesmen who promote the idea, and Connectors who know many different kinds of people. You must take on the roles of Maven, Salesman, and Connector to the greatest extent possible and engage others who can help. Even if you are a Maven, you will still need people who can help you keep up with the latest information. You may find Early Adopters who are good Salesmen, and the more Connectors you enlist the better.

Introducing a new idea is a gradual, learn-as-you-go process that will have setbacks and small successes along the way. We recommend that you start slowly and expect that your efforts will require time and patience. The journey cannot be successfully undertaken without some understanding of yourself, your culture, and the people within it. This understanding will enable you to make the most effective use of our guidebook. Above all, *enjoy the process*. As Steve Jobs of Apple Computer said, "The journey is the reward!" Bon voyage!

CHAPTER TWO

Strategies or Patterns

How many books, articles, memos, e-mails, and Web sites do you struggle to read each year? Even if you read them all, how much can you remember? All the highlighters and yellow stickies in the world won't ensure that you can recall the information when you need it. In this chapter we introduce you to patterns and try to show how they can solve some of the problems you face in today's overloaded society. The name of a pattern captures the essence of the idea you want to remember. A collection of related pattern names creates a special "language." We think you'll soon be "speaking" patterns!

We're not trying to add to your information load; we're just trying to help you put good ideas to use. To this end, we have documented the strategies in this book as **patterns**, which are a form of knowledge management. We have seen how effective patterns are for sharing information. When you know a pattern and use its name, a lot of information is communicated with just that single word or short phrase. When you know a collection of patterns, for example, patterns for introducing new ideas, the names of the patterns in the collection give you a vocabulary or language to talk about strategies for introducing change. That's our goal. We want you to be able to speak this language.

You can certainly apply the ideas in this book, even if you don't know much about patterns. We include a short introduction to patterns in this chapter and, if you want to learn more, we encourage you to check out the pattern books in the list of References for more information.

In short, a pattern is a way to capture expertise. The word "pattern" refers to a recurring best practice documented as a solution to a problem in a given environment. We feel it's important to note that patterns do not simply document good ideas, but rather strategies that have been shown to work well for a variety of people in a variety of circumstances. When patterns work together to solve problems in a particular area, these patterns are called a **pattern language**. Our patterns work together to solve problems in the area of introducing new ideas into organizations.

Pattern Formats

There are several pattern formats, but nearly all of them include the following components: Name, Context, Forces, Problem, Solution, Rationale, and Resulting Context. We use a variation of the format originally proposed by Christopher Alexander, a building architect, who used patterns to document successful practices in constructing buildings and towns.

The following example pattern illustrates the format we use.

Pattern Name: Innovator

Opening story:

Roger lived next door, so every time he bought the newest, coolest gadget, I would hear all about it. He would get so excited about his purchases, even when the items were much too overpriced. But if he convinced me that something was really useful, I would wait and buy it months later when the cost came down to less than half of what Roger paid.

Summary:

When you begin the change initiative, ask for help from colleagues who like new ideas.

Context:

You are a new Evangelist(144) or Dedicated Champion(129) just starting to introduce a new idea into your organization.

Problem:

You need people to jumpstart the new idea in your organization.

Forces:

You can't interest everyone in a new idea all at once, but you need to start somewhere. A community of even a few people who share your interest and want to work together will make a world of difference in the confusion and inconsistencies that invariably arise. Virtually every significant change initiative starts with a small number of deeply committed individuals, often as few as two or three.

It's easier to begin with those people who will be most receptive to the new idea. Innovators make up a small percentage of the population. They get intrigued and excited about something just because it is new. They don't need much convincing, just a little information. They enjoy trying to figure out how the latest thing works. This puts them in a good position to help launch the new idea into the organization.

Therefore:

Essence of the solution:

Find the people who are quick to adopt new ideas. Talk to them about the innovation and ask for help in sparking an interest for it in the organization.

More about the solution:

Look for Innovators among those who attend early Brown Bags(113) and other meetings where new ideas are being introduced. Some of them will come to you once you start talking about the new idea.

Encourage these individuals to take on the role of gatekeepers. Invite them to Test the Waters(237) by using Just Do It(177) and doing an early evaluation. Ask for their feedback about the innovation and listen to their suggestions for appealing to the larger community. Because they are the first to come on board with a new idea, perhaps they could lead one of the first Study Groups(228) for other people who are curious about learning more. Those who are especially enthusiastic may become Evangelists(144) in their own groups.

Resulting Context (positive and negative consequences):

This pattern establishes support from a group who can help get a new idea going in the organization. It doesn't take a lot of work to interest them and then you won't feel so alone. Since they are willing to accept some of the uncertainty that comes with a new idea, they ease the risk for later adopters.

However, you may not be able to depend on them in the long term. Their interest in new ideas makes them move from one thing to another. In addition, their willingness to quickly accept new ideas causes others to be suspicious of their claims. Therefore, they generally aren't good opinion leaders. Count on their help as gatekeepers in the short term. If they offer more, consider that a bonus.

Known Uses:

Bill's eyebrows seem to rise to his hairline when he hears about something new. So he was one of the first people Julie talked with about the new idea. He tried it, reported the results, and helped Julie plan a few events to pass the word. His enthusiasm was just what she needed to keep her going in the early days of trying to convince other people whose eyebrows did not rise as quickly.

Some people know when you've returned from a conference and drop by to see what new books you've bought or new techniques you've seen. They wanted to be there but couldn't take the time. So Sam always tries to bring something back for them. It is fun to watch how happy these people get about anything because their need to be in on the "latest and greatest" is almost physical. Sam knows what his boss means when he says, "Sure, you can go to the conference, but bring something back for the team!" He is thinking about these guys.

Using Patterns

When you first see all the information in a pattern, you might think it's overkill. That's how Linda felt early in her pattern experience when she participated in a workshop on software architecture. The workshop leader outlined the task for the session—look at some common problems software architects encounter, document solutions for those problems, and also identify elements of the environment where the solution would be most appropriate. To a "patterns person" that sounded very much like Problem, Solution, and Context. Linda suggested that they use patterns to document their ideas. Since most of the participants didn't know what patterns were, she gave them a quick overview but only included the components they needed, that is, Problem, Solution, and Context. She thought that trying to deal with the other pattern elements, for example, Forces and Resulting Context, would take too much time and was probably not necessary.

The group began to work and immediately ran into a snag. A fellow from one company said, "I think that anyone who uses this solution should be aware that there are some problems with it. Should that go in the Solution?" "Actually," Linda replied, "there is an additional section for concerns like that. It's called the Resulting Context." She explained further and they added Resulting Context to their list of pattern elements. Gradually, additional information was revealed that needed to be included to help those who would use the techniques. In a relatively short time, all the pattern components had been added. It was a significant moment for Linda. Suddenly she saw all the pattern components as essential for capturing and communicating the knowledge needed to solve a problem.

It's like your mother always told you: "Haste makes waste." That means if you hurry, you'll mess up, so take your time. However, your mother also said: "A stitch in time saves nine." That means you shouldn't let things go or you'll be sorry. Well, which is it? Your wise mother understood the context and the forces and the resulting context but forgot to pass along all that helpful information. When we know the wisdom, it's easy to simply summarize a solution for an inquiring novice. The rest, we think, is easy—just do it! However, novices who find only a summary of a technique are often at a loss about when and how to apply the solution and what the consequences will be when they do. Patterns supply this essential information.

A topic for considerable debate among pattern writers is whether or not a solution that has worked well in a particular context to solve a particular problem really is a pattern or whether it is just a general heuristic or guideline. The fallback response to this question has historically been: What does the pattern "build?" The origin of this response is the work of Christopher Alexander, an architect who builds structures. His patterns describe concrete changes in the real world. Since our patterns describe organizational solutions, the result is tangible but usually not structural. Therefore, we have taken extra care to include both an opening story to provide an image for the intent of the pattern and also to include text that describes what we feel the pattern "builds"—that is, what the positive and negative results of applying the pattern will be. Stories mean different things to different readers. If our opening story strikes a chord with you, then the name and story may be enough for you to understand what the pattern is all about.

Another important component in our patterns is the Known Uses. We've found that many people read these stories first and are convinced by the compelling accounts. Research in cognitive science shows that humans have evolved to hear stories as the way to learn important lessons. We believe that patterns should be based on stories from experts. In fact, we might say that if there isn't a story behind the pattern—a startling success or a shocking failure—then maybe the pattern shouldn't be written.

The name of the pattern is of critical importance. When pattern names are used in a community, the individuals speak a common language. For example, when using the patterns in this book, one of the first that may become part of the common language is Do Food(132). Everyone immediately understands this pattern because they know food makes meetings more enjoyable. Therefore, once they have read the name Do Food, they use it in conversation without explanation because they feel sure everyone will get the meaning.

In "speaking" a pattern language, the pattern names can be used naturally in conversation or in text. In this book, we use the pattern names conversationally. You will find that after quickly reading the pattern summaries that you will understand what the pattern reference means, even if you haven't read all the information. That's an effective test for a pattern name. If it can be used and the people working in the area understand what you mean, then the name is probably a good one. We find that change agents across the globe are starting to use the names of our patterns when they talk about strategies for introducing new ideas. For example, most call themselves Evangelists(144) and talk about giving Brown Bags(113) or inviting Big Jolt(107) speakers and trying to find a Local Sponsor(186) or a Corporate Angel(123). Some names are more evocative than others, but after a quick glance through the summaries in the

Appendix table, we hope that the names will become part of your conversations about change.

The context or setting in which a pattern can be applied is a vital component. The Latin root of the word *context* signifies a "joining together," and the conventional modern meaning refers to the parts that immediately follow or precede a piece of writing and determine its meaning. Hence, a phrase taken "out of context" is one whose meaning has changed or become difficult to understand because it is not part of its original setting. This is also true for a pattern. Each pattern gets its meaning as a result of applying other patterns. The context of an individual pattern not only weaves it into a pattern language, but also ties it to the situation in which it is most applicable. Pattern readers who apply a solution and find that it doesn't work may feel the pattern is useless, when it's more likely that they are using the pattern in the wrong context. The context, or appropriate setting, for our collection of patterns or pattern language is an organization of any size where you are attempting to introduce a new idea. Experts apply their knowledge by calling on their experiences in many different contexts. They seem to recognize when it's appropriate to apply the solution. They are using patterns—even if they don't always have a name for the particular solution they are using. The expert knows when it's appropriate to use a particular pattern and when it doesn't apply. This is what defines expertise, and what we hope our patterns will communicate to you.

Patterns provide solutions to problems. It's hard for people to buy into the solution if they don't understand that they are facing a problem and what that problem is. For example, one change agent saw this in her experiences trying to get policy changes in her organization. She noted, "When I took the time to explain the problem, the proposed policy (which contained the solution) met less resistance and passed."

Some people may read a pattern and say, "Why, that's just common sense!" And, of course, many times they are right. Since a pattern is an expert's solution for a recurring problem, it might appear obvious, especially to others with experience in the same area. The power of documenting "common sense" as a pattern is that, sad but true, "common sense is so uncommon." If this were not the case, no one would ever make the same mistake twice. You would simply apply the wisdom of your experience or "common sense" and become more and more perfect as you age. Unfortunately, we live in stressful times (everyone has always lived in stressful times!). Under stress, we tend to forget even those hard-won lessons that could help us solve recurring problems.

Mary Lynn sees this every semester when her students participate in a fast-paced simulation of a software system development process. In the weeks prior to this exercise, the students learn many concepts about managing and implementing software development. They are tested on the concepts and they review everything during the days before. Once the simulation begins, the students get so involved in completing the task that they seem to forget many of the good practices they studied. When they reflect on the experience, their response is always the same—yes, we knew we should have done <this> and not have done <that>, but in the heat of the simulation we forgot what we knew.

Just as in this simulation, most of us have such hectic lives that we need help recalling and applying those things we have learned and, yes, even our "common sense."

To give you an idea of the power of patterns, here's a story about a friend of Linda's, Frances Blaker, a professional recorder player. Frances and members of her group, The Farallon Recorder Quartet, were visiting in Phoenix recently and started talking about patterns. Linda gave Frances a copy of her book, *The Patterns Handbook*. A short time later, Linda received this e-mail from Frances.

> Hi Linda,
>
> I have been reading your book and finding it very interesting. Already patterns are appearing. I have been stressed with many different projects and deadlines, but decided a way to handle it was just to take 15 minutes for any one thing rather than get in too deep with one thing and have no time for any of the others. When feeling most stressed I say "15 minutes." This is an example of patterns and names, isn't it?
>
> Anyway, good work. I am happy to have discovered a new way of thinking of things, and discovered a whole world of people doing this.
>
> Frances

We often say we have a "disease"—we see patterns everywhere. Then, in our enthusiasm, we "infect" others! We believe that "15 Minutes" could be documented as a pattern. Frances obviously knows the right Context and Forces for applying this Solution and it helps her solve the Problem of having too much to do and not enough time to do it. A second e-mail from Frances says something else about patterns.

> Hi Linda,
>
> I ran my whole day yesterday based on the 15-minute pattern and was therefore able to accomplish more in one day than in a long time. Good thing, since I have to go out of town tomorrow and had lots of things to get done.
>
> Frances

Now that Frances has identified this helpful pattern, she can apply it. In the past, she would have struggled as she faced this problem over and over again, and since the problem always arises in stressful settings, she might not have remembered what she already knows about solving it. Does this sound familiar?

We have seen teams wrestle with problems and sink deeper and deeper in the mud, getting hopelessly lost. But when they heard someone say the name of a pattern, it's as though a light had been switched on to show the way in the darkness. That little tap on the shoulder called everyone back to sanity. Of course we know how to solve this; we've done it a million times! Why didn't we think of that? The answer to this question is that without a handy way to reference your accumulated wisdom, you don't always remember what you know. Patterns can help. The names of the patterns work together to give you a vocabulary to talk about problems in a particular area and help you overcome the obstacles in your path.

We're not prescribing a fixed sequence for using our collection of patterns that will be effective in every situation. How you use this pattern language will depend on your goals, the needs of your organization, your organization's culture, and the people in it. We will provide some examples of specific sequences of pattern uses throughout and in the experience reports in Part II. These will give you some good ideas, but you will need to discover what is appropriate for you and your organization.

In our work we provide training sessions to teach people our patterns. In one of the exercises, the participants form small teams and develop a plan for introducing a new idea into an organization. The purpose of the exercise, of course, is not to create the plan, but to allow the teams to learn more about the patterns. It's much more fun and much more effective than listening to a lecture!

During the exercise we provide each team with a collection of index cards. Each card contains the name of one of our patterns and a brief description. The teams interact with the cards and with each other. They pick up cards and move them around on a table or the floor. They create sequences of patterns as they work. Usually the plan develops to fit the framework described in the following chapters—with variations depending on the group, their perceived organization, and the idea they want to introduce.

We've tried to capture the results of that exercise for you. You can find the file with the pattern abstracts on http://www. awprofessional.com. You could use a similar set of cards to develop your strategy because we think that you will want to discover what fits your style and your organization. Using the cards also means that you can easily adjust to your experiences. Learn as you go. You can't anticipate everything. Once you accept that, everything becomes less of a struggle.

Since we know how difficult introducing new ideas can be, we are careful not to oversell our patterns. Even though they've been road-tested by many people in many organizations, we remember what Henry Petroski, author of *To Engineer Is Human*, said in his keynote speech at a recent conference: "Nothing can be designed so that it has no limitations."

So, that's "patterns in a nutshell." The chapters that follow describe the infrastructure—framework—for the patterns in our collection. Each chapter presents a small slice of the pattern collection as you might use them to introduce change in your organization. The first question you might be asking yourself is, "Where do I start?"

CHAPTER THREE

Where Do I Start?

Maybe you attended a seminar, read a book, or heard about a new approach from a friend. You're excited because you think it can help your organization, but you don't know where to start. This chapter describes the very important pattern Evangelist(144) and a small package of patterns to always carry with you on your journey: Test the Waters(237), Time for Reflection(240), Small Successes(216), and Step by Step(224).

Think about how important it is when building a house to first decide where to build it. Only then can you make intelligent decisions about the house itself. In the same way, some of our patterns are better when applied before others. However, there isn't a strict ordering on the entire collection.

We have created a framework that provides some structure for using the patterns but it does not impose a rigid plan for you. The framework suggests rather than dictates. It's a springboard for action that you can adapt to your own organization and culture.

We believe that an effective change agent begins as an Evangelist(144). That is, we see this pattern with this name as the starting point for the rest of the pattern language. The name has a religious flavor and there's a good reason for that: We've found that unless you are truly passionate about the new idea, others will not be convinced to leave the tried and true ways and follow you. There's another piece to this rationale. If you don't have faith in your proposal, then you won't survive the bumpy road to grassroots adoption. There will be successes and failures along the way, and you must celebrate the former and withstand the latter. Only a sincere and abiding belief will carry you through all this turmoil. You must have passion and share that with others. At the same time, you should guard against being overzealous because, as you can imagine, there's a difference between having passion and being a fanatic. A fanatic is likely to turn people off.

Mark Twain said, "You know, I'm all for progress. It's change I object to." That's not true for everyone all the time, of course. Sometimes you're excited by change and look forward to it, but even when you welcome it, change is hard. Some people always seem to resist it. Research has shown that people are more easily convinced by those they like, those who are enthusiastic. As Ralph Waldo Emerson observed, "Nothing great was ever achieved without enthusiasm."

We found the following testimony to the Evangelist pattern in *Agents of Change* by Barbara Bouldin.

> *Several years ago, I set out on a crusade. Management declared me a missionary and commanded me to go forth and convert everyone in our organization. I was spreading the word about the need to embrace the concept of productivity in the form of an automated software tool called Excelerator. As far as I can tell, management selected me because I was a true believer; in other words, I was the first convert.**

---

*Bouldin, B.M., *Agents of Change*, Yourdon Press, 1989.

Evangelism Is Critical for Success

We strongly believe in the importance of this pattern for another reason. We have known change agents who were "hired guns" brought in from outside. We have a pattern called Dedicated Champion(129) (introduced in more detail in Chapter 8). This pattern recognizes that you can't effectively spread the word without having some part of your job dedicated to the task. In other words, a volunteer change agent is limited by lack of resources—particularly the time and energy for the required tasks.

We've talked to several who were hired to fill the role of a Dedicated Champion. We believe that those who weren't successful failed because they felt that since they were paid for introducing the innovation, they didn't have to be concerned about the sales aspect of the task. In other words, they thought they could bypass the evangelism. We've discovered that without the essential elements of passion, enthusiasm, belief, and commitment, a change agent who is "just doing his job" is not likely to be successful. So, even for a person who immediately dons the mantle of a Dedicated Champion, even if you are in a management position, becoming an Evangelist is critical.

A manager at one large company told us:

> The important thing about new product development is that the champion of a new product develops a passion for that product and inspires passion in others. It's like a new business venture. People who have a passion for something find the time to work on it, at lunchtime, before or after work, weekends, whenever.

So the answer to the question "Where do I start?" is "Use the Evangelist pattern."

A Small Package of Patterns

We know how you feel as you embark upon this journey. You're passionate about getting started, but you have so little time, no resources, and no management support.

We do hope, however, that you have a goal for your innovation, a vision for its ultimate adoption. Yes, this is important; you must have vision, but in our experience there is no need for a detailed master plan.

To help you better understand what will work in your environment, we provide a small package of patterns: Test the Waters, Time for Reflection, Small Successes, and Step by Step. Have these in your "carry-on bag" as you embark on your journey. You will use them, not just at the start, but throughout, to be applied at each turn and each new juncture.

The first pattern in the package, Test the Waters(237), enables you to fit your strategy to your setting. Each company has is own character and its own culture. We don't advise throwing out the old and wholesale bringing in the new. Rather, we recommend a gradual, experimental strategy that begins with a little investigating and experimenting to see if your idea has a chance in your environment. Some of the patterns you can use for experiments to Test the Waters are described in Chapters 4 and 5: Ask for Help(104), Innovators(170), Brown Bag(113), Piggyback(201), and Do Food(132). These patterns require minimal investment on your part and the feedback will help you decide what steps to take next.

The pattern Time for Reflection(240) suggests taking time out to learn from your experiments so that you can decide what patterns to apply next. It may not seem obvious that this is necessary. It's one of the great illusions in any endeavor that you learn "on the fly," that somehow, lessons from your experiences are automatically carried forward in life. In reality, you need to dedicate time for this activity—to ask the questions: What worked well? What should be done differently? What still puzzles me? Without careful consideration of these questions and an attempt to find answers, you risk failing to learn.

Mary Lynn tells the following story about reflection.

> My students asked me if I would consider "extra credit" in the quantitative analysis course this semester. I replied, "I'll put that on my list of things to think about." One student replied, "That's funny. I make lists of things to do but I never heard of making a list of things to think about." I suddenly saw myself at her age, moving from one activity to another, rarely taking the time to reflect.

One change agent reported this use of Time for Reflection:

> At our company, retrospective data was used to document patterns for software design, system test, and customer interaction. When data from successful teams showed that a team size of no more than ten was a factor in the successes of the projects and when those results are backed up by observations and the literature,

this is an important pattern. Capturing this information and giving the pattern the name "No More Than Ten" was a useful way to ensure that this knowledge was not lost.

One of the results of this exercise, of course, is that you could decide not to continue your effort. Here's a comment from one change agent we interviewed:

*I went from successfully introducing <a new idea> at a medium-sized company to attempting the same thing at a small company. Even though the support of a **Local Sponsor(186)** and **Corporate Angel(123)** were easy to get and the developers were enthusiastic, most had no time to attend **Brown Bags(113)**. The company had no resources for training or conferences, so despite all the support, I got tired and gave up. I realized that some companies with tight schedules, especially small ones, have no "slack" for investing in innovation.*

The third pattern in the package, **Small Successes(216)**, reminds us to celebrate even the small things along the way, instead of being overwhelmed with all the challenges and potential disappointments that are ahead of us. Eamon Kelly, president of Tulane University, featured in the film *The Journey*, observed, "My success resulted from moving from one failure to another failure with enthusiasm." Celebrate the moving forward!

Robert Schaffer tells the following story in his book *The Breakthrough Strategy*.

At Amstar Corporation, maker of Domino Sugar, all of the refinery's departments needed improvement, but trying to tackle everything at once would have been an overwhelming task. Instead, they chose to focus on the packaging area, where a lot of sugar was lost when bags were overfilled or broke while being filled. The first project included only one supervisor and seven hourly employees and was launched with a few short-term goals: making adjustments to the weighing scales, identifying damaged bags before they could break; resolving packaging problems caused by one kind of sugar. In 6 weeks, the team had reached its initial goals and 3 months later had reduced breakage by 80% and overfills by 56%. The process was extended to other packaging lines and, over the next several years, to every department in the refinery. The first success led to far-reaching improvements as they learned how to achieve significant, immediate results and new work patterns. They used their initial successes as stepping-stones to sustained improvement.

The Amstar story also illustrates the last pattern in this package, Step by Step(224), which cautions against doing too much and expecting results quickly. We have all heard the observation from the oft-quoted Lao Tzu, "The longest journey begins with a single step." Vincent van Gogh wisely noted, "Great things are not done by impulse, but by a series of small things brought together." When your focus is on the long-term goal, it's hard to maintain enthusiasm day after day. A common mistake we all make is to take on more than we can handle. Innovations are best spread slowly and quietly, so you can learn from your failures and build on your successes. The risk in adopting everything at once, rather than incrementally, is that your effort may overwhelm project members.

The five patterns introduced in this chapter work together. We recommend that you use the pattern Test the Waters to conduct an experiment by trying a few patterns from this book. Then use the pattern Time for Reflection to consider what worked well and what should be done differently. Don't forget to use the pattern Small Successes; this will help you stay focused on the good things that are happening instead of being overwhelmed by setbacks. Finally, use the pattern Step by Step to continue to make small changes that move you closer and closer to your final goal.

Colonel David Hackworth writes in *Steel My Soldiers' Hearts*, his compelling account of change in Vietnam:

> *Some command principles are just common sense. Good small-unit leaders make for good battalions, so I fired two small-unit leaders and replaced them with my men. A thousand other changes needed to be made, but I didn't want to bury my staff on our first day together. If I'd ordered all shortcomings squared away immediately, I'd have sent them into overload. I approached the conversion the same way I'd train a pup. Just a few tricks at a time. "Starting now, we're going to follow the two-rule plan," I said. "I'll tell you what the two new rules are and you'll make them happen. Once your troops have mastered the first two rules, we'll add two more and we'll keep doing that until we're squared away. First we'll crawl, then we'll walk and then we'll run. Just stay with me—because we're going to run faster and faster every day."**

---

*Hackworth, D.H., and E. England, *Steel My Soldiers' Hearts: The hopeless to hardcore transformation of U.S. Army, 4th Battalion, 39th Infantry, Vietnam*, Rugged Land, LLC, 2002.

We hope you feel ready to begin your journey. You're enthusiastic (Evangelist(144)) but you know that just having a dream isn't enough. You need to check out the lay of the land (Test the Waters(237)), learning from your experience (Time for Reflection(240)), celebrating each win (Small Successes(216)), and moving gradually forward (Step by Step(224)). Once this foundation is in place, never lose it. Now you're ready to take those initial steps. The next chapter will provide some patterns you can apply without spending resources and taking a lot of your own valuable time. After all, at this point, you're still a volunteer!

CHAPTER FOUR

What Do I Do Next?

You're off and running. You're becoming known in your own small circle as an Evangelist for your new idea. You have confidence that it's worth your time and energy to go forward because you've been using that package of patterns we described in the previous chapter. In this chapter, you will spark some influential support for the new idea with Connector(119), Guru on Your Side(158), and Innovator(170). You will recognize the power of Ask for Help(104) and Just Say Thanks(183).

We hope you have been especially faithful in applying the pattern Small Successes(216), because if your goal is to see real change across a larger organization rather than only your own team or staff, you must be prepared for setbacks. Focusing on the good things that will likely come your way will help you weather the storms.

Linda was attending a conference recently, listening to a very compelling speaker talk about his discouraging experiences trying to introduce agile software development practices into his organization. He all but described himself as a Don Quixote, doing battle against the fierce "old-style-process" windmills. She thought that at any moment he was going to break into song, "To dream, the impossible dream...," but instead he seemed to be saying that his effort was wasted, that people didn't appreciate what he clearly pointed out to them as "The Way" to solve their problems. Only he, in his infinite wisdom, could see the path clearly.

Yes, it's easy to get carried away. Yes, you know that to introduce a new approach you have to be enthusiastic and apply all the sales techniques you can muster. Yes, there will be dark days; two steps forward and one step back. But playing the lone hero is not the way to win friends and influence people.

It was all Linda could do to stay in her seat and not jump up to say, "Did you ask anyone for help?" The presentation used up the question period, so she resolved to talk to him later. The answer she received was the expected one. No, he had not asked for help. In fact, he had not even thought of asking for help. He believed that the responsibility for the success or failure of getting his venture going was solely his.

It's surprising how many change agents make the mistake of trying to go it alone. Somehow, it adds to the challenge, but it's not the strategy that leads to the successful introduction of new ideas. The pattern Ask for Help(104) outlines the reasons for this. The risk with introducing anything is that you can get caught up in the passion you feel for your vision and pretty soon others see this as "all about you." Right from the beginning, enlist others to help you avoid this trap. You may have to hand over some credit for the idea in order to get it going. If you truly believe that adoption of the new approach is the right thing to do, this should be a step you are willing to take.

Many people who are enthusiastic about the introduction of new ideas have no intention of being the final owner of the implementation in their companies. On their list, right near the top, is to find someone who will ultimately be responsible for it and will be the official owner, perhaps the Dedicated Champion, the one whose job it is to make it happen. The Evangelist is only the messenger. For these people, asking for help is a matter of course. They hit the ground running, reaching out for assistance from others.

A critical component of this pattern is ownership. How many meetings have you attended where a proposal was made and the rest of the time was spent hashing and rehashing the details, recasting elements to essentially produce the same thing? "Why," you may wonder, "do we have to reword and restate and argue over things that really don't matter? The end result is pretty much the same as it was when we started." The answer is—ownership. People resist change because of many reasons, but one powerful way to overcome their resistance is ownership. When people feel that they have contributed to the implementation, even in a small way, they have "marked" the new thing so it's theirs. They want to have input. Instead of having new stuff forced down their throats, they want a say in what happens and, especially, how it happens to them.

Mary Lynn has seen this many times: Even when her colleagues agree with a suggestion, they can be extremely critical of it if they are not given a role in deciding when and how it will become part of their everyday work. Over the years, she has watched many administrators arrive believing that their role is to make decisions and begin to implement those decisions alone. However, they soon suffer at the hands of all those who were never given an opportunity to provide input and help. Take the time to ask for help so that others won't see the idea as "all about you," and they'll be able to take ownership for part of the effort. Every person you bring in will help you understand the idea, how it can be improved, and what other techniques you might apply to get the innovation going in your environment. The pool of ideas for making yours a success story will improve with every new person you bring in. Such a deal!

Donald Keough, former president of Coca-Cola, was interviewed in the movie *The Journey*. He observed, "What separates those who achieve and those who do not is in direct proportion to their ability to ask for help. If you shut off honest communication—I want to know what you know; I didn't understand that; Will you help? —you'll have an empty tank at the end of the day."

Anne Lamott in her book *Bird by Bird* advises:

> *There are an enormous number of people out there with valuable information to share with you, and all you have to do is pick up the phone. They love it when you*

do, just as you love it when people ask if they can pick your brain about something you happen to know a great deal about—or, as in my case, have a number of impassioned opinions on.*

The movie *The Journey* also features John Popper, the lead singer of Blues Traveler, who said, "If you actually ask for help out loud, it comes." Using the pattern Ask for Help not only brings others on board to take some of the work off your shoulders, but it allows others around you to shine. Use their skills and energy and give them full credit for their contributions.

To bring in help, talk to everyone you know, even if you're an independent, self-reliant individual. The task of introducing a new idea depends on your enlisting the support of as many people as possible. Tom Kelley, general manager of Ideo Product Development, states:

The social ecology at many American companies says that when you're stuck, you're supposed to go back to your desk and think harder, because you are hired for your skills. At Ideo, the culture is exactly the opposite. You have a social obligation to get help.**

Target Groups to Ask for Help

Chapter 1 described some of the special people you might target: Connectors, Mavens, and Salesmen. The Connector(119) pattern describes those people who are valuable assets because they know "everybody" (well, at least they know a lot of people!). They are members of several diverse groups and, as a result, can spread the word about anything very quickly. In most organizations, secretaries, especially those who have been with the company a long time, are valuable people to get on board. They are the ones who make things happen and they know the people and the people who know the people. Be very happy to have them on your side.

We realize that we are both Connectors. Connectors are people who know and talk with many different people on a regular basis. So when someone tells

---

*Lamott, A., *Bird by Bird: Some Instructions on Writing and Life*, Anchor Books, 1995.
**Rischler, L., "Seven Secrets to Good Brainstorming," *Fast Company*, March 2001.

us something interesting, it isn't long before we have shared the news with many others. When Mary Lynn had a party recently, approximately 25 people showed up. Most of them were her regular friends who she socializes with in separate groups. At one point, she looked around the room and thought, "My, what a diverse group of people. They would probably not have the opportunity to know each other if it weren't for me."

Another small group or, in some organizations, a single person, is described in the pattern Guru on Your Side(158). One of the fundamental influence principles is respect for authority. In times of uncertainty, we rely on trusted experts to help us decide among difficult alternatives. Once you have a guru on your side, many who might have been skeptics up to that point will at least show interest in the approach and will be more open to what you have to say.

Linda likes to call the guru "Fred." When Fred is on your side, others will listen. Here's how you can approach him. "Fred, I've just read an article about <Big Idea> and I know you have probably heard about it. What do you think? How would this work for us? I've been thinking I might have an information meeting to tell the team about it. Would you be willing to show up and add your input? Here are a couple of things I think would be good to share...." Always have a short, two-minute "elevator speech" in your back pocket for those times when you happen to run into a guru. Keep it low key. Be prepared to ask questions, and don't threaten him by overwhelming him with information. Keep your approach humble. Never make him (we keep saying "him," but of course the guru could be a "her") feel that you are trying to take over in some way. Power is always an issue! Your goal is to win Fred's support. In some organizations what Fred says can make or break you. If he shows up at your meeting and nods a couple of times, you're set.

Another important group to target for help is described in the pattern Innovator(170). The pattern tells us that a small percentage of the population likes new ideas and, therefore, is likely to take up the cause and eagerly do what they can to help you. Geoffrey Moore, author of *Crossing the Chasm*, observed that "Enthusiasts are like kindling: They start a fire." He describes the role played by Innovators in the introduction of Post-it notes. The inventor gave early prototypes of the sticky notes to the secretaries. Some of the secretaries tried them out to see how they could work and became enthusiasts. They were key in keeping the idea alive during the early use of Post-it notes.

It's Important to Say "Thanks!"

Never forget the help you get from Connectors, Gurus, Innovators, or anyone else who joins your team. The pattern Just Say Thanks(183) is unbelievably critical. We never forget how important this is. When we lead project retrospectives for organizations, we use "Offer Appreciations," one of the exercises from Norm Kerth's excellent book, *Project Retrospectives*. In the exercise, team members simply say to each other, "<Name of appreciated person>, I know you've spent the last three months working overtime and weekends to get this product out the door. I just want to say thanks for that. I appreciate your hard work." Then someone else will offer an appreciation. It gets going. It has a life of its own. It's wonderful to be in the middle of that. You don't need to wait until the end of a long delivery schedule; you can do it every day, and the difference it will make in your lives is hard to explain to anyone who hasn't seen it. It costs so little and the return is so great. Just say thanks!

Since we wrote this pattern, we've been making a real effort to thank people for everything and anything, and we've noticed something interesting—it's fun to thank people when they don't expect it. When people do something they consider quite ordinary or part of their job and you take time to thank them, they seem quite pleased. You'll find that you really enjoy that.

Here's a story about these patterns from one Evangelist:

> I was just like you. I was so excited by my new idea that I told everybody. I mean everybody. I believed that all I had to do was tell the reasonable folks who worked with me why my idea was a good one and they would just sign up. That's honestly what I believed. Well, I've learned along the way that it's not so easy. I got discouraged, but I kept on talking. Not just about my idea, but also about why I couldn't get others to see the benefits. I was following the "three-foot rule," you know, telling everyone within three feet of me about what I was trying to do! As we were gathering for a department meeting, I happened to sit next to one of the administrative assistants. She said, "Why don't you go see Greg or Paul? They've been with the company forever." Sure enough, I stopped by Greg's cubicle and he gave me a few minutes. He said, "Come to our team meeting and I'll introduce you." After that meeting I felt like Alice in Wonderland. Someone had opened a magic door and bingo! All of a sudden, people were asking about my new idea. They wanted me to come to their team meetings and then one department manager suggested I give a talk to his staff. Now that I know these patterns I can see that I was using **Ask for**

Help, Connector, Guru on Your Side, *and* Innovator. *And I always thanked everyone along the way. Powerful stuff, patterns!*

The patterns we outlined in this chapter, Ask for Help(104), Connector(119), Guru on Your Side(158), Innovator(170), and Just Say Thanks(183), will not require a lot of effort on your part, but they will get you off to a good start. In the next chapter you'll find other patterns that require a little more time, but which will pay off handsomely as you continue your journey.

CHAPTER FIVE

Meetings and More

One way to ask for help from Innovators, Connectors, gurus and other colleagues is to hold a meeting. Here are some effective meeting patterns that can be used in this phase of your work: Piggyback(201), Brown Bag(113), Do Food(132), The Right Time(207), Plant the Seeds(204), External Validation(148), Next Steps(195), Stay in Touch(221), e-Forum(135), and Group Identity(155).

We're all busy, and one of the worst time-wasters we face is meetings. But if a meeting or other event is optional and the purpose is just to tell people about your new idea, you can bring in attendees by using some of the patterns in our collection. First, the Piggyback(201) pattern recommends that you don't do any work you don't have to. Instead, give your presentation as part of a regularly scheduled activity. This way you avoid the effort of finding and reserving a room and advertising the meeting time. One company we visited held monthly Tech Forums where a multitude of technical topics were presented. This was a good place to introduce new ideas.

The Piggyback pattern is useful for other activities in addition to meetings. Taking advantage of an existing practice to bring your new idea in "the back door" is a good way to introduce change without disturbing the way things are normally done. As German author Jean Paul Richter advises, "Do not wait for extraordinary situations to do good; try to use ordinary situations."

Linda remembers when a small group was struggling to attract participants for a new conference. One of the planners had the idea of scheduling the fledgling event immediately after another conference, a big international gathering that would draw folks who might stay a couple of extra days to attend the newer conference and also be magnets for other potential attendees. This proved to be an effective way to get the new conference going, so that even now, several years after its inception, the small conference still piggybacks on the larger one.

Let's Meet!

If you do decide to schedule your own meeting, try the pattern Brown Bag(113) and have your gathering over lunchtime, when most people are free. Attendees bring their lunch and eat during the meeting. Here's a cut from an advertisement for a Brown Bag at one company that calls the gatherings "Lunch and Learn."

> "OK, so you've heard of food for thought, right? Well, how about Food AND Thought?"

This practice seems to extend across organizations and across cultures. Linda attended a seminar in Japan and during lunch bento boxes were delivered to a nearby conference room. This allowed the group to continue discussions over lunch.

The pattern Do Food(132) recommends using food because it is a powerful influencer. In her article "Seven Secrets to Good Brainstorming," Linda Rischler wisely observes, "Cookies always spur creativity." Research has shown that people are more favorably inclined to ideas that are presented while they are eating. Indeed, sharing food has long been associated with building friendship and community. In French, the word *compagnon* means "companion" or "people belonging to the same community of craftspeople." The Latin origin of the word means "sharing bread."

Mary Lynn tells the story of suggesting that a regular committee meeting be held over breakfast one week. It was amazing to watch the transformation in the members. They relaxed and even joked a bit. The work still got done that week, in an atmosphere that was much more pleasant than a sterile meeting room with no food.

A tradition at one company is the "Food Place." One department has its own kitchen, another its famous espresso room. One company we visited was built on acres of nature preserve and the inside was as beautiful as the outside. There were conversation nooks with coffee and tea bars—places to gather to get away from the office and enjoy a moment, contemplating nature and sipping a comforting beverage. It reminds the visitor of Christopher Alexander's pattern, Alcoves. You are immediately drawn to those places.

At this point in your effort you probably won't have resources, but if you use Do Food and, for example, buy cookies with your own money, you can enhance the influence principle and community building effects. It shows people that you believe the idea is important enough to invest your own time and money.

The Right Time(207) is another pattern to keep in mind. For example, there are always better times than hitting a team right before a deadline. Mary Lynn saw this when she worked in industry. She learned never to ask the software developers for anything in the last few months before they were due to release a product. Now in academia, she has observed that faculty members are more open to volunteering for a task or listening to a new idea in the beginning or at the end of a semester rather than in the middle when their workloads have heated up.

This simple recommendation can help you in the beginning when you are sensitive to the constraints of your target audience. As you venture forth into the larger organization it may not be possible to always consider timing, but certainly December in almost any organization is not a good choice. As the Cowboy's Guide to Life Web site* wisely notes, "Timing has a lot to do with the outcome of a rain dance."

At the end of every event, consider the pattern Next Steps(195). Give people something to hang on to. Wolf's Law of Meetings states, "The only important result of a meeting is agreement about next steps." In our training classes, we use the last 30 minutes to lead the attendees in brainstorming what they would like to do next in their organizations.

Using Information That's Out There

If you have some interesting books or interesting articles about your new idea, use the pattern Plant the Seeds(204) and bring these materials (seeds) to the meeting. Some of these seeds will take root; that is, they will be picked up, read, and spark the interest of some people. This comment by Winston Ledet, author of a chapter in Peter Senge's book, *The Fifth Discipline*, describes this phenomenon:

> I looked out my hotel window and noticed that the grass was littered with pinecones. Nature, I realized, doesn't put all its resources into one or two seedlings, and expect them to take root. It drops myriad seeds, like those pinecones, over as broad an area as possible. Most of them may die, but enough survive to generate a whole forest.**

We heard this story from one Evangelist:

> I remember bringing books about patterns to a project retrospective session. They generated curiosity and questions about patterns. Funny story: One of the participants picked up one of the collections of patterns during a break. When he put the book back on the table he told the others, "Hey, guys! You should check out this book—it has a great ending!"

---

*http://members.tripod .com/cavanaughc/a_cowboys_guide_to_life.htm
**Senge, P., *The Fifth Discipline*, Doubleday/Currency, 1990.

The pattern External Validation(148) is closely related to Plant the Seeds. When you begin to introduce the idea, there is little evidence for the validity of the new idea in the organization. So you must look for evidence from the outside. People will usually pay more attention to anything in writing, and will be more impressed if the external source has a good reputation. Successful entrepreneur and author Robert Sullivan writes, "How do you react when reading an advertisement versus an article? You are suspicious of the advertisement but reading about the same product or service in the body of an article gives it instant credibility. Clearly the author is an 'expert.'"

Mary Lynn tells this story of introducing patterns into one organization:

> When the book *Patterns in Java* hit the market, I showed it to many Java developers. It caused many of them to become interested in patterns and they started coming to me with their questions.

Stay Connected

As you collect a list of interested people, think of good ways to use the pattern Stay in Touch(221). Author and Buddhist monk Jack Kornfield reminds us that "When we get too caught up in the busyness of the world we lose connection with one another—and ourselves."

One way to stay in touch is to use the pattern e-Forum(135). Creating an electronic forum will allow you to communicate with a large group of people on a regular basis. But be careful with this over-used medium. As one Wall Street wag stated, "What do you mean we don't communicate? Just yesterday I faxed you a reply to the recorded message you left on my answering machine."

If there is sufficient interest, at an appropriate point use the pattern Group Identity(155). Assigning an identity to your change initiative helps people become aware that it exists and what it is trying to do. Baseball legend Casey Stengel quipped, "Finding good players is easy. Getting them to play as a team is another story." In our training sessions, participants form teams. We ask them to choose a name for themselves, because we've learned how this simple step gets them to work closer together. At the conclusion of the exercise, we ask the teams to tell us about their strategies. They always begin their brief summaries by saying, "We're <incredible team name>!" and this is usually accompanied by a rousing cheer.

A change agent at Hewlett Packard tells the following story:

> *I wanted to do something at the corporate level with a focused topic: thermal cooling in computers. I only knew six people who were interested but each of them knew another six, and so on. Ninety people showed up at the first meeting—the beginning of an annual thermal cooling conference. The "COOL TEAM" now meets weekly by phone, e-mail, and conference call. The technology developed out of this conversation delivers tens of millions of dollars to the bottom line, and, with regard to cooling, leaves our competitors behind.**

If you've been able to apply the patterns in this chapter, you've been busy! You've had a meeting using the pattern Piggyback(201) or Brown Bag(113). Perhaps you were able to Do Food(132) and you scheduled the meeting at The Right Time(207). You brought some interesting books or articles, hoping to Plant the Seeds(204) and point to External Validation(148) for your new idea. You talked about the Next Steps(195) for your fledgling effort and maybe you used e-Forum(135) to help Stay in Touch(221) with people who are getting interested in your work. If you were really lucky, your collection of like-minded folks has started to form a Group Identity(155). If you have more time and want to see your change effort really take off, have a look at the patterns in the next chapter.

---

*Waugh, B., and M.S. Forrest, *Soul in the Computer*, Inner Ocean, 2001.

CHAPTER SIX

Take Action!

You've started to grow a community and now you're ready for action.
Just Do It(177), Study Group(228), and Mentor(192) are the patterns
we offer for your next bold step.

Linda recently received an e-mail from an old friend. He knows that she's written three books and has another in progress. He's thinking about writing one so he asked her advice. They exchanged some e-mails. He asked about the format for the proposal **and** whether he should have most of the book written before he contacted the publisher **and** if his idea was too broad or whether he should focus on just one part of it **and**.... Finally Linda said, "Brad, I've got a great pattern that you might think about applying at this point in your writing adventure. It's called Just Do It(177)."

We can understand why Brad wanted to consider every detail before he started his book. In his profession, product development, this condition is often the death knell for complex projects. It's called "analysis paralysis." Engineering types tend to wallow in details. They need to plan strategies to anticipate every problem before it occurs and (here comes the killer) strive for perfection. Someone once explained the difference between perfection and excellence (because it's easy to get them confused). People striving for perfection try to make things "perfect," that is, without errors. On the other hand, people striving for excellence know that it's impossible to avoid mistakes.

Thomas Edison understood this. He said, "The secret is not the 71 times you fail, but to persevere to the 72nd time, in which you succeed." Gandhi observed, "Only a fool expects perfection. A wise man seeks learning." So what should you do to learn? Our answer is in the pattern Just Do It. Take a step on the path to your goal. As Goethe observed, "Whatever you can do, or dream you can, begin it. Boldness has genius, power, and magic in it." Just do it!

This is especially true now during the current chaotic upheaval of change and transition we are all experiencing. If you're interested in innovation and taking on the role of a change agent, you will likely make more headway pursuing excellence than perfection. So, the best advice for Brad, the writer, and for you, someone interested in introducing new ideas into your organization, is—just do it. You don't have to do it all at once, just take Goethe's advice and begin it. Remember that package of patterns we introduced in Chapter 3? Just stick a toe in the water—use the pattern Test the Waters(237). Once you begin, take time to learn from your experience—use the pattern Time for Reflection(240), and then use the pattern Step by Step(224) to reach your goal of excellence. The result will be better than if you had tried to plan everything up front because you will be learning and improving as you go.

Anne Lamott is talking to writers in her book *Bird by Bird*, but the advice applies to anyone starting any kind of journey:

> You get your confidence and intuition back by trusting yourself, by being militantly on your own side. You need to trust yourself, especially on a first draft, where amid the anxiety and self-doubt, there should be a real sense of your imagination and your memories walking and wool-gathering, tramping the hills, romping all over the place. Trust them. Don't look at your feet to see if you are doing it right. Just dance.*

The best way to take action is in your own work. You may not be an expert in the innovation (there probably are few experts!). When something is just getting off the ground there are lots of opportunities to experiment. Trying out the new approach for yourself will give you a chance to see the costs and benefits. When you have some experience, you can do a better job of convincing others that there are real gains to using your new idea.

E. M. Rogers, author of *Diffusion of Innovations*, has written that lack of experience is easy for resistors to attack while positive experience is more difficult to refute. In addition, an understanding of the innovation's limitations helps you avoid overselling and provides insight into approaches that will work.

One change agent asked, "How do I sell my executive team on doing this stuff?" The answer from internationally known consultant, Jim Highsmith, "Don't. Just do it. They don't know what you're doing anyway."

Other Ways to Learn

Eric Hoffer, American social philosopher and winner of the Presidential Medal of Freedom, said, "In a time of drastic change it is the learners who inherit the future. The learned usually find themselves equipped to live in a world that no longer exists." Yet a change agent can get caught in a Catch-22: You don't know enough to do much, but until you do something how can you learn? One way out of this vicious cycle is to find a small group of like-minded folks who are

---

*Lamott, A., *Bird by Bird: Some Instructions on Writing and Life*, Anchor Books, 1995.

willing to help you use the pattern Study Group(228). As psychologist Carl Rogers has observed, "The only kind of learning which significantly influences behavior is self-discovered or self-appropriated learning—truth that has been assimilated in experience." This is especially true for adult learners.

Study groups have been used to support adult learning in Sweden for over a hundred years. The practice began with the establishment of the first folk high schools and "study circles" to provide education for the children of farm families who often could not attend school because they were needed to work on the farms.

Study groups are interesting learning models because no expert is present. Each member of the group takes turns leading a session and preparing a "lesson." When eight people read a section or a chapter, it's astounding to see the eight different interpretations that show up at each meeting. Even more astounding is how much you learn from hearing the different views of your colleagues. It's bootstrapping at its best!

Spreading out the learning over several weeks means that participants have time to digest the ideas. We once heard someone compare week-long training sessions to "trying to drink from a fire hose." In contrast, a study group takes a small bite each week and rotates the role of leader. This offers a slower pace for the learning, which means that there's time for insight and deeper understanding to develop.

We've known many organizations that sponsor study groups. The company buys the books and, in some cases, also buys lunch for the participants. Mary Lynn's organization offers a small stipend to group participants as a way to show that their time is valued. Even with these expenses, study groups are more cost effective than in-house or offsite training of any kind.

While you are learning, you can begin to help others using the Mentor(192) pattern. When teams are just beginning to apply an innovation, it can be invaluable to have someone around that knows more than they do, even if it is only a little more. Mentoring will make it more likely that the team's experiment with the innovation will be successful and less frustrating along the way. This is important because the early experiences people have will be a strong influence on their decision to continue using it. And, of course, the benefit for you is that no one learns as much as the mentor, especially in the early days.

Fellow Evangelist Steven Newton shows how he "just did it" and was then able to offer mentoring in his experience as a change agent leading the introduction of JUnit, a new method of unit testing in developing software.

I thought our software development team should do more unit testing and, to do this, we had to start using testing tools. I was playing the role of **Evangelist** *but I wasn't an expert on testing. So I played with the tools and was then able to talk with the team leader and give a presentation to the group about the tools. Everyone thought it was a good idea. We decided that rather than have the team lead mandate it, we would just start using the tools. This would allow us to learn more and would show us whether or not the tools were worthwhile.*

Teams started asking me for mentoring and demonstrations because they recognized the quality of my work. When I was consulting with teams on specific projects, I would give one-on-one assistance, especially to those new to unit testing. When they asked for details and help with their issues, I used that as a "teaching moment" and brought up the topic of unit testing. The following is a common scenario.

Co-worker: *I can't figure out how to fix this bug.*
Steven: *Have you written a unit test to isolate the error?*
Co-worker: *How do I do that?*
Steven: *Let me show you JUnit....*

In addition to the action-oriented patterns we've introduced in this chapter—Just Do It(177), Mentor(192), and Study Group(228)—you'll need some influence strategies. The next chapter provides some patterns to help you with that.

CHAPTER SEVEN

It's All About People

Throughout the change process, yes, every step of the way, you're going to be interacting with people, and that means communication. People want to know what's in it for them. The pattern Personal Touch(198) will help you interact with individuals. The pattern Tailor Made(234) targets organizations. You will also need the pattern Shoulder to Cry On(213) since your interactions can be hard at times!

L inda directs a recorder consort. The recorder is the precursor of the modern-day flute, but that has nothing to do with the success of this group of five people. They have been making music together for over seven years, and they're still going and still friends. Linda feels that things work well for them because early on she sensed that each member of the consort had different expectations. None of this was explicit, but here's how she followed up on her intuition.

Karen is the virtuoso of the group. She studied flute and easily picked up the recorder. She likes challenge and has the best tone of all the players. Linda always tries to give Karen the more difficult parts and feature her if a solo is required. Rick can sing and prefers the guitar, but he also plays recorder. He likes "jamming" and has an excellent ear. He's not as interested in difficult recorder parts and, in fact, often resists if the piece is too much for him. Karen, on the other hand, relishes tackling parts like that!

Anne and Karl are pretty good. They like a certain amount of challenge, but not too much. They are both fair musicians. They can both sing and Anne can play keyboard. They're flexible and don't mind playing supporting roles for Karen's solos. They're solid. Linda is bossy! She likes to organize and plan and also likes the recorder, keyboard, and singing. She has found a group of people who, within limits, allow her to lead and work well together. She uses a personal touch to make sure each player gets as much satisfaction from the group as possible. Her reward is the incredible sound the group makes, which gets better and better over time.

When you use the pattern Personal Touch(198), you help each individual understand how the innovation can be useful in his own environment to solve his problems. As consultants, we use this pattern to first understand where the frustrations lie and then find ways to help ease those frustrations. When first encountering any innovation, people tend to think about what it can do for them. In one company, someone said that she would adopt the new approach if it would "help me do my work faster, cheaper, easier because that is something that will be of value to me."

We have both served on program committees for conferences where our job was to encourage quality submissions. To do this, we personally contacted key individuals to ask them what they wanted to accomplish, for example, write a book or paper, form a user group, bring in potential graduate students, or expand their research network. We would work with them to show how the conference could help achieve their goals.

Part of the message in this pattern is that it's important to listen to what individuals are saying when they hear about your new idea. It takes effort, but you can get better over time at hearing and understanding what people need. Ask questions if they seem reluctant. They won't become supporters unless they understand how your proposal can be useful to them in solving their personal struggles.

What's in it for the Organization?

The pattern Tailor Made(234) addresses the same concern as Personal Touch but at a different level. Your message is more powerful when it has meaning for those who want to see how the innovation can meet the business needs of the organization. Lee Iacocca reflected, "It's important to talk to people in their own language. If you do it well, they'll say, 'God, he said exactly what I was thinking.' And when they begin to respect you, they'll follow you to the death. The reason they're following you is not because you're providing some mysterious leadership. It's because you're following them."

It's important to select the right information and develop an effective format for a specific audience. You're not just a mover of data. Instead, you should mold the message in your preparation and in your delivery. You must target each audience carefully to persuade listeners.

The following is one of Stephen Covey's memorable stories in *The 7 Habits of Highly Effective People*:

> "To make an effective presentation, you've got to empathize with the listener. You've got to get into his frame of mind. You've got to make your point simply and visually and describe what he is in favor of better than he can himself." After hearing this, one change agent started by saying, "Let me see if I understand what your objectives and your concerns are about this presentation and my recommendation." He did it slowly, gradually, demonstrating his depth of understanding and respect for their point of view. In the middle of his presentation, one senior manager turned to another, nodded, turned back to the presenter and said, "You've got your money."*

---

*Covey, S.R., *The 7 Habits of Highly Effective People*, Simon & Schuster, 1989.

When Linda started talking about a new idea in her organization, she knew that her managers and executives would ask about the stance of the parent company, since her organization was a subsidiary of a large, powerful corporation. She did her homework and found that her idea was already being used in several areas of the parent company's product development. She featured this information in her initial presentation and could sense that it had considerable impact on the support she received.

Of course, we would argue that you need both the Personal Touch and the Tailor Made patterns. They work together. As you focus on larger issues, for example, improved performance of your team or increased profit for the company, remember how important it is to consider the personal needs of individuals.

Each of us has come to a crossroad—one path leading to what's best for the company and another separate path leading to what's best for us. Someone once said, "All interest is self-interest." That's not a bad thing. Effective change agents know how to bring both interests together to work toward meaningful change at all levels.

You Have Feelings, Too!

Even with all the patterns we have been describing, your journey is not going to be an easy one. You will have successes, but you will also have difficult times. It's always easier to face struggles if you can find others who are trying to do the same thing in their organizations. We offer the pattern Shoulder to Cry On(213) because we believe in what baseball Hall of Famer Satchel Paige asserted, "Never let your head hang down. Never give up and sit down and grieve. Find another way."

Sometimes "another way" can't be discovered on your own. You may find that other like-minded individuals can help, not only to listen but also to help thrash out possible solutions to your problems.

Linda founded her own local support group. It was comprised of others throughout Phoenix who were interested in her new idea. Some of them were trying to introduce the idea to their organizations, but others were just Innovators who wanted to learn more. They met once a month and Linda looked forward to reporting in and sharing stories of successes and setbacks. She also used an online listserve to reach similar kinds of folks. The wonderful thing about an online group is that someone is always there regardless of the time of day you decide to log in!

Mary Lynn learned the power of the patterns introduced in this chapter when she joined a research unit of a large telecommunications company for seven months. She was hired to build a knowledge management database of patterns that would capture the organization's best practices in software development. To really make the patterns repository work, though, she knew that she had to make patterns a part of how developers did their work and, to do that, she had to convince them that patterns would help them do their jobs better.

> *I was already enthusiastic about patterns and had lots of friends in the patterns community who had experience bringing patterns into their organizations. I relied on them and actively sought their advice and counsel as I started to work in my organization. I wasn't always sure whether I was doing the right thing. If it hadn't been for an electronic discussion list, I would have had a harder time. The people on that patterns listserve were supportive and helpful. They always had good suggestions and provided an ear when I needed it.*
>
> *As I targeted the guys in the trenches, that is, everyone and anyone who would listen, I tried to frame my pitch to match their struggles. This wasn't always easy, since I was the "new kid on the block." I took every opportunity to chat with people during lunch or breaks. I also attended as many project meetings as possible to hear what was going on inside the development teams. This allowed me to talk about how patterns could be useful to the individuals, the teams, and to the organization.*

Even with the powerful patterns in this chapter—Personal Touch(198), Tailor Made(234) and Shoulder to Cry On(213)—you won't get far as a volunteer. To have real impact, the change effort must become part of your job. We'll explore how you can make that happen and how you begin to take on that role as we introduce the patterns in the next chapter.

CHAPTER EIGHT

A New Role:
Now You're Dedicated!

The good news is, you are making some progress in the change effort. The bad news is, you still have to get all your other work done! The patterns in this chapter will help as you move to take the next big step—making the change effort part of your job. The patterns are Dedicated Champion(129), Local Sponsor(186), Corporate Angel(123), Early Adopter(138), and Early Majority(141).

Each Evangelist makes his or her own way through this pattern language. For a host of reasons, it may be that the patterns we have described so far will be all that you have a chance to apply. This is not necessarily a bad thing. Many times you can have limited success by just spreading the word about something new to a few innovative colleagues and giving a couple of presentations to others in your organizations. After that, the idea may be adopted to a certain extent and then your attention is drawn elsewhere. But if you'd like to take the new idea further and make it a part of your job, read on.

The patterns we describe in this chapter require resources and commitment from management. To make real headway, you will have to be able to apply the pattern Dedicated Champion(129), that is, the change initiative must become part of your job description. The "dedication" we are talking about involves two things. The first is the passion for the innovation—you still have to keep the enthusiasm articulated in the Evangelist pattern. The second, newer component, essential for real impact, is the support of the organization for you to continue your work. The recognition that the change initiative is deserving of this attention will probably come from your boss. We describe this role in the pattern Local Sponsor(186).

When we give presentations and tutorials about this material, the most frequently asked question is, "How can I convince my manager to let me become a Dedicated Champion?" The answer, of course, is patterns! Start by devoting your own time as an Evangelist. To become convinced that the new idea has value for your organization, use the other patterns described in Chapter 3: Test the Waters, Time for Reflection, Small Successes, and Step by Step. Begin to accumulate data. Determine, as best you can, how many people are using the new approach and capture the results they are seeing. Document the testimonials, especially if you use the pattern Guru on Your Side (introduced in Chapter 4). Count the number of people who show up when you use the pattern Brown Bag (introduced in Chapter 5), who sign up when you use the pattern Study Group (introduced in Chapter 6), and who are on your list when you use the pattern e-Forum (introduced in Chapter 5). Track the people who ask for copies of articles or books when you use Plant the Seeds or External Validation (both introduced in Chapter 5).

Scour the publications your management favors to find references that will be meaningful. Trade publications that feature your competitors are also powerful persuaders. Use Tailor Made (introduced in Chapter 7) and speak the language your managers understand.

At some point you will also need the pattern Corporate Angel(123), so look for opportunities to capture the interest of a high-level executive, who can ensure that your work is aligned with business needs. This is the role described by popular speaker and author Lew Losoncy:"The most vital task of the leader is to motivate, inspire, empower and encourage the team's primary resource—the unlimited, creative human potential to find better ways."

Once you have enlisted the support of management at any level, don't forget them and don't let them forget you. Remember the pattern Stay in Touch (introduced in Chapter 5). David Baum describes the importance of this in his entertaining book on change, *Lightning in a Bottle*.

> *Let's briefly examine the issue of communication. What's needed can be summed up in one word—more! Communication is usually underexecuted by a factor of ten. Finding proactive ways to keep information flowing is essential. The last thing you want is for your [management] to feel embarrassed because they lack information. It doesn't take long for embarrassment to turn to frustration and frustration to anger. Your attempts to keep a communication link with your [management] will pay off handsomely in the end.**

You Have Convinced Them!—You Are a Dedicated Champion

When the three patterns Dedicated Champion, Local Sponsor, and Corporate Angel are in place, you should have the time to reach the wider community and not just the Innovators. You must capture the support of those described in the patterns Early Adopters(138) and Early Majority(141), because as Geoffrey Moore writes in *Crossing the Chasm*, "The real news is the deep and dividing chasm that separates the Early Adopters from the Early Majority. This is by far the most formidable and unforgiving transition in the Technology Adoption Life Cycle, and it is all the more dangerous because it typically goes unrecognized."

---

*Baum, D., *Lightning in a Bottle: Proven Lessons for Leading Change*, Dearborn, 2000.

It will take more work to attract Early Adopters and those in the Early Majority. The Innovators "come for free" because they like new ideas. Early Adopters need to be convinced that the idea is useful to the organization, while those in the Early Majority need to see that others have been successful before they are influenced to try the innovation.

From David Baum's *Lightning in a Bottle* again:

> If your change process is like most, about 15% of your folks are going to be thrilled and will only want to know what took you so long. About 15% will utterly reject the need to change, and won't be happy no matter what you do. The remaining 70% will sit on the fence and quietly watch to see who's winning.
>
> This middle 70% is where you need to put most of your time and energy. That is where the victories really count. The 15% who are positively excited will need very little support and encouragement. They are already motivated by the change. For the negative 15%, there may be nothing you can do.*

Linda worked at AG Communication Systems for five years. It was from her experience that many of the patterns were initially created. At the time Linda was applying them, she didn't even know they were patterns!

> I was just back from a conference and I had been talking about some new ideas I had picked up. I was surprised when my boss asked me to give a presentation to our vice-president at his next staff meeting. I thought this was a chance to tell our management about a good idea. I had no grand plans for spreading the word about my ideas or anything more than conveying development information. To my surprise, the executive team was very enthusiastic about patterns and could clearly see the long-term benefit to the company of sharing good design solutions and other aspects of the telecommunications business. They were obviously more farsighted than I was. That was the beginning of a new adventure for me. I was moved to a new department with a very supportive manager and the corporate world suddenly opened up. I saw firsthand what high-level sponsorship and management can do.
>
> The downside was that instead of using my spare time and giving a couple of Brown Bags to interested Innovators, I had to show benefit to the more pragmatic developers in our company. People began stopping by and asking for infor-

---

*Baum, D., *Lightning in a Bottle: Proven Lessons for Leading Change*, Dearborn, 2000.

mation. I was called upon to give more presentations and mentoring to groups who wanted to try the new technology. My manager followed my work pretty closely at first and I had the feeling that he was checking things off to report to his boss. Things went well, but it was a change from the old Evangelist *mode to more serious business.*

Even if you're successful in becoming a Dedicated Champion, you still need to convince people to try the new idea. The patterns in the next chapter will help you do that. They require more time and effort on your part, but you can tackle these because the change initiative is now part of your job.

CHAPTER NINE

Convince the Masses

We know our organizations must be agile enough to make changes when necessary. But we also know that's easier said than done. In this chapter we present the patterns Trial Run(245), Guru Review(161), Big Jolt(107), and Royal Audience(210), which you can use to convince others that change is good.

A friend called Linda the other day. He's one of those unfortunates who has inherited a tendency for high cholesterol and he knew that she had had some luck lowering her cholesterol with diet. "But I can't imagine life without bananas and potatoes!" he wailed.

Linda assured him that many of the tenets proposed by diet gurus were not based on rocket science. Some popular rationales like the values in the glycemic index were the result of limited observation and there was precious little science to back up the claims of the diet hawkers.

"Think of this as an experiment," she suggested. "Try making a few changes and see what happens. Everyone is unique. Everyone has a different approach to eating and exercise. Try a few things and find out what works for you."

Her friend calmed down. Linda offered, "After you try some things for awhile, then see your doctor for another test, say six months from now. When you get the results, you'll know more about what works for you and you can decide what the next steps will be."

He was much happier than when they had started their conversation. "Okay! Maybe I don't need a banana every day; I'll try it out. I'll let you know how things go."

"Great!" she said, "Stay in touch."

After their phone conversation, Linda remarked to herself that it was amazing how little it had taken on her part to move her friend from panic and resistance to a calmer, more accepting state. What she had applied was an influence strategy that has been captured in our pattern Trial Run(245). Why is it such a valuable technique? Because most of the time, for most of us, change is difficult. It's especially difficult when our jobs are threatened, as in these tough economic times. It's really, really difficult when it means giving up something that is a highlight in our day, that special dessert, for instance. Even when we rationally know that improving our skills or watching our diet is good and good for us, we often resist making changes.

The magic is in seeing the change as "temporary." Suddenly, the new approach becomes a smaller threat. We are less resistant and more open when we think of the change as an experiment, just something we're going to try on for size.

The Trial Run pattern can help you keep your sanity and your patience when you're facing an endless stream of objections to the new idea. Instead of trying to address each and every concern, suggest that the critics try out the new idea for a limited time. You know, just like a test drive—if you don't like it you can bring it back, no questions asked, no problem. This makes even skeptics more open to the new approach because they know they're just taking it for a spin without a long-term commitment.

To make the technique even more powerful, throw in an unexpected or unusual twist. This enhances the influence strategy and lowers resistance. In a recent experiment, students posing as beggars found that they received a small amount of money 44% of the time when they just asked for cash. When they asked for a precise sum that was a single coin (25 cents), they got it 64% of the time. But when they asked for an apparently arbitrary number (37 cents) they got it 75% of the time. The more unusual the request, the more likely it was to be satisfied.

So when you suggest a Trial Run of a new idea, you might give a specific and unexpected spin on the "let's try it" approach. For instance, you might say, "Let's try it for the next two quarters and then see how things are going." The brain loves to whirl around on complex instructions like "the next two quarters." Vocal skeptics start churning possibilities in their minds while plans are being made for the experiment. It keeps them from presenting major objections and gives you a chance to get things off the ground.

Getting people to change can be difficult. It's usually easy, however, to get them to try an experiment. We have seen so many resistors turn around when the innovation is proposed as a Trial Run. They feel the risk is much lower because they don't have to commit to anything. If they're not happy, they can return to the old ways. No one is trying to push something on them; they're just taking it for a "test drive."

Enlist Gurus and Famous People

Sometimes resistors want data. To show that your idea has benefit for the organization, you can ask some respected individuals or gurus to evaluate it. This is the Guru Review(161) pattern. Mary Lynn remembers how effective this was when one administrator wanted to make significant changes in the academic organizational structure. He formed a task force of five representatives from the faculty senate who reviewed his proposal and made suggestions. After this body of professors gave their approval, it was much easier for the administrator to sell the changes to the rest of the faculty senate.

There are many ways to gather the gurus. For example, you can ask impacted managers to submit names of influential people in their areas. Keep the review period to a minimum, but be sure to allow enough time for a satisfactory evaluation. If things go your way, it will make your journey easier. It's an important stamp of approval that you can always carry with you.

When you have resources, you can apply the Big Jolt(107) pattern and bring in an outside speaker. This allows you to take advantage of the considerable influence of well-known people. As Marlon Brando once noted, "The power and influence of a movie star is curious. I didn't ask for it or take it; people gave it to me. Simply because you're a movie star, people empower you with special rights and privileges."

Big Jolt does not suggest that you bring in a movie star! You just need to look for someone who will capture the attention of the people you want to influence in your organization. We have seen interest and inquiries increase significantly after a visit by a well-known person who supports a new idea. It seems obvious, but be aware that the same credentials will not impress everyone. Different visitors may be needed to influence the different target audiences: technical people, business people, managers, and executives.

When you combine a Big Jolt visit with the pattern Royal Audience(210), you provide the opportunity for people to personally interact with the famous visitor. This allows you to thank some of your supporters as well as influence newcomers. A prominent visitor who is willing to meet with team leaders, managers, and executives can help win support for decision makers at all levels.

We heard a little of Linda's story in the previous chapter. When she became a Dedicated Champion her responsibilities changed, but she also acquired resources and management support. Here's what happened next.

I got a request from the vice president. He was still excited about patterns, but his staff wanted a little more evidence. Each of his executives had named a department member to be on an evaluation team for the new idea. They wanted me to give a short course in the material and outline some ideas about how it would apply to our business. I was happy, but a little afraid to get up in front of that gathering of gurus. As it turned out, they were open and listened to what I had to say. I suggested that some of them just try a few patterns and see how they worked.

About this time I was lucky enough to run into a fellow at Bell Labs who offered to visit and give a talk about what his department was doing with patterns. Since my company was a partially owned subsidiary of Lucent, that talk had considerable impact on the gurus, the management, and everyone else. What really helped was having the Bell Labs guy hang around after the talk and have lunch with some interested folks and, later, a bunch of us went out for dinner. The results of the evaluation went well. I'd like to think it was my presentation, but I think it was really the guy from Bell Labs!

You're on a roll now! If you've been enlisting the help of gurus and inviting famous Big Jolt speakers, your change effort has really taken off. The next chapter presents a handful of patterns that document influence strategies. Again, they require some effort. Because you're now a Dedicated Champion, remember to keep your initial enthusiasm and concern for the benefits to individuals and your organization as you apply these patterns.

CHAPTER TEN

More Influence Strategies

Even though you now have resources, your enthusiasm will still be tested daily. So you will need to continually expand your bag of influence strategies. In this chapter we introduce Hometown Story(164), Smell of Success(219), Just Enough(180), In Your Space(167), Token(243), and Location, Location, Location(189) to add to your toolbox.

A wise observer once said, "People will always do what you want them to do if what you want them to do is what they want to do." But if you are proposing something that people aren't eager to do, the act of convincing may mean you must present a logical argument with cold hard facts. Unfortunately, research has shown that most of us make decisions based on emotion and then justify those decisions with facts. Your effectiveness as a change agent will rest on more than your ability to talk to people, whether you're doing that one-on-one using the pattern Personal Touch(198) or in front of a group using the pattern Brown Bag(113). You'll also need to learn as much as you can from the successes of others.

Leonardo da Vinci cautioned, "Flee the advice of these speculators whose reasons have not been confirmed by experience." Everyone likes to hear stories of risk-taking and will take them to heart if they respect the teller. This is especially true for people who are in the Early Majority(141). When they hear what others are trying, they think to themselves, "This is what some people are paying attention to; maybe we should, too!"

In Chapter 9, you learned how to convince teams to do a Trial Run(245) so you might have some Early Adopters(138) who have tried the innovation. Take advantage of their experience and use the Hometown Story(164) pattern. Ask people to share their story in an informal forum where they can just talk about their experience and then interact in a question and answer session.

We have seen amazing things happen at these sessions. Some people who have been holding back will suddenly perk up because they see that their colleagues have tried the new idea, survived, and found real benefit in it. As the saying goes, "Nothing succeeds like success."

The Smell of Success(219) pattern recognizes that people will be drawn to the innovation when they hear about positive results. Thus there will be an increasing number of people who will have questions and requests for more information. Most of us have seen those movies about someone who has a good idea but is not having much luck convincing others. The innovator may even be seen as crazy in the beginning. But then the plot takes a turn, the new idea solves a big problem—maybe the whole town or the company is saved—and things start to look up. Skeptics are suddenly interested and new supporters step forward.

Okay, your experiences are not likely to be as dramatic, but even when small successes appear, people will take notice. They will want to find out what's going on and become a part of it. The pattern Smell of Success advises you to treat their inquiries as a "teaching moment." You can apply the pattern Personal Touch(198) to help them understand how the new idea can be useful for them.

The other pattern to keep in mind during these encounters is Just Enough(180). You're not talking to Innovators or Early Adopters at this point. The new arrivals are typically members of the Early Majority. They are a bit more reluctant. They're not resistant, just hesitant, and there's probably a good reason for that. Maybe they've been burned in the past. Maybe they're just too busy to follow every promise of another so-called silver bullet.

As the Dedicated Champion, your job is to tell them what they need to know when they need to know it; no more, no less. Don't browbeat or overwhelm them. Encourage and support them. As Hall of Fame basketball coach Morgan Wootten has said, "A lighthouse doesn't blow a horn, it shines a light." Do the same for all those struggling to understand the new idea. Give them just enough information and let them know you'll be around when they're ready for more.

Keep Things Visible

When people are asking questions and things are happening, it's a good idea to keep the work-in-progress visible using the pattern In Your Space(167). Making sure the new idea is seen throughout your organization will have a positive impact on the rate at which people adopt it. There are many ways to do this. Mary Lynn posted a small sign on her workstation that said "Ask me about patterns." That prompted quite a few questions! She also put a whiteboard in a high traffic area and displayed the "Pattern of the Week." The space was an active one because it included some room for anyone to record comments and questions. One week they played "Pattern Jeopardy" on the board. The postings drew attention to the patterns effort and stimulated conversation as people passed by.

The popular book *Fish!* describes the best practices of the successful Pike Place Fish Market in Seattle. The importance of play in the workplace is emphasized as a core value. The book tells a story about a company that tried to bring more playfulness into the workplace by starting a "Joke-of-the-month" contest on its own bulletin board.

Another Evangelist who devised a new process for prioritizing work in the company used a corkboard to display cards with major tasks. The board was placed in a central location so that anyone in the office could see the plan at any time. It was portable so it could be carried to a weekly team meeting.

You can also use electronic media. In one company we visited, an electronic newsletter was sent out several times a week with timely notices. Important activities pertaining to the latest and greatest were always advertised and any related publications described. This kept the news of innovative approaches in front of everyone, especially management.

It's Just a Token

Another way to keep something alive in people's minds is to use the Token(243) pattern. This simple influence strategy suggests that you hand out something for the participants to take with them when they attend an event related to the new idea. You can do this without much effort, because even small trinkets make events more memorable. For example, we're all familiar with the distribution of certificates at the end of a course, but people may be more likely to keep something that is just a bit more creative and usual.

Mary Lynn has participated in countless sessions at a variety of conferences. Yet she still remembers a particular workshop in 2000 because she came away with a small stuffed animal that she keeps on her desk. Most people have one or two, or even more, of those simple things displayed in their homes or offices. Despite the fact that the tokens are usually small and inexpensive, and sometimes silly, they still remind us of some special event, and that is what matters.

Location Also Counts

As you schedule meetings related to the innovation, consider the important pattern Location, Location, Location(189). What's true for real estate is also true for events. Linda facilitates retrospectives. One company she visited held a two-day retrospective at a local country club. The facility was beautiful and the snacks and lunch were just right. She kept thinking during the entire experience, "The company really cares about this and the people seem to feel that. They don't seem as frazzled as some teams do at the end of a project." We are all impacted by our surroundings. Christopher Alexander's patterns began because he was concerned about what he called the "quality without a name" that he feels is disappearing from our lives. This quality is something we sense, sometimes without knowing it, but it is a powerful influencer on how happy we are with our work and other aspects of our lives, including new ideas.

Mary Lynn's department holds its yearly retreats away from their usual place of business. It's a nice site, but nothing special. The important thing is that it keeps the department members focused on learning, brainstorming ideas, and planning for the future rather than on all the work that is sitting on their desks back at the office.

Even in these days of corporate belt-tightening, teams can find creative ways to make the location special. A member of one team we knew lived across the street from the company. Since the company was in Phoenix, this fellow, like many Phoenix residents, had a pool in his back yard. It was common for the team to adjourn across the street and sit around the pool on late Friday afternoons for status meetings. As a result, the Friday afternoons were more productive because the team members took an hour away in a place that was more relaxing and less stress provoking than the four walls of a corporate meeting room.

Things Are Humming

Your experience with the patterns in this chapter may be similar to John's, a colleague who shared his story with us:

It took awhile to get to this point, but finally a few colleagues who had tried out the innovation agreed to share their experiences. So I scheduled a room, bought a few bagels, and arranged the chairs in a circle to encourage informal conversation. It was a pleasant surprise to see that some of the attendees were people who had been quite skeptical, but they asked a lot of questions and seemed to come away with a more positive attitude. A few weeks later, I scheduled a similar session led by another person who had seen some possibilities during a trial run. I gave everyone who attended one of these talks a hand-made star inscribed, "Reach for the stars."
It was interesting to see how my work changed after these two events. Rather than constantly seeking out people who might be convinced, I spent more time with people who contacted me. At first I eagerly told them everything I knew. I soon realized that I was overwhelming these more cautious latecomers, so I just answered their immediate concerns and reminded them that I was available if they had more questions.

One of the ways I kept them involved was to transform a rarely used bulletin board into a space to publicize the latest happenings. There was a place for scribbling comments and questions, so the board was alive with discussion and replies to the questions. After a few months, we got permission to hold a planning session in a popular hotel restaurant. In this time of tight budgets, each of us paid for our own lunch, but it was still nice to spend the time in a comfortable surrounding away from the office.

Now that you've applied nearly all our patterns, it would be easy to rest on your laurels and think that everything is fine without your interference. What we've seen, however, is the importance of the two patterns we've saved for last (well, almost last). In the next chapter, you'll realize that you still need to expend energy and resources to keep it going.

CHAPTER ELEVEN

Keep It Going

You're becoming a successful change agent. Many people are using the innovation, and even those who aren't are talking about it. The patterns in this chapter—Involve Everyone(173) and Sustained Momentum(231)—remind you that it's important to keep it going.

To continue your successful journey, you must share your good idea with as many members of your organization as possible. Use the pattern Involve Everyone(173) to bring in even those who might not have been a part of your original target population. Martin Luther King, Jr. observed that "Everybody can be great…because anybody can serve." When everyone is involved it's surprising how much commonality there is and how much everyone understands the problems outside their own domains. Legendary UCLA basketball coach John Wooden commented, "It's amazing what gets accomplished when no one cares who gets the credit." And, of course, when you have involvement, you also get buy-in. Increasing support from as many people as possible means spreading the responsibility and the ownership of the innovation.

The manager of the shipping department of one company realized the power of this pattern when he brought all of his hourly employees together. He described his performance goal and asked for any improvement ideas. The number of suggestions that were contributed overwhelmed him. Obviously, these were ideas the workers had thought of long before but had kept to themselves. Commenting on the meeting later, the manager said, "I'm sure those people went home that night and told their families that they had been asked their opinion for the first time." You can get a lot of movement in the right direction and valuable suggestions for improving your business when you involve everyone.

In her book *Soul in the Computer*, Barbara Waugh suggests that you "Ask people everywhere what they see. In the aggregate, people have a better picture of the system than any expert inside or outside the organization can provide." She learned this lesson in 1993, when Joel Birnbaum, senior vice president of research and development for Hewlett-Packard, inquired, "Why does no one out there consider HP Labs the best industrial research lab in the world?" Waugh was directed to hire a consultant to find the answer. She was unhappy with the answers from initial contacts with several firms and returned with the suggestion, "Why don't we just ask HP employees?" They decided to add the following four questions to the annual employee survey.

+ What would it take to become world's best?
+ Why aren't we?
+ Is what you are working on world class? If not, why not?
+ What do you need to be your best?

Instead of declaring a vision, as many leaders do, this course of action invited the collaboration of every employee as an equal voice. The result was an organization-wide vision.

In the very beginning, when you took on the role of an Evangelist and contributed your free time to the change effort, you couldn't really work to Involve

Everyone. You were focused on your own team or on the small group of Innovators and Early Adopters who attended your Brown Bag seminars. It takes time and energy to reach out to those in the wider organization, and an interest on your part in the work of the entire company, not just your small part of it. Involve Everyone is an important pattern, but because of the effort required, we don't mention it until the end game. It's a pattern that ideally should be applied from the start, but as one observer noted, "It's like packing the trunk of your car for a trip. You want to put everything in last so you can get to it easily!" So, in our setting, we feel that all our patterns are useful in the beginning, but we also realize that even the most enthusiastic Evangelist or Dedicated Champion has only 24 hours in each day.

Be Proactive!

The second, equally important pattern in this chapter advises that you'll need to keep a Sustained Momentum(231). Our natural tendency is to stop and rest once things are underway, but we run the risk of losing everything if we don't keep it going. In David Baum's book on change, *Lightning in a Bottle*, he relays this appropriate comment from Glendon Johnson, former CEO of John Alden Insurance: "A cow never stays milked." Even a small action just to show that the idea is still alive can make a tremendous difference. Henry Kissinger noted that "History knows no resting places and no plateaus."

Even the billionaire founders of the Google search engine recognize this. While observing the company at work, a news crew wondered why the many employees were so busy even though Google had already reached the status of the world's largest search engine. "What is there left to do?" they asked. One founder replied that any successful idea must continue to get attention or it will not survive.

Similarly, your idea faces competition from a never-ending stream of things that demand the attention of even your most solid supporters, so you must treat your change initiative as a living thing; it needs tending if it is to survive. Some days it just takes a little watering, other days, a major repotting is required, but if those around you see that the effort has gone to seed and is dying from lack of attention, they'll start to lose interest. Momentum is hard to regain once you've lost it.

This key pattern is really a natural extension of your initial and continuing role of Evangelist. If you retain your enthusiasm, it will naturally spill over into your daily activities. Tell those around you about that intriguing article you read and offer to make copies for anyone who's interested. Loan that new book you just finished. In other words, use the patterns Plant the Seeds(204) and External Validation(148). Continue holding Brown Bags(113) and keep the Study Groups(228) going strong. When you hear about a success story, encourage a Hometown Story(164) to spread the word. Stay in Touch(221) with all your key supporters. At one company where Linda worked, they called her the "patterns princess," because she was always talking about patterns. She wasn't heavy-handed, but her enthusiasm was contagious. Most of us like to be with people who are interesting and interested in what's happening around them.

Mary Lynn knows the value of the two patterns introduced in this chapter.

> I've been in academia for a long time, so I've seen many students attempt to finish a master's thesis or doctoral dissertation. It seems clear to me that there are two things that separate those who succeed from those who don't. The first is to involve as many different types of people as possible. Don't simply ask their advice now and then (although that is important too), but also keep them regularly informed of your progress. They will feel a part of the project and are likely to offer their assistance at unexpected times. Their reward is the realization that the final product would not have happened without them.
>
> The second important factor is to keep a steady pace. You will eventually be successful at this large project if you do something every day, rather than work only when you feel inspired or find a large block of time. To keep the task alive in your mind, you have to keep it going. If you leave it alone too long, it loses meaning for you and becomes harder and harder to resurrect.

You have momentum going and a variety of people involved in it. The next chapter contains the collection of patterns we have documented for dealing with resistance. We saved these patterns for the last of these introductory chapters because we don't want you to concentrate on them. Focus on making small changes where you can. We know you'll meet resistance, but *Fearless Change* is the name of this book and also captures our attitude toward resistors. We recommend that you use criticism to your advantage.

CHAPTER TWELVE

Dealing with Resistance

You're going to run up against those who are less than enthusiastic about the innovation. Some of these are hardliners, but most are just hesitant. Usually we tend to avoid these roadblocks, but we need to see them in a more positive light. **Fear Less(151)**, **Bridge-Builder(110)**, **Champion Skeptic(116)**, **Corridor Politics(126)**, and **Whisper in the General's Ear(248)** will help you overcome resistance.

W e have a colleague, a sturdily built, strong-willed individual we'll call "Michael." He's very bright and takes great pains when he presents something new at meetings. He does a thorough job of arguing his case, but if someone disagrees with any of his points, he often flies off the handle and storms out of the room muttering, "These people are morons!"

Do you know Michael or someone just like him? We all face resistance on many levels, but we usually don't see it as a good thing. Yet it forces us to be realistic about our brilliant ideas. It leads us to see all sides, if we are open to hearing what critics have to say.

In *The Passionate Organization*, James Lucas observes:

> *Every idea has flaws. There are no perfect plans. Pressure reveals clearly where we are missing wisdom, truth, knowledge, information, data, or passion. It provides an opportunity to fill in the gaps, stop the game until we can learn the rules, or quit the game entirely. The usual response is to scapegoat: Who messed up our plan? The classier and passionate response is to grow: How do we find what we're missing?**

Of course, all this is easier said than done. To help, we provide a few patterns for dealing with resistors. The first, Fear Less(151), urges you to use the skeptics as resources. As Stephen Covey suggests, "Seek first to understand, then to be understood." Listen with an open mind to those who don't think your idea is the greatest thing since sliced bread. Many times these people can be more help to your cause than your most fervent supporter. They can help you broaden the appeal to more than just the Innovators. Listen to them; take notes. Like good lawyers, use this data to anticipate questions and prepare answers for presentations.

As one scientist explained:

> *I used to believe that if my ideas were valid, then "killer experiments" could be done that would be so persuasive they would sweep away all opposition and quell every argument. That reflected my idealized view of science—that scientists are completely rational creatures who, when faced with data, respond as objectively as a computer and "do the right thing." I no longer believe this, because I have learned*

---

*Lucas, J.R., *The Passionate Organization: Igniting the Fire of Employee Commitment*, American Management Association, 1999.

that my idealized image of science was wrong. Scientists are not unemotional com-
puters. They can be as biased and ornery as anyone else, particularly when ventur-
ing outside their field. As one respected scientist said when asked to review a
*scientific paper, "This is the sort of thing I would not believe, even if it were true."**

Popular inspirational author Brian Biro observes, "In our culture we are con-
ditioned to push differences away. When we speak of having differences with
another person it means we are in conflict, not getting along. This cultural con-
ditioning often leads to a position of defensiveness and distrust."

But consider how silent resistance can be more difficult to overcome than
vocal resistance. Don't you feel better when you've had a chance to voice your
criticism? We all want our side of the story to be told. We all want to feel that
our input matters. We all have a point of view that can help others understand
the larger issues. The pattern Fear Less advises us to hear the other side and take
the message to heart. No idea is perfect. We need to learn as we go and what
better way than by hearing from everyone around us.

Build Bridges

Sometimes, however, resistance has nothing to do with the idea and everything
to do with the proponent of the idea. You need help from others to make inroads, and overcoming resistance is definitely one of those areas where outside
support is critical. Using the pattern Bridge-Builder(110) to find the right person
to "adopt" a skeptic can allow you to reach those who don't find you credible. Eric
Saperston, the creator of the film *The Journey*, said, "I don't claim to be an expert.
I want to be a conduit between people in my generation and the one before."

This pattern requires us to take a realistic view of ourselves. We have to accept that we're not perfect and that in some settings we are not credible. Mary
Lynn remembers when one Evangelist of a new initiative in her organization
tried to convince her to be a part of it. "Look," she said, "I need you. People know
you and like you and so you can convince them when I can't." This Evangelist
was aware of how important a bridge-builder was for the initiative—she accepted the fact that she couldn't reach everyone and understood the value in
asking for help from others who could reach a wider community.

---

*Dossey, L., *Reinventing Medicine*, HarperSanFrancisco, 1999.

Sometimes you're held back because you're the new kid on the block. Whatever it is about your experience or your personality, realize that you are not the idea and ask for help from someone who has the required credentials. The helper can build a bridge to the skeptic and bring him over to your side.

A Champion Skeptic

Being open to resistance allows you to examine it honestly and fairly. As Henry Ford noted, "If there is any one secret to success, it lies in the ability to get the other person's point of view and see things from that person's angle as well as from your own." To make sure you have the objections of the skeptics before you, use the pattern Champion Skeptic(116). Recognize the contribution of a person who is good at looking at the negative side by officially giving him that duty. Tom DeMarco recommends this in his book *Slack*:

> You have to directly acknowledge the Can't Do possibilities. One solution is to have a Can't Do specialist. Explain at the outset, "Lillian is our Can't Do specialist, our risk manager. It's her job to focus on the uglies, all the could-go-wrongs that might interfere with our plans. All the rest of you will succeed if you achieve your ambitious goals. Lillian succeeds if she warns me of every possible eventuality that might reasonably be expected to thwart us. She fails if I get blindsided by anything she hasn't warned me about."*

You can go overboard with this. Select a Champion Skeptic carefully to make sure you're not creating a monster. Some people can really get into this role and make your life miserable. It takes creativity to use this pattern wisely.

It's All About Politics

When there are important decisions to be made, consider the pattern Corridor Politics(126). Politics are here to stay, and experienced change agents know that before a big vote is taken they should contact each individual who is voting to

---

*DeMarco, T., *Slack: Getting Past Burnout, Busywork, and the Myth of Total Efficiency*, Broadway Books, 2001.

address any concerns or questions. Sometimes all it takes is a few words in the hallway. Start by talking to those who are more open, and when you have them on your side, use this to leverage influence with those who are more resistant. Don't make any promises you can't keep and always remember the important pattern Just Say Thanks(183) for support. All of this effort before a vote will help to ensure that things will go your way.

Mary Lynn understands very well what can happen when you don't use this pattern. She still has unpleasant memories of sitting in a committee meeting and listening to the members chew up and spit out a new idea she had just presented. The thought ringing in her head was, "Gee, I know better. I should have used Corridor Politics!"

In addition to Corridor Politics, use the pattern Whisper in the General's Ear(248) to convince reluctant managers. It's been said that gaining management confidence is 70% politics and 30% facts. The primary reason for using this approach is to begin to build a relationship with a high-level manager. While he may never become an enthusiastic supporter, at least he is less likely to block your efforts. High-level management may be sensitive to asking questions in front of others. Meet with the manager in his office at his convenience and promise that you will keep the conversation in confidence. Protect his vulnerability. If you succeed, he may come to rely on you in the future. This pattern, when properly used, can give you an enormous advantage.

We heard from one Evangelist who said:

> I like the way these patterns for skeptics all fit together. Here's how I use them on my team when I want to bring in something new. I talk with Brian and Don one-on-one. I use Fear Less—I listen and work their suggestions into my plan. When they're satisfied, I use Bridge-Builder because Brian is a good buddy of Tom and Paul, and Roger respects Don. This is also a bit of Corridor Politics because now I can bring up the idea in a team meeting and it flies. It's never unanimous because there's always Steve. Nothing much works with him but he really likes being the Champion Skeptic. If he gets too rowdy, we let him have it, but it's amazing how many good ideas he comes up with when he knows we will take him seriously rather than treating him like a bozo. And Whisper in the General's Ear—I save that for when we really need our team lead to back us up. He's a good guy, but he doesn't always understand the technical details. I just have a quiet minute with him and I never mention it to the rest of the guys. It works.

Good luck with those skeptics! Above all, listen to them so that you can use their ideas to help rather than to hinder you.

Now that all the patterns have been introduced, we hope you're encouraged to read the experience reports in Part II from other Evangelists who used our patterns—whether they knew it or not. These stories will give you more ideas about how these patterns work together to introduce new ideas in a variety of environments.

PART TWO

Experiences

Most of us prefer to learn new ways of doing things by hearing stories. In fact, most human conversation is really story telling. We not only tell stories to each other to explain ideas and relationships, but we also exchange technical expertise in this manner. One researcher found that Xerox copier maintenance personnel shared expertise and helped peers by telling "war stories" of maintenance adventures. We seem to understand how the world works by hearing a story about a specific experience. One study found that people were better able to remember a list of instructions when it was presented as a story.

The usual approach of organizing material into categories not only takes time and effort, but the result is a structure that may be more difficult to understand than a story.

Therefore, we present the following stories, or experience reports, in this section to illustrate how our patterns can be used to introduce something new.

- Multiple Sclerosis Society—One woman's effort to build an international organization involved in research and support for patients with MS.
- UNCA—A medium-sized university introducing a new general education curriculum.
- Sun Core J2EE Patterns—Sun Microsystems, provider of hardware, software, and services, introducing a specialized collection of design patterns.
- Customer Training—Introduction of a new approach at a large avionics company.

We have included these stories for several reasons. First, we want to show you how some people have applied the patterns, in many instances, without knowing they were using them. These experience reports let you read a story about *how* the patterns are used instead of struggling to make sense of a category, scheme, or diagram. Also, we hope to illustrate, especially if you're not familiar with patterns, how the use of one pattern can lead to the application of another; in other words, to illustrate a sequence or path through the collection of patterns. Finally, these diverse experience reports demonstrate that people can apply the patterns to fit their own contexts and that the resulting sequence of patterns reflects the individual and the organization. It's clear that these patterns are useful in many domains. We don't know anyone who has used *all* the patterns, but we are happy to be able to include the many different accounts.

Multiple Sclerosis Society Experience Report

Linda's daughter, Amy Brown, is the programs director for the MS Society in Tennessee. Amy gave her mother a copy of *Courage*, the biography of Sylvia Lawry, the founder of the MS Society, as a Christmas present in 2001. At that time, most of our patterns had been written and tested in workshops. As Linda read the book, she was gratified to see that Sylvia Lawry had been an unaware user of many of the patterns.

Sylvia Lawry's story began more than five decades ago. On May 1, 1945, she placed the following ad in *The New York Times* [Just Do It, Ask for Help, Test the Waters]:

> *Multiple sclerosis. Will anyone recovered from it please communicate with patient.*

Sylvia's brother, Bernard, had been diagnosed with multiple sclerosis. They were desperate for answers to help treat his disease. Sylvia received 54 responses from MS sufferers or their family members. None spoke of a cure. Most wanted information about the disease and asked her to send any information she uncovered. All were seeking some shred of hope.

---

*Trubo, R., *Courage*, Ivan R. Dee, 2001.

Little was known about MS in 1945, even though it was and still is one of the most common diseases of the central nervous system. It is believed that people inherit a genetic susceptibility to MS and that it is triggered by any number of yet unknown environmental factors, possibly connected to viral agents. It is an autoimmune disorder, where the immune system attacks the myelin sheathing that protects the nerve fibers of the brain and spinal cord. When the myelin is attacked, nerve impulses to and from the brain may be distorted or interrupted. Some may never be transmitted. This triggers MS symptoms, which may be hardly noticeable, while other symptoms are so severe that the individual may be incapacitated. Though not considered terminal, MS can shorten lifespan—and the disease never disappears.

Sylvia suggested to the respondents to her *Times* ad that they meet, so about a dozen of them [Innovator] started getting together regularly [Brown Bag]. They shared their experiences [Hometown Story] and discussed the search for possible solutions. They leaned on one another for support, and at times, shed tears together [Shoulder to Cry On]. They began from their first meeting to discuss the creation of an organization to support research into MS [Group Identity].

For Sylvia, the challenge of launching an organization to seek a cure for the disease seemed an impossible undertaking. Were Bernard not so seriously ill, she might not have done it. She reflected later, "I felt it was something I had to do, even though I wasn't sure where it would lead" [Evangelist, Step by Step].

In Sylvia's reading, she repeatedly came across the name of Dr. Tracy Putnam, director of the Neurological Institute of New York. She met with him and asked if he would become the chairman of a medical advisory board [Guru on Your Side]. Dr. Putnam agreed to create a list of prominent neurologists around the country [Connector] and Sylvia would invite them to serve on the board. If the board wanted, he would serve as chairman. All but one of the physicians accepted.

Sylvia then persuaded attorney Irving Berkelhammer to draw up papers of incorporation [Group Identity]. He had responded to her ad because his brother had MS. She also convinced officials at the Academy of Medicine to donate a small office at its headquarters. She said, "It's amazing how far you can get just by asking. By nature, I can't ask favors of people, let alone ask for money. But I found it easy to ask for funds for MS, because the need was so urgent, and the pain was so great" [Ask for Help].

She was advised to recruit a board of directors of people whose names could create public confidence in the organization and get attention from the press.

Sylvia had a difficult time with this assignment until Dr. Putnam introduced her to Otto Frohnknecht [Corporate Angel], founder and chairman of the board of the International Minerals and Metals Corporation. His daughter had MS. He was looking for some way to deal with the disease. With Frohnknecht's help [Connector], several of his high-powered colleagues were recruited.

On October 3, 1946, a press release announced the formation of the new organization [Group Identity]. This gave MS the highest visibility it had enjoyed up to that time. Nearly 10,000 letters from around the world flooded the organization's tiny office.

Not all of the feedback was positive. Sylvia received an angry phone call from a New York resident who shouted through the entire conversation. "It sounds like you are trying to get money from MS patients," he fumed. "Can't you just leave us alone?" The man's attack shook Sylvia, but she let the man talk [Fear Less]. Finally she said, "I'd like to meet with you to explain what the organization is all about." He quieted down and invited her to his home. Sylvia found a paralyzed man living alone. He conducted an insurance business over the phone. He was quite remarkable. As she explained her dreams for the society and what she hoped to accomplish, she began to win him over [Personal Touch]. Before Sylvia left, he told her he would help any way he could. Over the next few years, he became one of the most active members.

When Sylvia asked Carl Owen to become president of the new organization, he took a wait-and-see attitude. He suggested placing ads in the Boston newspapers to see how widespread interest in MS really was [Test the Waters]. Carl felt that if the ads generated a significant response he'd seriously consider assuming the presidency. The ads ran for just one day in *The Boston Globe* and *The Boston Herald*, but it was enough to generate a flood of mail. Letters arrived from physicians, scientists, and from families of individuals with MS, emotional pleas for help. Within 10 days, 5,000 letters had overrun Sylvia Lawry's desk [External Validation]. She was stunned by the response—and so was Carl Owen [Smell of Success]. He said, "I'd be honored to serve as the first president."

The new organization began holding monthly meetings in an auditorium in the New York Academy of Medicine that attracted standing-room only crowds [Early Adopter, Early Majority]. It was a social evening where people with MS and their families could interact with others living with the disease [Shoulder to Cry On]. Sylvia invited neurologists [Big Jolt] to speak and answer questions. For the first time many MS families had a source of reliable information about the disease. As word of the meetings spread, people came from all parts of New York, New Jersey, Connecticut, and even farther away [Involve Everyone].

In 1947, Carl Owen approached a prominent fundraising organization for help in raising $100,000. His request was declined with the following explanation:"We couldn't raise $100,000 for you. MS is not like cancer or heart disease; most people have never heard of it and you don't have sufficient volunteers in place to benefit from our guidance."

Owen was incensed by the rejection. "I'm going to raise the $100,000 myself!" [Just Do It]. In the weeks that followed, Owen asked everyone he encountered for contributions [Evangelist, Connector, Involve Everyone]. Once he explained the effects of MS, no one said no. Before the end of the year he had reached his goal and had done it single-handedly [Small Successes].

In 1949 Sylvia met Edward Bernays, called by *The New York Times* "the father of public relations." He was a professional opinion maker whose client list included General Electric, Procter & Gamble, and other large corporations. Bernays suggested using "MS" because it was easier to remember than multiple sclerosis [Group Identity].

U.S. Senator Charles Tobey of New Hampshire had a daughter who had just been diagnosed with MS. He called Sylvia to ask what he could do to help. Sylvia had been looking for a way to enlist government support. Since most members of congress had never heard of MS, they were reluctant to support Tobey's bill for a government-sponsored MS institute. Sylvia gathered a group of experts to testify before the senate subcommittee [Guru on Your Side]. However, her star witness was Eleanor Gehrig [Big Jolt], widow of the famed New York Yankee first baseman, who had been forced to retire because of amyotrophic lateral sclerosis, which, like MS, was a demyelinating disease. Eleanor told senators how her husband's illness had undermined his career and shattered his life. She described the importance of research to reduce human suffering. Her testimony made headlines, including a *New York Times* article entitled "Mrs. Gehrig Backs Sclerosis Aid Bill" [External Validation]. In August 1950, Congress voted to create a Neurological Institute.

Information was beginning to surface about the disease [Small Successes]. In an epidemiological study by Mayo Clinic researchers, MS was found to be more common in countries distant from the equator. Most cases of MS are diagnosed when the patient is between the ages of 20 and 40. A patient with MS may be so disabled that he is unable to get out of his bed or wheelchair and yet within a period of days or weeks be walking again. The chemical or physical change that causes this must hold a clue to the answer to this disease.

Sylvia wanted to extend the MS Society to the United Kingdom [Involve Everyone]. Dr. Putnam put her in touch with Dr. MacDonald Critchley, one of the leading neurologists in England [Guru on Your Side]. When Sylvia visited Critchley, he was intrigued with the idea of an MS society in the U.K. and offered to host a reception and invite the U.K.'s leading neurologists, including those from Scotland and Ireland. The day of the reception, however, showed an empty meeting room. When finally one of the invited physicians, Dr. Allison, showed up, he told Sylvia why no one had been at the event. Dr. Douglas McAlpine considered himself to be England's foremost MS authority. He was upset that Sylvia had first approached Dr. Critchley and not him. He had urged his colleagues to ignore the event. Dr. Allison arranged for Sylvia to meet Dr. McAlpine. She convinced him of her sincerity [Fear Less, Whisper in the General's Ear] and won his support.

When Sylvia called a meeting to create an international MS organization, European countries felt that the United States would dominate the organization. Sylvia offered to provide $100,000 in seed money. She contacted people all over the world to convince the European delegates that an international organization would be a good idea. The crucial speaker, however, was Shirley Temple Black [Big Jolt]. Moments before the vote was to be taken, she rose to her feet and asked, "What have you got to lose? We're all here for the same reason and that's to wipe out multiple sclerosis." The result was a unanimous vote in favor of the global organization. Someone commented afterward, "We shouldn't underestimate the credit that Shirley Temple Black deserves in this. All these brilliant, gray-bearded scientists wanted to meet Shirley. They remembered her from when she was a little kid in the movies. They were nearly tripping over one another to have their picture taken with her. It was really something."

In 1996, the National MS Society marked its fiftieth year of service to individuals with MS and their families. Those who lived with MS a half-century earlier fought their battles alone, with nowhere to turn for information, support, and treatment. Today the National MS Society meets the standards of all major agencies that rate not-for-profit groups in the United States. Through the Society's 50-state network of chapters and divisions, assistance is provided to over a million people annually. Two million volunteers, supporters, and friends carry out its mission to end the devastating effects of MS. Since its founding in 1946, the Society has invested more than $320 million in research [Small Successes].

Trent Sickles drove Sylvia to the airport after one of her long trips. He could see the exhaustion in her face. When she was about to board the plane, Sickles remarked to her in Swedish, "Nicht legg lo," which means "Never give up" [Sustained Momentum].

Sylvia Lawry was a woman with a vision, a true Evangelist. Even though she never saw her dream fulfilled, she improved the lives of those with MS and their families. After a lifetime of struggle, she died on February 24, 2001. Though Sylvia Lawry's commitment to finding a solution to MS never faltered, she died without knowing the answers to key questions. The cause of MS remains unknown.

UNCA Experience Report

Edward Katz is an Associate Professor in the Department of Litera-
ture and Language at the University of North Carolina at Asheville
(UNCA). In the Fall of 1999, as the University was preparing for re-
accreditation, Ed was asked to serve as Chair [Dedicated Champion]
of the General Education Review Subcommittee (GERS). This is his
story of leading the faculty toward a change in the general education
curriculum.

GERS was originally comprised of 22 faculty and student members. We
began our work in the spring of 2000 by discussing student development
issues, reflecting on our experiences with students at UNCA [Time for Reflec-
tion], talking about our own college years, and studying trends in general education and curricular reform [Study Group]. In a series of meetings with a large
group of colleagues, we wrote mission statements for our project and our idea of
general education [Group Identity] and recommendations for revising and ad-
ministering a new curriculum. I created a Web site to share our work with the
faculty, staff, administration, and students [In Your Space] that became a clear-
inghouse for a variety of information: meeting minutes, documents, reports,
and links to publications on curricular development and revision.

At the end of re-accreditation, the Vice Chancellor of Academic Affairs
[Corporate Angel] asked us to continue by revising the present curriculum.

This assignment turned out to be very controversial. Because UNCA has a strong tradition of governance by its Faculty Senate, some felt that Academic Affairs had overstepped its authority by asking us to work on curricular revision. Over the next several weeks, I met with members of the Faculty Senate to hear their concerns [Fear Less, Corridor Politics]. We had some heated discussions, but the Senate finally decided to authorize the subcommittee, renamed the General Education Review Task Force (GERTF), to do a program review and revision [Group Identity]. I agreed to make status reports each semester to the Senate [Stay in Touch]. We were taking important steps and the reports became a great way to keep our forward momentum [Sustained Momentum].

We initially reviewed all Senate Academic Policy Committee reports and investigated general education reform [Study Group]. Some members researched professional journals and books on curricular reform in the liberal arts [External Validation].

In June 2000, several of us attended the Asheville Institute on General Education, a nationally recognized forum on general education programming and curricular reform [Location, Location, Location]. We consulted with experts [Mentor] and talked with other teams about the programs they had developed and the problems they had encountered [Shoulder to Cry On]. By the end of the institute, the team had come together around our mission, shaping an eight-point plan for continuing its work [Group Identity]. We were now convinced that an innovative curricular revision was possible, and we were excited about working to gain faculty buy-in [Small Successes].

Team members wanted to get right to curricular design, but I held them back to allow for development of a campus-wide overview [Just Enough]. This was frustrating for those who wanted to finish the task and some were openly skeptical about whether a revision was even possible. I countered this negativity with humor and end-of-semester gatherings at a local pub, as a reward for their energy and hard work [Do Food, Just Say Thanks]. Even so, two members withdrew from the group citing other commitments, two students graduated, and one of the alumni moved away from Asheville. I used this opportunity to pull a smaller task force of 17 together around a sense of ownership of this project [Group Identity].

Starting campus-wide discussion was difficult. An online Web forum failed, and I worried that this might undermine our morale. At the Asheville Institute, I had thought of conducting a Listening Project based on focus-group approaches. Though everyone agreed that would be a lot of work, the idea energized the team. So we went in pairs to departments or programs contributing to the general education requirements. The pairs met with faculty and recorded their responses to questions we'd given them in advance [Personal Touch].

The responses were anonymous and posted on a Web site. A social scientist and natural scientist on the task force [Ask for Help] studied the data and prepared a Summary Analysis Report. Faculty members were encouraged to read this summary to identify recurring issues and themes [In Your Space]. This work took over a semester, but the faculty could see that we wanted to reach out to them and understand their perspective. Faculty across campus reported feeling part of a public, community process [Involve Everyone], and team members were excited about talking to colleagues about curricular innovation [Small Successes]. The Listening Project replaced the failed Web forum and gave the impression of a discussion [e-Forum].

The Listening Project also helped us formulate a Statement of Institutional Principles for Design [Tailor Made]. The principles became discussion topics, so that faculty and staff could begin defining the way they wanted to develop a new curriculum.

During this period, I spent time with people who were excited about what we were doing [Innovator]. They energized me when the going got tough. I discovered several professors who were already using some of the cutting-edge teaching approaches envisioned for the new program [Piggyback]. Others were supportive of the revised program, which featured flexibility that they found especially attractive. I began to identify a small group of colleagues who were voicing support for the effort [Early Adopter].

To crystallize faculty interest and increase buy-in [Involve Everyone], we scheduled another campus-wide discussion in the Faculty Forum series [Piggyback] to discuss the Institutional Principles. We provided food and wine [Do Food] so the event would be special. I contacted about 150 colleagues [Corridor Politics]. I explained that our process had been organic [Step by Step], faculty driven [Involve Everyone], and based on quantitative and qualitative data [External Validation] from the beginning. The time I spent really paid off—attendance was around 90, nearly two-thirds of our full-time faculty, and several colleagues publicly expressed support. This was a key moment—the faculty enthusiasm turned the skepticism of those who doubted a revision could ever happen [Small Successes].

After the forum, I split the team into three groups: a Design Team (DT), a Curriculum Research Team, and a Resource Research Team, and provided members with clear roles [Group Identity]. The DT used the two research teams to study curricular and resource issues both internally at UNCA and at other schools [External Validation]. These teams drafted reports, which I posted on the Web site [Stay in Touch]. This reinforced the public nature of the process [Involve Everyone] and assured faculty that we were being thorough. Often, faculty would e-mail us to offer feedback or other resources. The Web site was becoming a learning tool for the campus community [In Your Space].

I held the DT back from discussing specifics. They started with a study of the principles, since they would have to be familiar with these to shape a program that met these requirements [Just Enough]. As we discussed the principles, we asked the research teams for specific data or information [External Validation]. I kept in touch with faculty, the Senate [Connectors], and the Vice Chancellor of Academic Affairs [Corporate Angel, Stay in Touch].

As the DT moved from general to specific curricular issues [Step by Step], I reminded everyone about faculty wishes for more flexibility in the curriculum. We considered "topical clusters"—sets of courses that might be designed around a larger topic or subject, and "intensives"—courses that would give students enhanced experiences in key skill and content areas. Our aim was to shape a structure that would reflect our institutional culture and faculty needs, concerns, and interests [Tailor Made].

We analyzed several models, looking for common and divergent elements. This was an exciting moment for the team. We allowed ample time for debate. The team was so engrossed in its work and had developed such intimacy that we were not afraid of conflict [Fear Less]. We were able to work through our differences and come to consensus on a single curriculum that we could enthusiastically support.

The DT's next step was to get input and approval from the entire GERTF [Guru Review]. I started with the most influential member, a key member of the university faculty [Whisper in the General's Ear]. Without her support, the plan would most likely fail. After hearing her initial reaction, I realized that our materials were not clear enough, so I explained what this plan would offer her as a chairperson of an important department and to other departments like hers [Personal Touch]. This captured her interest. I asked if she would be willing to work with me to create more effective documents to introduce the concept to others [Ask for Help]. She agreed. I then showed the new materials we created to other key players [Guru on Your Side], to expose GERTF members, one by one, to the new curriculum [Corridor Politics].

When we finally took the model to the entire GERTF team, my work in preparation really paid big dividends. GERTF spent two sessions discussing and refining elements of the architecture and the phrasing of documents, coming, for the most part, to quick agreement. Two or three difficult issues were resolved. Several DT members [Connectors] became mediators for the rest of the GERTF, helping the entire group reach agreement. By the end of the second meeting we were ready to take the model public.

Before going to the full campus, I met with key department chairs, program heads, and other faculty who might be seriously affected by the changes we were proposing [Personal Touch, Corridor Politics]. Other GERTF members talked with colleagues opposed to certain innovations, to convert them or at least reduce the threat of resistance [Bridge-Builder]. We went from office to office to talk with faculty who had different ideas about what was appropriate for the general education program at UNCA.

This next phase was conducted as the earlier portion of the process had been—as an open, faculty-driven stage of an ongoing conversation about curricular reform [Involve Everyone]. GERTF held five faculty focus groups on elements of the model and two student-faculty forums on diversity in the curriculum. At the end of the week, we led another faculty meeting on general education, where we presented the proposed model. Again, I contacted individuals before the meeting [Corridor Politics]. About 95 people attended the forum. The response to the proposal was favorable, though concerns about particular changes persisted, as we expected. We assured our critics that we were happy to adapt the model to address any problems and that flexibility would continue to be fundamental, as it had been throughout the process [Fear Less].

The plan was sent to the Academic Policies Committee of the Faculty Senate for approval [Guru Review]. Following their recommendation, the proposed architecture for the new curriculum passed the Senate, which gave us the authorization we needed to advance to the implementation phase [Small Successes]. We plan to build on the approach we have taken so far as we move to make the revision a reality in our university's curriculum [Step by Step].

> Following approval of the new curriculum architecture, Ed was appointed Associate Vice Chancellor for University Programs. The announcement memo by the university Vice Chancellor spoke of Ed in this way: "…he has become identified on campus as an energetic, thoughtful, principled, and purposeful force for general education reform that also retains the best of our existing programs."

Sun Core J2EE Patterns
Experience Report

John Crupi is a Distinguished Engineer and Chief Java Architect for Sun Service Java Center at Sun Microsystems. He has 15 years of experience in distributed object design and development. John is a co-author of *Core J2EE Patterns*. The popularity of the J2EE standard in developing distributed applications led to the need to disseminate the lessons of successful design efforts. This is John's story of this project.

In 1998, we developed one of our first J2EE applications. J2EE, or *Java 2 Platform Enterprise Edition*, is a platform-independent, Java-centric environment from Sun for developing, building, and deploying Web-based enterprise applications online. We sensed that there was rapidly growing interest in J2EE. Customers were jumping on the technology faster than we had anticipated. Since this technology was new and Sun was the source, we suspected that our global Professional Services organization would be very busy in the upcoming years doing J2EE architecture, design, and implementation. As it turns out, we were right, and luckily we were prepared.

Our idea in 1998 was to document the J2EE patterns we discovered in our early customer engagements. We believed that since we are a global organization, we needed a way to communicate and exchange our successes. We felt that design patterns would be the best way to capture and share our design experience. We also felt that once the patterns were documented, we could share them with our customers to efficiently convey our design decisions [Evangelist].

Consulting organizations are usually hired to solve a specific problem: in our case, to architect and design J2EE applications. In our early engagements, we wanted to capture the patterns we were using to solve our customers' design problems. There were two immediate challenges. First, we had a good understanding of the *Design Patterns* book and there were several good books on software architecture, but these patterns were not tied to a specific platform. Even though we were not sure whether we could accomplish our goal, we were ready to try [Just Do It]. The second problem we faced was lack of time to document the patterns given our workload. Since patterns capture solutions that have solved problems over and over we knew that we needed to generalize the specific designs captured from our engagements. We solved this problem by convincing our customers of the value they would realize from the patterns we created [Tailor Made].

After a year of designing successful J2EE applications, we had identified some potential patterns [Small Successes]. I told my boss [Connector] about my ideas for J2EE patterns and said that I wanted to show them to our group. At one of our semi-annual offsite team gatherings of 200 Java architects from around the world [Location, Location, Location], my boss told me to present my ideas to the team after dinner [Piggyback, Guru Review]. I grabbed Danny Malks, a pattern-savvy J2EE expert [Guru on Your Side] who was interested in the patterns [Ask for Help]. We created a presentation that described four designs we thought reflected some of the patterns we had seen [Hometown Story].

We presented our ideas to the group to get their feedback not only on the four candidate patterns but also on the idea of capturing other J2EE patterns [Test the Waters]. The pattern concept was well received; many said it was a good idea [Innovator, Early Adopter]. We got approval from our manager [Local Sponsor] to continue the patterns work and write a book [Dedicated Champion].

I recruited Danny to work on the presentation-tier patterns [Ask for Help]. Danny had experience with design patterns and Servlet/Java Server Pages (JSP) and also appreciated the challenge in doing this work. We recruited some of our architects [Guru on Your Side] who weren't currently working on projects to help us write the patterns. Even though Danny and I were well versed in the Enterprise Java Beans (EJB) and the Servlet/JSP side of J2EE, we felt we needed an additional resource who was patterns savvy and smart in EJB. Serendipitously, I got a call from Deepak Alur. He said he had some questions about our patterns and wanted to share his ideas. After about an hour of conversation, it was clear that Deepak was our guy [Guru on Your Side].

The next step was to begin documenting the patterns [Step by Step]. Initially we had identified about 120 patterns, but many turned out to be variations on the same theme, so we added "strategies" to our pattern template to capture these implementation variations. We weren't sure how to best present the abstractions in the patterns. We discovered that some people can think at an abstract level, while others think best at a more concrete level. We spent about two years documenting the patterns and held five workshops with internal colleagues along the way [Guru Review].

Throughout most of the review processes [Time for Reflection], about half the reviewers were supportive [Innovator, Early Adopter, Early Majority], about a third saw no value, and the rest were indifferent. In the Sun Java Center, most of our architects are senior to very senior, so, they may not be representative of the developer community at large, but they gave us a good critical perspective [Champion Skeptic].

We released the patterns on our Web site [In Your Space, e-Forum] before the book was published. The only negative feedback we received from both the community and book reviewers was that there were no source code examples on the Web site. A common comment was, "Without source code, these patterns are useless." It's interesting that some developers need source code examples to see the value in the patterns, while others don't. This experience reinforced our earlier observation that some people can see abstractions and understand how to realize them, while others need to see concrete applications to find the deeper, more general structures.

We listened to our critics [Fear Less] and when the book was finally released in June 2001, it had many source code examples. The second edition was released in 2003. There has been real interest in the J2EE patterns, primarily through the acceptance of our work outside Sun [External Validation].

> The book remained in the Amazon.com top 100 technical books for quite a while, and a presentation of the patterns at the international JavaOne convention drew over 4,000 attendees. The Sun Professional Services organization has been winning lucrative services engagements based on industry adoption of the patterns. Respect for this particular piece of Sun Intellectual Property has grown, and the authors have been invited to many customer sites where organizations have standardized on the patterns.

Customer Training Experience Report

The following story is from a colleague who wishes to remain anonymous.

The customer training department of a major avionics company hired me to create an online version of their traditional classroom training [Dedicated Champion]. Although they really weren't sure what their online avionics training would look like, they seemed to think that it would probably be some kind of self-paced, computer-based training delivered over the Internet. I had something different in mind. I began to talk about the notion of a virtual classroom.

I wasn't sure they really understood what I was talking about, so I arranged for some of our instructors to visit a company that specializes in technical training delivered in online classrooms [Personal Touch]. The helpful folks at this company guided us through their studios and explained how their online courses are structured and delivered. They have a very successful instructional model that they can apply to any topic they are teaching [External Validation].

Our instructors were very impressed with what they had seen. When we returned to our workplace, they talked about how we might be able to develop live online classes. They talked about scheduling meetings to explore the concept.

They talked about forming a committee to create a proposal that could be presented to our management. At that point I stepped into the discussion and said, "No, guys. We're just gonna do it" [Just Do It].

We already had all the technology we needed. We had computers, Internet access, telephones, and most importantly, a corporate license for a robust online meeting tool. We had a seldom-used CBT lab that could be easily restructured for delivering virtual classes. It was to become our eLearning Broadcast Studio [Piggyback].

Working with our facilities staff, I cleared out a corner of the lab and we configured some modular office furniture to create a studio environment spacious enough for two instructors and a producer to interact comfortably. I added four computers, four telephones with headsets, an array of wall clocks to represent world times, and some custom lighting for atmosphere. As a final touch, I asked our graphic artists to create some custom artwork to further define the space and give it character [Ask for Help]. Because I was able to repurpose computers we already owned, the total bill was under $4,000.

The next step was to develop an instructional model that would work for our courses [Tailor Made]. I designed an interactive modular format that took its inspiration from the company we had visited earlier. I focused my efforts on creating a very tight instructional design, high-quality presentation of content, and a high-energy delivery that would hold students' interest. Since the learner is online, boredom is death for the virtual classroom.

Working without fanfare, it took a couple of months to get the studio in place and our first class designed and piloted. It was only after we began delivering online courses that I gradually introduced my management to the concept of eLearning and virtual classrooms [Step by Step, Just Enough]. I never told them what we were going to do. I told them only what we had done. I didn't tell them about vision. I talked about successes [Small Successes]. Within six months, we developed a full curriculum of eLearning modules for one of our products and were delivering them to customers worldwide.

> The vice-president of our Customer Services organization [Corporate Angel] has become a big fan of our work. In fact, he now conducts all of his Global Leadership meetings and all-employee meetings online using our eLearning Broadcast Studio. We continue to expand our offerings. And you know what? We never did form a committee. We never did ask or get permission. We just did it.

PART THREE

The Patterns

This part contains the patterns. Each pattern includes:

+ The Opening Story (in italics)
+ Summary (in bold)
+ Context (in body text)
+ Problem (in bold)
+ Forces (in body text)
+ Essence of the Solution (prefaced by "Therefore")
+ More on the Solution (in body text)
+ Resulting Context (in body text)
+ Known Uses (in italics)

Patterns from other sources are underlined and are referenced at the end of this part.

Ask for Help

Markita Andrews has generated more than $80,00 selling Girl Scout cookies since she was seven years old. She does not propose to be smarter or more extroverted than other people. Rather, she claims the difference is that she has discovered the secret of selling: Ask, Ask, Ask! The fear of rejection causes many people to fail before they begin because they don't just ask for what they want.

Since the task of introducing a new idea into an organization is a big job, look for people and resources to help your efforts.

◆◆◆

You are an Evangelist(144) or Dedicated Champion(129) working to introduce a new idea into your organization.

The job of introducing a new idea into an organization is too big for one person, especially a newcomer who doesn't know the ropes.

The single biggest failing of many change agents is that they do not look for help. They believe they can do it themselves, or they feel they can't ask for help because this would reveal their own inadequacies. Yet the likelihood of success is directly related to their ability to ask others for help.

David Baum, author of *Lightning in a Bottle*, has observed that a leader who appears invulnerable, never showing anything but complete confidence and certainty, will eventually create a workforce with a somewhat warped view of reality. On the other hand, a leader who admits his vulnerability will find that people will move toward him in surprising and generous ways.

We all need help at times. People who set a high goal will eventually find that they cannot achieve it without other people. It can take effort to find help but the return can be worth it. Taking the steps to identify what resources are available will allow you to take advantage of them.

Often we feel it would be easier to just do it ourselves, but involving others will bring extra benefits in addition to the help. Involvement leads to growing support for your new idea. It can also encourage people to take partial or complete ownership of the project—this is especially valuable for a change agent who hopes to spark the idea and then pass it on to others to implement.

Some people are not quick to volunteer their help or advice. It could be because no one ever asked them. Most people are more likely to help when they are asked. Most people want to be connected, invited, and involved. Most people will have energy and commitment if they are given the opportunity to be players and to influence an initiative's outcome.

Therefore:

Ask as many people as you can for help when you need it. Don't try to do it alone.

Get the help, advice, and resources of people who care about you and/or the things you care about. Look around you and talk to everyone about the innovation. You may think you don't know anyone who can help you with your dream but keep talking and then talk some more. Ask them at The Right Time(207) and remember to Just Say Thanks(183).

Sometimes it takes digging—you might have to talk to someone who knows someone, and so on, before you get the help you need. Every organization provides some kind of support: Web development, graphic design, special printing, free advertising, corporate publications, secretaries, and assistants. Help can be there for the asking. Look around. Sometimes just wandering over to a support area and stopping at someone's desk can help you discover what's available.

If a person is hesitant to agree to your request for help, turn it around. Explain how this opportunity can be an advantage to him, such as allowing him to learn something new, make new contacts, or even add a line to his end-of-year report.

Don't become discouraged if the help is slow in coming. Even a small start can help you promote your ideas, leading to more resources in the future.

= = = = = = = = =

This pattern builds support from people who will now feel part of the effort. Small contributions from a variety of individuals can create Small Successes(216) and can add up to significant results. Most importantly, each time you ask for help, you'll bring in more interested individuals.

The risk is that asking for help can be seen as a sign of incompetence, especially if you are part of an organization that fosters a "You should be able do it yourself" image. You can overcome this difficulty by creating a Group Identity(155) and involving everyone who has contributed to the initiative.

Someone told Samantha, "No one knows you. If you talk to Mark or Greg, they know how to get things done and I'm sure they'll help you." He was right, and it made a big difference. Mark told her how to reach the editor of the online daily newsletter to announce upcoming events. Greg introduced her to the tech support person who could set up a bulletin board for the new idea. They were both available when she had questions. She felt like she had a chance at it after that.

Writing computer programs in pairs is part of a new agile software development approach. Programmers say that pairing makes it easier to admit they don't know something. In the pair programming relationship, individuals lose the embarrassment that typifies the lone cowboy coder who would rather try to muddle through on his own. Asking for help has become a natural part of the software development process.

Big Jolt

I was invited to give a presentation at a company in another city. Afterwards the local Evangelist said, "You didn't say anything I couldn't have, but more people will listen to you. Your talk will have greater impact than mine would and then they'll come to me for more information."

To provide more visibility for the change effort, invite a high profile person into your organization to talk about the new idea.

You are a Dedicated Champion(129) working to introduce a new idea into your organization.

You've been carrying out some activities to give your new idea some visibility in your organization, but at some point you need to attract more attention to the effort.

Some people might be too busy to attend your presentation, but they will take time to hear an expert in the field. When a speaker has credibility, people are influenced by what he has to say.

Even those who have adopted the innovation need to have their interest reinforced. They need something to re-energize their interest and strengthen their commitment; otherwise, they may fall back into old habits or forget the new approach.

Therefore:

Arrange for a high-profile person who can talk about the new idea to do a presentation in your organization.

If funding is not available, entice the expert by pointing out that his visit is an opportunity for publicity for his latest project or book. Increase the probability of significant audience at his presentation with lots of publicity before the event and by personally inviting and reminding people. Tell Connectors(119). "Big name" people usually expect a big audience and may consider it an insult if they don't get one at your organization. This is especially important if the speaker is not being paid.

Schedule a pre-event meeting so the speaker can tailor his talk to the needs of the company. Give him some insight into the attitudes surrounding the new idea, the local power structure, and the organization's true priorities. Make certain he understands the types of individuals he will be speaking to. Well-known experts may wish to talk about something that most people in the organization are not prepared to understand, so encourage him to use Just Enough(180) to speak at a level the organization can absorb.

When advertising and introducing the speaker, highlight his experiences that relate to the innovation. This is likely to impress even the people who are not familiar with his name and make them more interested in what he has to say.

If the speaker will agree to do more than just a presentation, arrange a Royal Audience(210) to reward those who have helped with your new idea in the organization and to make an impression on a Corporate Angel(123) or Local Sponsor(186).

Get permission to videotape the presentation for people who can't be there to hear the speaker live. Later, you can schedule some group viewings—be there to answer questions. Use both the presentation and the video sessions as an opportunity to Plant the Seeds(204).

= = = = = = = = =

This pattern creates an event that will increase awareness of an innovation and provide some training for it. A big name speaker will catch the attention of even the busiest people and will raise your credibility since you arranged for this person to visit the organization. Even those who cannot attend may be influenced by the publicity before the event and the talk about it afterwards.

The risk is that it can create more enthusiasm than you can handle. Make sure you have people to help you after the speaker has gone. Without appropriate follow-up, the enthusiasm is likely to fizzle. Also, dealing with the visitor may involve a lot of extra overhead, divert resources, and distract you from higher-priority tasks and may not contribute to your long-term community development. Make sure this event is held in the context of a larger plan.

Barb invited a well-known speaker to talk about a new idea in her organization. Immediately following his visit, she saw a difference between those who had heard the talk and those who did not. Most of those who attended were willing to hear more, while most of the others were still skeptical.

David said, "We use this as much as we can. For some reason, people don't believe the in-house experts as much as a visiting 'dignitary.' We've had several big name speakers pay us a visit and it never ceases to amaze me the number of new people who sign up afterwards. It's not like we don't have our own in-house training or resident mentors. I'm learning about the impact of outsiders!"

Bridge-Builder

I knew better than to try to convince the guys in Human Resources that our proposal for increased minority hiring would help the company in the long run. All I had to do was walk into that meeting room and our hopes were dead. Instead, I sent Bob to represent our team. He wore a suit and was our Ivy League recruiter. He didn't have the reputation for being a "bleeding heart" like the rest of us. He could speak their language. They listened and our proposal was accepted, no problem.

Pair those who have accepted the new idea with those who have not.

You are an Evangelist(144) or Dedicated Champion(129) working to introduce a new idea into your organization. Some people in the organization have accepted the new idea, while others have not.

Some won't listen to even the most enthusiastic proponent if it's someone they don't know or trust.

In many cases, people may be suspicious of the Evangelist and not the idea itself. Many hard-boiled veterans will not listen to a newcomer, no matter how knowledgeable that person may be. Veterans need to hear from one of their own, someone they trust. People like people who are similar in opinion, personality, background, or lifestyle. They enjoy interacting with others who understand where they're coming from.

Even trivial similarities between individuals have been shown to create a greater openness to new ideas and a willingness to try new approaches.

People are often skeptical because they see the world differently than the person who is talking about a new idea. Those who have already accepted the new idea can help with this, especially if these adopters are considered to be thoughtful and discerning in their decision making.

Therefore:

Ask for help from Early Adopters(138), Connectors(119), or gurus who have already adopted the innovation. Introduce them to people who have interests similar to theirs and encourage them to discuss how they found the innovation useful.

Match a skeptic with an adopter he knows and respects. Ask the adopter to use Personal Touch(198) to inform and address questions of his more skeptical friend. While his goal is to try to convince the non-adopter, this may not be possible when talking with a strong skeptic. In this case, it may be just as important for the Bridge-Builder to allow the person's viewpoint to be heard by someone he respects.

It can take a lot of time and energy to find the right Bridge-Builder for everyone, so you may want to reserve use of this pattern for only the key people. On the other hand, if you know someone who is "hot" on the innovation who has a buddy that is a skeptic, you might just simply ask, "Will you talk to <skeptic> about your experiences with <the innovation>?"

Don't become discouraged if this pattern does not work for everyone. The last to come around, the Laggards, usually accept an innovation only after most or all of their co-workers have adopted it. Even then they may only do so under pressure. Therefore it might be the best use of your limited resources to simply wait for them to come around, if they ever do, rather than putting a lot of effort into trying to persuade them.

When someone takes on the challenge of being a Bridge-Builder, remember to Just Say Thanks(183).

= = = = = = = = =

This pattern builds a bridge between two people who can talk about the new idea. Someone who wasn't receptive to you is now more informed, thanks to the help of someone he will listen to. In addition, the person you asked to be the Bridge-Builder becomes a stronger part of the effort because of the contribution he is making.

The risk is that a strong skeptic may make the adopter think twice about the innovation and you may lose both of them. Make sure that the Bridge-Builder is someone who is truly convinced of the innovation and strong enough to work with a potentially argumentative skeptic.

I was a Dedicated Champion, with a cubicle right next door to a skeptic whose opinions were respected in the organization. I tried to influence him without success. Finally I found someone the skeptic respected, someone he had worked with at the company for a long time, who supported the change initiative. I asked for her help in convincing the skeptic. She agreed, and now the former skeptic is a supporter.

Lisa needed a favor from Bill, and although she knew she could probably get what she wanted by asking him, she also knew he really liked a good friend of hers. So she asked the friend to solicit the favor. Not only could Lisa be sure that the favor would be forthcoming, but she knew it would make Bill happier to do it for the friend—and that's exactly what happened!

Brown Bag

One of the engineers stopped by my cubicle the other day. "You've had such great success with <the innovation>—I wonder if you would help me. I have an idea but I don't know how to get started." I told him that I got things going by announcing a Brown Bag and talking to people who showed up. It was a small beginning, but the people who came were interested in the topic and were willing to help me take the next steps.

Use the time when people normally eat lunch to provide a convenient and relaxed setting for hearing about the new idea.

You are an Evangelist(144) or Dedicated Champion(129) who would like to call a meeting to introduce a new idea. Members of the user community are free to attend or not.

People can be too busy to attend optional meetings held during work hours.

There is always other, more important work to be done. Even though most people have a natural curiosity to hear about new ideas, it can be hard to take time during the workday to sit and learn. This makes it difficult to find a time when people can attend discretionary meetings. But since almost everyone eats in the middle of the day, a meeting over lunch will often find more people with time available. Lunchtime meetings are not as likely to be viewed as wasting time that could be spent doing "real" work, since the time would be spent eating anyway.

Therefore:

Hold the meeting in the middle of the day and invite attendees to bring their own lunches.

You can increase attendance if you find The Right Time(207). Consider spending a little of your own money to Do Food(132) to make the event special. Advertise the event in an e-Forum(135) or In Your Space(167). Talk it up with Connectors(119) or a friendly guru.

Use Next Steps(195) near the end of the event to help keep interest alive, and don't hesitate to Ask for Help(104). Tell people where they can find more information and who is using the innovation in the organization.

Hand out a Token(243) to help people remember the new idea that was discussed during the session.

= = = = = = = = = =

This pattern creates more awareness for the innovation in the organization. When the participants take time and bring their own food, it shows a willingness to invest a little of themselves that can grow over time.

While a noontime meeting can attract more people than a meeting at mid-morning or mid-afternoon, there will be others who won't attend because they view lunchtime as their break time. You will need to arrange other events for these people. Also, some cultures are not open to having meetings over lunch. If you are not familiar with the corporate culture, make sure that people will accept the idea of a Brown Bag before you begin your plans.

Brown Bag lunch discussions started in Brian's organization so testers could network, share ideas, and learn more about testing topics. The events are held bi-weekly from noon until 1:00 p.m. The meetings range from free-form discussions to formal presentations. Topics have included demonstrations of products they test and how they test them, conference experiences, software testing certifications, what kind of testers they are, and the organization's testing process.

Initially Brian came up with a few topics, but he soon began asking for feedback from peers. At the year mark, he formed a committee to request topic ideas from peers, set up agendas, find speakers, and bring in snacks and supplementary materials. In the beginning, most attendees were testers. Information about upcoming Brown Bags was sent to everyone in the company, in addition to those who received a notice of the meeting. The events have attracted a variety of people—managers, developers, and others who are interested in software testing.

David organizes Brown Bag conferences. His recommendations:

- *Have a presentation every day at lunchtime for one to two weeks.*
- *Ask for help to create a program committee to organize the event.*
- *Invite attendees to bring their own lunches.*
- *Draw presenters primarily from inside the organization.*
- *Invite corporate executives to host a session and introduce the speaker.*
- *Advertise the conference so it is perceived as an event.*
- *Track who signs up and attends each session.*
- *Send reminders to participants who registered.*
- *Have tokens or door prizes and snacks at each session.*
- *Take time to reflect and ask attendees to evaluate each session.*

Champion Skeptic

Astronomer Carl Sagan said that we need a balance between two conflicting needs—the most skeptical scrutiny of all hypotheses that are served up to us and a great openness to new ideas. If you are only skeptical, then you never learn anything new. You become a crotchety old person convinced that nonsense is ruling the world. (There is, of course, much data to support you.) On the other hand, if you are open to the point of gullibility and have not an ounce of skeptical sense in you, then you cannot distinguish useful ideas from the worthless ones.

Ask for help from strong opinion leaders, who are skeptical of your new idea, to play the role of "official skeptic." Use their comments to improve your effort, even if you don't change their minds.

You are an Evangelist(144) or Dedicated Champion(129) trying to Involve Everyone(173). You are using Fear Less(151) and Bridge-Builder(110) to try to interest skeptics in your new idea.

Some of the resistors to the new idea are strong opinion leaders in your organization.

Skeptics who are both gurus and Connectors(119) know and talk with many people across the organization. If they are vocal about their reluctance to accept your new idea, this will stifle your efforts unless you change their minds, limit their impact, or ask them to help you. The first option may not be possible—you may not be able to bring them to your side. But if they are offered a role in the initiative, they could change from a skeptical outsider to an insider who could make a positive contribution. They do this by bringing a "devil's advocate" approach to decision making: a solid argument is made and then subjected to grilling by another person or group. Proponents report that it allows only the best plans to survive.

A certain amount of opposition can be beneficial. If there are several strong opinions that provide different points of view, there is likely to be more thought and discussion. As a result, you can work toward a consensus of all the ideas.

Therefore:

Ask for help from a skeptical opinion leader to play the role of "official skeptic" or "official realist."

Encourage him to point out the problems he sees with the new idea. Invite him to all meetings and presentations, but if he can't attend, give him an opportunity to talk with you personally. Make sure he understands that his opinions should not stand in the way of progress. Rather, explain that his role is to anticipate problems so that these issues can then be addressed.

Use the information the Champion Skeptic provides. For example, when you talk about the new idea, mention the problems that still need to be tackled so that people know you have a complete view of the new idea. The information can also help set realistic goals that deliver real value.

Just Say Thanks(183) when some point you hadn't thought of is brought to your attention. It may be your opportunity to be corrected before you make a serious mistake.

Don't take the idea of Champion Skeptic to extreme. A moderate amount of disagreement is all right, but avoid people with strong personalities who are openly hostile.

If there is more than one skeptic who should be involved, you might consider creating a "Greek Chorus," a forum where skepticism is featured. This could be a one-time workshop or a group of people who regularly contribute to meetings.

= = = = = = = = = =

This pattern creates a relationship with a vocal, influential skeptic who can't be included in any other way. The invitation to become a Champion Skeptic will encourage the skeptic's involvement and the opportunity for him to learn more about the innovation. Assigning this role can also feed the skeptic's ego. Recognizing and validating the ideas of an argumentative person will give him positive reinforcement, and may possibly make it no longer as much fun for him to argue.

If the skeptics are a strong influence in the organization, amplifying their objections could result in the non-adoption of your idea. You must be resilient— be prepared to handle criticism and negative statements.

A couple of people in Dave's firm are good at "being critical." Even though they are difficult people to please, they are highly respected throughout the organization. So Dave makes a point of having at least one of these folks on any steering group. He says that they keep him from getting carried away.

When one department has a meeting or discussion, they expect Susan to take the negative side. No matter what she truly believes, she is excellent at playing devil's advocate. She seems to hate everything, but once she starts to use something she usually likes it. Her initial skepticism but openness in the long run makes her credible. Susan has an important role. Although the team sometimes feels like she is working against them, she keeps them honest in the long run. Without her insights, the other department members might not consider all the possibilities.

Connector

When I'm in search of something or someone in my large, complicated organization, I know who to ask: Mary. She seems to know everyone, or at least someone, in all the divisions and departments. When I explain my problem to her, she seems to think for less than a second and then replies, "Oh, yeah, you need to talk with...." It always saves me a lot of time to ask Mary first.

To help you spread the word about the innovation, ask for help from people who have connections with many others in the organization.

You are an Evangelist(144) or Dedicated Champion(129) trying to introduce a new idea into your organization. You're doing some things to give exposure to a new idea, but you know there are others who might be interested.

Your organization is too big for you to personally contact everyone.

Studies have consistently pointed to the importance of informal networks. This is how people learn about new ideas, coach one another, and share practical tips and lessons over time. The information that passes through these networks has credibility. When people we know talk about something new, we naturally pay attention.

Over 25 years of research shows that many people are more likely to turn to friends, family, and other personal experts than to use traditional media for ideas and information on a range of topics. Making a decision means having a conversation.

Word-of-mouth epidemics are created when Connectors talk with others. These special people see possibilities in everyone they meet. They know many types of people in different social circles and have a gift for bringing the world together. The closer an idea comes to this type of person, the more opportunity it has.

Researchers have identified a special subgroup of Connectors, the Influentials. They comprise about 10% of the adult population in the U.S. They are interested in many subjects and are connected to many groups. They know how to express themselves. Because of their connections in the community, workplace, and society, their opinions are heard and they can influence decisions among many people. Almost certainly you know one. Chances are you seek out an Influential when you have an important decision to make. They often know the answer to the question you have. If they don't, they know someone who does. Influentials tend to be two to five years ahead of the rest of us on many important trends, such as the adoption of major technologies or new ideas.

If word of mouth is like a radio signal broadcast over the country, Influentials are the strategically placed transmitters that amplify the signal, multiplying dramatically the number of people who hear it. The signal becomes stronger and stronger as it is beamed from Influential to Influential and then broadcast to the nation as a whole.

You have to work in the formal structure of your organization, but you can't overlook the ability of other communication networks to spread the word. You'll improve your chances for success by taking advantage of the many informal relationships in your organization.

Therefore:

Ask for help in spreading the word about the innovation from those who know and communicate with many others in your organization.

Look for individuals who can connect with others. They will be easy to locate because they know so many kinds of people, including you! You may be more likely to find them among the Early Adopters(138)—this group is generally more social than the Innovators(170) and more likely to be members of many different social circles.

Use Personal Touch(198) to convince them of the value in the new idea. If they are Innovators, it should be easy to persuade them. If not, it will be well worth the extra time, because once they become interested, their connection to others will decrease the effort you will need to spread the word. Connectors do not need to be close friends with everyone. They will have "strong ties" that typically share their interests or proximity, as well as many "weak ties" that link them to other social circles. Encourage them to talk with both their "strong" and "weak" ties about the new idea. Connectors will also know the skeptics, so ask them to be Bridge-Builders(110). Remember to Just Say Thanks(183) when they tell you about any contact they've made.

Be wary of Connectors who don't support the innovation. Connectors who are Influentials can spread the word about a new idea in persuasive ways. Few important trends reach the mainstream without passing through the Influentials in the early stages, but Influentials can stop a would-be trend in its tracks. They give the thumbs-up that propels a trend or the thumbs-down that relegates it to a short 15 minutes of fame. Consider giving Connectors with a thumbs-down attitude the special role of Champion Skeptic(116).

= = = = = = = = =

This pattern makes connections with people you might not otherwise reach on your own. Once the Connectors are convinced of the new idea, they will spread the word faster than you can by yourself.

But Connectors can also bring in more people than you have time to handle. So make sure you have interesting things to tell them and some plan of action in place so that the new people don't become intrigued only to find out that there really isn't anything interesting going on.

The people who were the most helpful to Pat when she started introducing a new idea were the secretaries. They know everybody and everything. They are the power behind the managers who make important decisions. They know who to talk to about any issue. They became Pat's most powerful resource.

There are many Connectors at one company because it funds organizations that encourage activities such as the music club, the flying club, and the golf club. The company also has a group that plays bridge at lunchtime and goes out for a meal every other week on payday. Most of these people have known each other for years—both at work and outside work—but even outside work, they talk about work, of course.

Corporate Angel

My boss stopped by my cubicle and said, "I hear you've been giving brown bags on <a new idea>. I think you should give a presentation to the vice president. His staff meeting is in a couple of weeks." I agreed, but I didn't understand why the high-level managers needed to hear about this particular idea. I thought it was a good idea for the technical people in the organization but that was it. I was so wrong. That presentation brought training and the purchase of cases of books and, eventually, a new job description for me that allowed me more time to work on introducing the innovation. My ideas wouldn't have gotten far without buy-in from upper management.

To help align the innovation with the goals of the organization, get support from a high-level executive.

You are an Evangelist(144) or a Dedicated Champion(129) trying to introduce a new idea into your organization. You've been giving Brown Bags(113) and have won the approval of your Local Sponsor(186).

Support from local management will provide some attention and resources for the new idea, but you need high-level support to have a more lasting impact.

Enthusiasm at the local level can only go so far. Big-ticket items—training, books, conferences, and visiting gurus, such as a Big Jolt(107) speaker or Mentor(192)—are needed if interest in the new idea is to grow. But resources can be limited because each level of management has authority to spend only in a certain area. A high-level supporter who believes in the importance of the innovation and will lend appropriate coaching and direction can make many inroads easier. In addition to resources, he can provide the collaboration and encouragement to align the new idea to the broader goals of the organization. This is vital to a successful change effort. It is this alignment that will make the initiatives last beyond any changes in local management.

The higher you go in your organization to reach and convince others, the more secure your effort will be. An analysis of the best technology-transfer practices of a broad cross section of government agencies, research institutions, and national and industrial laboratories identified the importance of *angels*, high-level executives who protect start-up projects until they mature.

Therefore:

Enlist the support of a high-level executive who has a special interest in the new idea and will provide direction and the resources to support it.

Talk to high-level executives about the new idea as early as possible. Explain how the innovation is Tailor Made(234) to match the needs of the organization. If the Corporate Angel (or his staff) is hesitant and wants more information, you might suggest that he call for a Guru Review(161).

Look for high-level supporters who are respected across their organization; otherwise their involvement could hurt your cause. The wrong kind of executive support can give the impression that the new idea is being "railroaded" through the organization. Be wary of those who embrace the new idea simply because of personal interest—the initiative may not survive if the executive moves to a different role or organization.

Make sure that the upper-level position is not brought in to dictate behavior. The role of Corporate Angel is similar to Peter Senge's "Executive Leader" —a protector, mentor, and thinking partner. This is not an authoritarian role. David Baum suggests that a simple statement from a leader such as "We're all going through an amazing amount of change," can create a sense that everyone in the organization is facing the struggles together. This alone can help.

Keep the Corporate Angel interested. Stay in Touch(221) and offer the chance for a Royal Audience(210) when an appropriate Big Jolt(107) visitor is planned.

= = = = = = = = = =

This pattern establishes high-level executive support for the innovation in the organization. The process of introducing the innovation becomes easier since lower-level managers and others in the organization are usually open to directives from the top. The Corporate Angel can also ensure that your interests and the plans of the Local Sponsor(186) are aligned with that of the organization to avoid competition and limit any confusion.

The risk is that high-level support can give the impression that the innovation is being imposed or is simply just the "buzzword of the week." If you suspect this could happen, it may be better to concentrate on growing more grassroots interest first.

The team that worked over a three-year period to earn Division I NCAA Certification for their university's Athletic Program found that the support of the Chancellor was vital. Although he was not involved in doing the large amount of paperwork, his occasional attendance at the team meetings was uplifting because it showed the hard-working members that he was willing to listen and participate in some of the discussions. He frequently mentioned the ongoing effort during campus meetings to the faculty that was not historically supportive of athletics. At the conclusion of the effort, when the Athletic Program received recertification and an outstanding report, the Chancellor continued marketing athletics on the campus by making the announcement and pointing out that the institution should be proud that they fared better than most institutions did.

Every time Helen brought a new proposal before her organization's decision makers, she faced a long discussion and a low probability that her proposal would pass on the first attempt. However, it was a different story when the vice president attended one meeting and took a few minutes to thank Helen for her hard work in making some needed changes in the organization. Her two proposals passed that day in a record amount of time.

Corridor Politics

I'm on the board of directors for several non-profit organizations, so it happens all the time. I know when I see the Caller ID of a fellow board member that I'm in for an earful. I learn a lot, though. I get the inside scoop, and in the end I almost always wind up supporting the guy who called me. I figure he's taken the time to call and thinks I'm open to his argument. Besides, next time I might be the one making the phone calls when I'm preparing for an upcoming vote on the board.

Informally work on decision makers and key influencers before an important vote to make sure they fully understand the consequences of the decision.

You are an Evangelist(144) or Dedicated Champion(129) facing an upcoming decision that will have an impact on your effort. The decision makers are peers, or at least approachable.

It's difficult to address the concerns of all decision makers when a new idea is raised in a large meeting.

If you go into a vote without having an idea what will happen, you risk an unfavorable outcome that may be impossible to change later. It's hard to change the decision of a group once it is made. Yet, decision makers are not likely to agree with a new idea immediately. Their automatic response is usually "no" if they hear about the idea for the first time during a meeting. They must first get the opportunity to voice their individual concerns and ask questions. This is difficult to do in a group meeting and much easier and more effective to do one-on-one.

Therefore:

Informally work on decision makers and key influencers one-on-one before the vote. Try to get the approval of anyone who can kill it.

Approach the decision maker gently by briefly explaining the issue and then asking if he has any questions. Listen to his concerns and address each one. After you've answered the questions that are foremost on his mind, give him additional details. Present the facts, not just your feelings. Be clear about what you hope will happen. Tell a story to make the issue real. Make sure all decision makers fully understand the problem and the consequences of the decision. Don't distort the facts just to win the vote; that will come back to haunt you later.

Let each person know if a decision maker who is a manager or a local guru has already given support. In many cases, if you talk to the most receptive people first, you can use these people as references for the next person you talk with.

Don't present the issue as controversial. No naming; no blaming. Don't use this pattern for personal issues (e.g., to have a specific individual put on a lay-off list—it then becomes a personal crusade and can lead to hard feelings). Don't use this pattern to get around a powerful person. Even if you win the votes and the decision goes your way, that powerful person may become angry if his perception is that the issue is being steamrolled past him. Use Whisper in the General's Ear(248) to enable a manager to look good in a group setting.

Use Fear Less(151) to calm skeptics. Even if your argument isn't convincing, you may turn down the heat on the other side.

Know when to compromise—it may be the best way to reach your ultimate goals. Don't be a fanatic. As long as it isn't seen as a trick, a concession will likely stimulate a return concession. Making concessions during an interaction is an effective way to win an argument.

Build a relationship with the decision maker. It may not be possible for a person who is new to the organization to use this pattern until a trusting relationship has been established with others.

If you are short on time, your key contacts should be the fence sitters, those who are uncommitted and could vote either way.

If the decision doesn't go your way, remember, "No permanent friends, no permanent enemies." Some day, on some other issue of importance to you, the decision maker may come through. In the meantime, don't allow a decision maker to become an active opponent. If you win support for your issue, Just Say Thanks(183) and pay your debts. If someone supports you, remember to listen when he has an issue that is important to him.

The importance of talking with people before an event is similar to fellow pattern writer, David Kane's <u>No Surprises</u> pattern, which stresses the need to talk with customers before any anticipated changes. In other words, rather than doing damage repair, anticipate what is about to happen and do risk management.

= = = = = = = = = =

This pattern creates one-on-one communication with decision makers. It helps you provide information before a meeting to encourage a vote to go your way. Since the issues are understood, the meeting time can be more efficient. There may be no need for discussion since all concerns have already been addressed.

The risk is that the people you talk with will expect a favor in the future. Also, one-on-one discussion before a meeting can be perceived as underhanded politics. You want to be as aboveboard as possible. Using this approach for purely selfish reasons is likely to backfire. The pattern is most effective when it is driven by what is best for the community.

When Bill's company decided to use the Rational Unified Process (RUP), some of the managers were tied to the old software process. So before they voted on the process decision, Bill talked with all the software managers. Then, at the meeting, the vote was taken without any discussion. Bill was certain that if he hadn't met with the managers individually they wouldn't have understood why the company needed to move to RUP and they would have automatically reacted against it. If the vote had been taken under those conditions, it would have been almost impossible to undo.

Lisa wanted mandatory training for all software developers, which had to be approved by management. She visited each manager in her area and described how the program would work and the costs and benefits. She explained how the training would reinforce the company values and would be useful in the short-term as well as over time. By the time Lisa brought it up at a manager's meeting, it was a done deal. There wasn't any discussion. They just voted.

Dedicated Champion

What allowed us to depart from our normal manner of business? I believe the most important element was a successful champion who engendered interest in process change. Our champion is a respected team member who is well known for getting work done and for his sincere desire to help lead the organization toward practical improvements.

To increase your effectiveness in introducing your new idea, make a case for having the work part of your job description.

You are an Evangelist(144) who has successfully enlisted a Local Sponsor(186) or Corporate Angel(123).

Effectively introducing a new idea into any organization is too much work for a volunteer.

Without the pro-active effort of someone whose job description includes championing the new idea, it can wither and die on the vine. A single, dedicated individual can bring a focus to the activities necessary to maintain a sufficient level of interest to keep the idea alive. A volunteer doesn't have enough time to do this. To get this time, the change effort needs to be recognized as part of your job.

Therefore:

Make a case for including the change initiative as part of your job description.

To convince your manager, consider the following suggestions. Managers are interested in metrics. Track the number of Brown Bags(113), the number and names of attendees, and those you have signed up for the e-Forum(135). If you have any findings, objective or subjective from your own experience applying Just Do It(177) or the experience of others, this is also convincing information. The support of a local guru will help, especially if it is someone your manager trusts. Offer to schedule a Guru Review(161) to provide an evaluation of the appropriateness of the idea for your organization.

External Validation(148) is also convincing, especially if the publications are in the domain the manager cares about or business-related books and articles. News about a competitor can make a big difference! A Big Jolt(107) visitor can be influential if he spends time in a Royal Audience(210) to address the manager's concerns.

You are "dedicated" if you have: (1) devotion to the cause and (2) time dedicated to the task of championing the new idea. You can start with a small percentage of your time and later use Tailor Made(234) to argue for expanding it if there are business reasons that will be compelling to your manager.

When you become the Dedicated Champion, keep your enthusiasm and don't neglect any of your current Evangelist activities. Even if you are hired as a Dedicated Champion, you must still take on the role of an Evangelist.

Realize that you do not own the success of the new idea. Too often, a Dedicated Champion, in his zeal to succeed, does all the work rather than facilitating and ensuring that others do their part. Use Involve Everyone(173) and Ask for Help(104). Measure success by how many tasks you encourage others to do. You must become comfortable with an emergence of the new idea in the organization, patient as teams struggle to find how the innovation helps them succeed, and secure enough to create opportunities for others to do their part.

= = = = = = = = = =

This pattern creates a role dedicated to leading the introduction of the innovation into the organization. The new idea is likely to grow in the organization because you now have time, and possibly additional resources, to carry out the necessary tasks in the change initiative.

However, the approval of this role may come with the expectation to succeed. If the success of the innovation is on your shoulders, it becomes important for you to justify your time, track the results and the small successes, and continually demonstrate the benefits. Metrics can be useful. If you note these as you go, you will have them in your "back pocket" in case your boss needs data to justify your new role.

Margaret's primary job in the organization was to introduce the innovation into the organization. Because of this, she had time to do things like talk with people individually, arrange special events, keep the idea visible, and have regular conversations about what is going on with the managers. In other words, the biggest and most important resource she had was time.

A newly hired vice chancellor noticed there were a few areas in the university that had been neglected and were in need of attention. So he appointed one faculty member to each of the areas with the task of making improvements. Because they were awarded some "reassigned time" from their teaching obligations, they had the time to examine the problems and lead the needed changes.

Do Food

Our small team had to prepare weekly status reports. We hated this job and the wasted meeting time it took each week. Someone told me that the next meeting was our team lead's birthday, so I bought chocolate chip cookies. As we gathered for the meeting I said, "I heard it's Tim's birthday today, so I brought cookies!" It was as though we'd been living in a cave and someone had turned on the lights. People smiled and began telling stories from their childhood. The meeting was fun. We joked about the report and the task we all hated. We finished early. All this from a few cookies.

Make an ordinary gathering a special event by including food.

You are an Evangelist(144) or Dedicated Champion(129) who has called a meeting to introduce a new idea. Members of the user community are free to attend or not. You have resources, your own personal contribution or those of a Local Sponsor(186) or Corporate Angel(123).

Usually a meeting is just another ordinary, impersonal event.

Research shows that we become fonder of people and things we experience while we are eating. Even in ancient times, you can find that people understood the importance of breaking bread together. In Christopher Alexander's pattern <u>Communal Eating</u>, sharing food plays a vital role in almost all human societies to bind people together and increase the feeling of group membership. Food turns a meeting into an event. "The mere act of eating together ... is by its very nature a sign of friendship...."*

Therefore:

Make food available at the meeting.

Mention the availability of food when you advertise the event. Ask for help from your Local Sponsor or Corporate Angel to furnish the food. This is an important sign to attendees that the organization supports the effort. If organizational funding is not available, you could buy some inexpensive snacks. Both your colleagues and management will be impressed that you believe in the idea enough to put your money where your mouth is.

Be sure you understand the role of food in the culture. In some settings, food and work don't mix and the idea of eating during a business-related meeting would not be accepted. Each company treats food in certain ways during the workday.

Try to be sensitive to health issues. People who struggle with weight problems may find that cookies on the table are too much of a temptation. Someone with an allergy to the one food you offer will feel left out. Think about offering a bit of variety and some healthier choices.

There is no need to be extravagant; the forces are resolved in this pattern even if the food is simple.

Food is also important in small meetings, even between two people.

= = = = = = = = =

This pattern turns an ordinary meeting into a special event and contributes to a feeling of community among the participants. Because everyone likes free food, it can draw people in. It will turn a mundane meeting, presentation, or other gathering into a more special event. If food is offered in the beginning, it

---

*Alexander, C.A. et al., *A Pattern Language*, Oxford University Press, 1977.

starts the meeting on a positive note. If the topic gets controversial, it can put people in a more relaxed mood—they can stand up and get a cup of tea or grab a cookie. Food holds people's attention if the meeting gets slow.

When you begin to regularly have food at events, people will expect it and be irritated when it doesn't appear. If the food budget is depleted, have a Brown Bag(113). There are other ways to make a meeting special, such as holding a meeting outside on a nice day, using a different meeting management technique that people are not used to, cutting the agenda in half and letting people go early, or holding the event in a special executive conference room arranged by your Corporate Angel.

When the company started cutting back on everything, the food budget was eliminated for meetings. So Sue started bringing some inexpensive sweets. Sometimes "scouts" went out before the meeting and reported back to the rest of the group if there was food. It made Sue realize how important food was for the success of the event. When a manager came to her and asked for a retrospective, she would say, "I think it's important to have food at the meeting, so I will personally pay for cookies for the team." The manager would always reply, "Okay, since you obviously think this is important, I'll personally pay for the Pepsi." It never failed. Yes, Sue had to spend a bit of her money every time, but the manager would always ante up his contribution and the team knew it. It actually was better than when the company's budget paid for everything.

When Rachel prepares for leading project retrospective sessions, she always reminds the organizers that they need to supply snacks and drinks during the day. She has noticed that participants often gather around the food for a friendly chat during breaktime and wander to the snack table when they need a break but can't leave the room. This is important, because it helps to relieve the strain and exhaustion that often develops during the intense retrospective work.

e-Forum

When I started on the South Beach diet, I thought, "Here I go again." I read the book and tried to clean out my pantry and refrigerator, but it didn't take long to really get tired of the food on the acceptable list. Then I discovered information about this diet on the Web site Prevention.com. I had been a reader of Prevention magazine for years, but the recipes and the tips that others shared on this Web site kept me going.

Set up an electronic bulletin board, distribution list, listserve, or writeable Web site for those who want to hear more.

You are an Evangelist(144) or Dedicated Champion(129) trying to introduce a new idea into your organization.

You need to initiate and maintain regular contact with people who might be interested in your new idea.

It's hard to get information to everyone. People are busy and overwhelmed by too many ideas. They may not find the time to attend every event, but they like to know what's going on. You are busy too. You want to Stay in Touch(221) but don't have the time to personally keep everyone informed about the latest and greatest happenings with the new idea.

Electronic forums allow people to keep in touch and keep a new idea on their minds. When you set up a mailing list for the enthusiasts or devotees, you'll get to know some of your most potentially valuable members and give them a chance to meet each other.

Therefore:

Create a publicly accessible electronic, interactive forum. Advertise its existence. Keep it alive, active, and growing.

This can be an electronic bulletin board, distribution list, listserve, or a writeable Web site. You may wish to use it to distribute electronic resources, announce upcoming events, and connect people who are doing similar things with the innovation across the organization. Create separate "announce" and "discussion" lists, since some people want to actively participate and others want to passively hear what's going on.

This is one way to Stay in Touch, but it should not be the only way. Post information In Your Space(167). Give regular status reports and tell people what's happening next. Use Connectors(119) to send information through their networks. Don't forget to maintain personal contact with individuals who are key to your efforts.

If you monitor the medium, you can use this data to convince a Local Sponsor(186) or Corporate Angel(123) that there is sufficient interest to take the next step in the change initiative.

= = = = = = = = =

This pattern creates a place to electronically share information and expectations about the new idea. It keeps you from becoming isolated from those who are interested in hearing about it. The virtual community will help you establish a real one.

If you use it too much, it can have an overdose effect and can even be viewed as spam. Don't get too accustomed to using electronic means. Know your community and what they are interested in seeing.

The first Brown Bag meetings Gary held were well attended but a few busy people stopped by and said, "I was held up and couldn't make the meeting. Do you have any handouts?" "Sure!" he replied, "I'll send them to you." While he was at it, he e-mailed notes to others he knew were interested. *That's how it started. The list grew as others heard he was e-mailing notices for meetings and other events. It was the beginning of the community that became involved in the new idea.*

Alison used an e-mail distribution list to draw attention to the activities surrounding the new idea. The initial list came from people who attended a *Hometown Story*. Later, when training courses were offered, attendees were added. The distribution list was used to advertise upcoming events, like *Big Jolt* visits, and other news surrounding the new idea. The list made the recipients feel special because they heard about something before the general population.

Early Adopter

Geoffrey Moore explains, " Visionaries are that rare breed of people who have the insight to match a [new idea] to a strategic opportunity, the temperament to translate that insight into a high-visibility project, and the charisma to get the rest of the organization to buy into that project."* They are the ones who can give your new idea its first break. Even though it is hard to plan for them, it's even harder to plan without them.

Win the support of the people who can be opinion leaders for the new idea.

You are an Evangelist(144) or Dedicated Champion(129) trying to introduce a new idea into your organization. You have a small group of Innovators(170) who support your new idea.

To create more impact for the new idea in an organization, interest must extend beyond the initial group of supporters.

Innovators are helpful as gatekeepers for the innovation, but they generally don't make good opinion leaders because people are wary of their attitude toward

---

*Moore, G.A., *Crossing the Chasm*, HarperCollins Publishers, Inc., 1999.

risk. Innovators tend to be effective opinion leaders only in highly innovative organizations. In other organizations, you need the help of people who are more practical, who have a reputation for being open-minded and sensible decision makers. These Early Adopters follow the Innovators on the normal curve of adopter categories. They are just ahead of the Early Majority(141) in their level of innovativeness and risk-taking.

Early Adopters are visionaries who care more about fundamental breakthroughs than simple improvements. Unlike the more enthusiastic Innovators who like an idea just because it's new, Early Adopters consider the usefulness of the idea and attempt to match it to a business goal. As a result, they often have the respect of their peers and make good opinion leaders. This is the reason they are generally sought by change agents to help speed up the diffusion process.

Therefore:

Look for the opinion leaders in your organization and ask for help from them.

You can find Early Adopters among people who have a reputation for discrete, successful use of new ideas. These are people who don't jump on a new idea, but instead react with an open mind and an interest to learn more. Give them as much information and training as possible to convince them of your idea. They are attracted by the Smell of Success(219).

Use Personal Touch(198) and encourage them to look to Innovators for experiences with the innovation. To cultivate their interest, you must use Tailor Made(234) and a down-to-earth approach and show the usefulness of the innovation to the organization. Be flexible and willing to work with them as they try to realize the business value the idea offers.

Once they are convinced of the new idea, encourage them to take on the role of Bridge-Builder(110). Ask them to lead a Study Group(228) or do a Hometown Story(164) after they get some experience using the innovation. They can also help land the support of a Local Sponsor(186) or Corporate Angel(123).

If you find an Early Adopter who becomes a Guru on Your Side(158), he may be interested in being part of a Guru Review(161).

Stay in Touch(221) and remember to Just Say Thanks(183).

= = = = = = = = =

This pattern establishes a group who can help serve as opinion leaders for your new idea in the organization. The support of these individuals will reduce the uncertainty that other people, such as the Early Majority and skeptics, have about the new idea.

The support of this group does not come for free. Unlike the Innovators who usually become excited after attending one event, Early Adopters will ask for more information before they become convinced. But this reaction to new ideas is what earns them a trusted reputation and, in turn, their role as opinion leaders. So any time you take with them is likely to pay off later.

Soon after Kathy started talking about a new idea in her organization, she noticed that Carol took the initiative to read one of the well-known books on the topic. So Kathy took her for coffee one day to answer her questions about what the idea could offer the organization. Carol was hooked. Because her work and her opinions were respected in the organization, Kathy asked her to talk with others about the new idea. And when Kathy planned an event, she always asked Carol for her opinion on the details.

The knowledge management initiative at one company targeted the software developers who would be interested in the long-term goal of building a repository to capture best practices in the organization. Those who were involved in the knowledge mining for the repository were the respected, down-to-earth developers who were open to new ideas, not those who were wildly enthusiastic just because it was a new thing.

Early Majority

Marketers of a high-tech product tell this story. In the first year of selling their product, the technology enthusiasts, Innovators, and some visionaries, Early Adopters, quickly jumped on board. During the second year, the company won over more visionaries and a handful of truly major deals. In the third year, the company expanded its sales force, increased its advertising budget, opened new district offices, and strengthened customer support. But the sales ended up being far less than expected and the growth in expenses was larger than the growth in revenue. What the company interpreted as a steadily emerging mainstream market was really an early market. The company failed to recognize that selling an idea to Innovators and Early Adopters is different from selling it to the Early Majority.

To create commitment to the new idea in the organization, you must convince the majority.

You are an Evangelist(144) or Dedicated Champion(129) trying to introduce a new idea into your organization. You have the support of Innovators(170) and Early Adopters(138).

The support of Innovators **and** Early Adopters **will spark the new idea in the organization, but you need much more to truly have impact.**

You begin to build your grassroots effort with Innovators who are gatekeepers and Early Adopters who are the early opinion leaders. But at some point you must win the support of the majority to allow the idea to thrive. The Early Majority represents about one-third of the population. Once this group is convinced, they are loyal and will often enforce organizational standards to help the innovation succeed.

The Early Majority are much more deliberate in their decision making. Before they commit to a new idea, they want to know how others have succeeded with it. They want the innovation to work properly and integrate well with the way things are done. Risk is viewed as a waste of time and money rather than a chance for opportunity or excitement. Unlike Innovators, the Early Majority adopts too late to take on the role of gatekeeper for the new idea. Unlike Early Adopters, they are followers and generally do not hold positions of opinion leadership. Yet, they provide the link between people that adopt early and those who are relatively late. This link bridges the gap or "chasm" between Early Adopters and the Early Majority. You must cross this chasm to get a new idea into the mainstream.

Therefore:

Expand the group that has adopted the new idea rapidly to include the more deliberate majority that will allow the new idea to establish a strong foothold in your organization.

Look for individuals who are practical and want incremental, measurable, predictable progress. Use Personal Touch(198) to show them that the risk is low while the value to their immediate needs is great. Show them the visible improvements that can be obtained with the innovation by applying Tailor Made(234). Demonstrate results with Just Do It(177) and share sources of External Validation(148). Connect them with Early Adopters and other peers who have already adopted the innovation. Encourage them to attend a Hometown Story(164).

Once they are convinced, encourage them to talk with their peers about the innovation. Since they are the link to the Late Majority, ask them to take on the role of Bridge-Builder(110) to connect with individuals who are more conservative than they are. Remember to Just Say Thanks(183).

= = = = = = = = =

This pattern establishes a grass roots majority for a new idea in the organization. Acceptance by the Early Majority defines the tipping point for the innovation. Gaining their support will accelerate the introduction of the new idea in the organization because the chasm has been crossed and the innovation is in the mainstream. In addition, unlike Innovators who usually move from one new idea to the next and Early Adopters who often see themselves on the fast track, the Early Majority can offer stability and long-term commitment.

But you can become frustrated with this group because they can be hard to reach by simply talking with them. Be patient. You must have successes before you can begin to convince them.

A faculty member in a neighboring department stopped by Karen's office seeking advice on a proposal he submitted for a new undergraduate major. He explained that he had been encouraged by the initial enthusiasm from some members of his department. So he moved forward with the planning and thought that the other members would eventually become convinced that it was a good thing to do. But this did not happen. The majority of the department was not behind him. Karen suggested that these people needed more assurance that his idea was not risky. So he talked with each individual about the advantages the new major would offer the department and provided evidence that it would not take large amounts of resources from other projects. It wasn't an overnight process, but eventually the majority agreed that he should move forward with the planning.

How do you know when you have built a culture surrounding a new idea? Randy thinks he knew that he had passed a significant point when a high-level manager stopped by his office late one evening. He sat down heavily and began to talk about some problems he was having and then asked, "So, do you think <the new idea> can help me?" This was a manager of a large legacy system. The new idea had never been "pitched" to his department and although anyone could take the training, most of the interest came from the new projects. If this manager was asking to use the new idea, clearly the majority was being won over.

Evangelist

Evangelist and author Barbara Waugh writes, "How I thought it worked was, if you were great, like Martin Luther King Jr., you had a dream. Since I wasn't great, I figured I had no dream and the best I could do was follow someone else's. Now I believe it works like this: It's having the dream that makes you great. It's the dream that produces the greatness. It's the dream that draws others around us and attracts the resources it takes to accomplish the dream."*

To begin to introduce the new idea into your organization, do everything you can to share your passion for it.

You're excited about a new idea. Maybe you went to a conference or read an article or book and, as a result, started learning more. You believe your idea will have value for your organization and you want to spread the word.

---

*Waugh, B. and M. S. Forrest, *Soul in the Computer*, Inner Ocean, 2001.

You want to get a new idea going in your organization but you don't know where to start.

It's hard to translate enthusiasm into action that has lasting impact. New ideas are always out there, more than we can handle. Even the best ideas still need to be sold. This depends on the enthusiasm of people who are the natural instigators of fresh ideas and practices. They are the ones who can grow an idea into real change for the organization.

Therefore:

To introduce a new idea into your organization, let your passion for this new idea drive you.

Invest yourself in your cause. In other words, the first person to convince is you. If you don't believe in your cause, it will be difficult to sell it to anyone else. If you're not convinced then you're not convincing. You must be likeable, believable, and open, but not a fanatic. This is not a role for the fainthearted. Look for possibilities in every situation; take advantage of even small opportunities to get your idea across.

Share your vision with others. Let them feel your enthusiasm. Tell your story—this is the driver for real change. Your story should convey your passion, excitement, and conviction and inspire others to feel the same way. It's a good idea to have a two-minute "elevator speech" targeted for different audiences, so you're ready when anyone asks you about your new idea. Show that there's value in your new idea. Don't preach—any improvements should just radiate from you and from your work. Hopefully others will notice and inquire.

Learn more about possibilities for the innovation in your organization with Just Do It(177). But realize that you are not the expert. Don't sell yourself that way or expect that you can play the expert role. A little humility goes a long way. Also, keep in mind that you are not the idea. You're a person who has a good idea but other people can share it. You don't lose anything if others become more knowledgeable, or if others also become Evangelists.

Don't worry if you don't have an all-encompassing strategy. Test the Waters(237) with a simple plan of action. Take Time for Reflection(240) and learn as you go. Celebrate Small Successes(216), be prepared for setbacks, and realize that real change takes time. Get beyond a quick-fix mindset, because progress can be slow. Proceed Step by Step, letting each stage build on the previous one.

Give Brown Bags(113) and use Plant the Seeds(204). Do Food(132) at events when you can. Begin to identify Innovators(170) and Connectors(119). Set up an e-Forum(135).

If there is interest, start a Study Group(228). If you have a well-known contact who will come in to your organization at no cost, bring in a Big Jolt(107).

Use Personal Touch(198) and remember to Just Say Thanks(183).

If you are seen as an Innovator, people are less likely to trust what you have to say, since you probably get excited about new things just because they are new. If you seen as are an Early Adopter(138), you are likely to be more effective in reaching the rest of the organization because of your reputation for being more down-to-earth in your decision making.

Research suggests that if you are naturally likeable and attractive, your job will be easier because people are unconsciously more open to people they like. If you are introverted or opinionated, people are not likely to trust you, even if you've got the best data in the world. You must be a strong communicator, someone who can build personal credibility. Fellow pattern writer Joe Bergin's Introvert - Extrovert pattern suggests that you can learn to play the role of an extrovert, so that an observer believes you are bold and outgoing. You must recognize when this role is appropriate, gather your resources, and play the part.

Ask for Help(104). It's hard to be a Salesman *and* a Connector(119) *and* a Maven, but all three roles are needed to lead a change initiative. Don't try to do it all. For example, a Guru on Your Side(158) is a good candidate for a Maven. Encourage others to be Evangelists in their own teams.

Your goal is to earn credibility. Others may not always agree with you, but they need to trust what you say. This is the most important part of being a change agent. Once you've earned credibility, you're in a good position to become a Dedicated Champion(129). Be on the lookout for possible managerial support. Real impact will require a Local Sponsor(186) and a Corporate Angel(123).

= = = = = = = = = =

This pattern establishes a role for an initial enthusiastic introduction of a new idea. It gets the new idea going in the organization and sparks some support from Innovators and possibly some interest among management.

The risk is that you can become too passionate about the new idea and turn some people off. Maintain the enthusiasm, but don't get carried away. Don't let your enthusiasm make you impatient. One of your most powerful qualities may be your ability to be patient and impatient at the same time. Keep in mind that most people need time before they will feel the same enthusiasm you do.

In 1999, after writing a book about improving long-term care for the elderly, Bill Thomas hit the road on a promotional tour. He spoke on radio and television. He also met with public officials, offering his perspective as a medical specialist on the care of the elderly. He stressed what was wrong with nursing homes: they were utterly devoid of hope, love, humor, meaning—the very stuff of life. He gave lectures on the changes he had in mind, but he also demonstrated why this was no ordinary book and this was no ordinary tour, and why he is certainly no ordinary doctor. It wasn't enough for Thomas to communicate his vision for better long-term care through an imaginative book. He also developed a one-man show based on the tale, traveling to 27 cities in 31 days. For him, the tour never ended. It can't. Not if he's going to fix long-term care in this country. It's an audacious mission and a truly big fix—one that requires more than just fresh ideas. Thomas advises, "You need to have people go a little nuts about what you want to do."

Walt Disney was good at conveying his vision for a new film. He would act out all the roles in front of a large group of his staff. Even though he was not a cartoonist, he knew what he wanted and could get his ideas across. He believed in these approaches: establish the vision; sell your dream, make it clear and alive; trust your people; don't interfere with their work; and give feedback at critical points.

External Validation

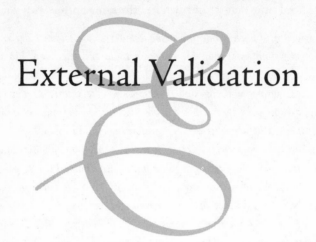

I've been trying to convince my dear friend Linda that my hometown of Asheville, North Carolina would be a great place for her husband and her to retire. She would just nod politely when I would tell her about all the things I thought the area has to offer. Then I pointed out some national publications in which the Asheville area appears as "best city" and "best place to retire." She now tells me that they have put Asheville on their list of cities to seriously consider.

To increase the credibility of the new idea, bring in information from sources external to the organization.

You are an Evangelist(144) or Dedicated Champion(129) working to introduce a new idea into your organization. People are writing and publishing on topics related to the new idea.

Before being persuaded to accept a new idea, people want assurance that the idea has validity outside the organization.

The innovation-decision process begins with knowledge. When people become aware of an innovation, they want to understand how it works. This information can come from within the organization but, initially, external sources of information are more important. External publications have more credibility than internal technical reports that are often write-only documents that are distributed widely but largely unread.

Most people want some evidence that the innovation is not just an impractical notion of a few individuals in the organization; therefore, endorsement from outside the organization will catch their eye. External sources of information are especially important for Innovators(170) and Early Adopters(138), typically the first to adopt an innovation, because at the time they are seeking knowledge there are few in the organization who have experience with the new idea.

Therefore:

Give people in the organization external sources of useful information about the new idea.

Mass media sources are a good place to start—books, articles, and Web pages with no-nonsense information. Include success stories when you can for those who appreciate the Smell of Success(219). Make sure the publications are trusted by the people you are trying to reach. For example, managers read business journals, not technical ones.

Look for opportunities to Plant the Seeds(204). Distribute the information one-on-one with Personal Touch(198) or on a wider basis with e-Forum(135) and In Your Space(167). In addition to the written word, bring in a Big Jolt(107) speaker.

Consider presenting your work externally in a venue that is recognized by your colleagues. Publish in journals read by the people you want to convince, especially Early Adopters and anyone who is a Guru on Your Side(158). You may even want to write a book and get it published by an external publisher.

Although external sources can and should be provided at any time, use this pattern especially in the early days of your efforts, when people need knowledge and there are few opinion leaders in the organization.

= = = = = = = = = =

This pattern generates some validation for a new idea in the organization. It shows that the innovation is not just a local phenomenon. Because this is what people need, it is effective in gaining awareness and raising credibility. Management might see this External Validation as a sign that the competition is gaining ground in this area. This can spur decision makers to support the innovation.

But the distribution of external sources throughout your organization can be seen as intellectual browbeating. Sending books or articles up and down the chain can make people feel inadequate because they can't keep up with the pace of reading. Use Just Enough(180) and state ideas as simple, authentic statements. Provide more background if anyone asks. External publishing also involves risks. Others across the organization might label your effort as "writing only and not working." Make your topics factual, relevant, and useful so your colleagues don't dismiss them as academic.

My manager never paid much attention to my research until one day I showed him a book that referenced one of my publications. He wasn't familiar with the topic of the book, but was extremely impressed that my name appeared in it. I did not expect such an enthusiastic reaction from him, but it showed me the power of external validation!

When we moved from Level 1 to Level 2 CMM (Capability Maturity Mode), we asked a few speakers from other companies at Level 2 and 3 to talk about the benefits they had realized in their organizations when they achieved these levels. This helped people to understand what could be achieved, and how these other organizations approached the changes.

Fear Less

In her book Soul in the Computer, *Barbara Waugh says, "I force myself to ask of every obstacle, 'What if this is a gift? What is it that this obstacle or setback is telling me?' Someone who is initially the most skeptical may become my best partner, constantly detecting the hype and fluff and unnecessary complexity in my thinking about what we are doing and what the next steps are."* *

Turn resistance to the new idea to your advantage.

You are an Evangelist(144) or Dedicated Champion(129) trying to introduce a new idea into your organization.

Any innovation is disruptive, so resistance is likely.

Every change agent complains about resistance, but if you think *this* is bad, consider the alternative. It's frightening to imagine a situation with no resistance at all. If that were the case, you would be solely responsible to be 100% correct, 100% of the time. Scary, isn't it? But nobody's perfect. We need resistance to test

---

*Waugh, B. and M.S. Forrest, *Soul in the Computer*, Inner Ocean, 2001.

our ideas. So, the first step in dealing with opposition is to appreciate it. Fortunately, it is universal. It's like fungus; it doesn't thrive in daylight. Therefore, once you suspect that there is resistance, your first step is to get it out in the open, rather than let it fester in the dark.

Skeptics can teach us a lot about what we are doing wrong. No matter how determined we are, how "righteous" our cause, we're going to run into obstacles. No course of action is perfect. Skeptics are a gift because they provide us with information about the route we've chosen and how to alter our approach and our goals.

You will eventually have to address fear, both the listener's and your own. Listeners may fear loss of position or status, loss of comfort, or being taken in by hype. Someone resists change because he is trying to avoid the pain he believes will result or the loss of something positive and enjoyable. Fears typically manifest themselves as resistance. Your reaction is likely to advocate your views harder. That too is motivated by fear: the fear of looking bad when everyone is watching, the fear that your ideas may, in fact, be wrong. The collision of two fearful people leads to an impasse. Resistance is not the primary reason why changes fail. It's the reaction to resistance that creates problems.

It's hard to listen to people when we don't agree with them. Usually we just elaborate our point of view or repeat what we've said. A better approach is to encourage the other person to say more about his point of view. Sometimes just hearing what another has to say will help each of you reach a better understanding.

Therefore:

Ask for help from resistors.

Listen, really listen, to what a skeptic has to say and learn from him. Try to appreciate the differences in opinion. When people disagree with you, stop and think about the value in seeing things from their perspective. Rather than hiding the potential problems, ask for input on ways to address them. When someone makes a critical comment, reply, "What would you recommend?" You don't have to agree with them; you can simply recognize them, and then seek to understand. Be sure the skeptic knows you are listening. Acknowledge and validate his expertise. Ask questions. Try to understand his arguments.

Bring the skeptic's concerns to light and address them before he has a chance to use them to stifle your efforts. Include his objections as limitations and topics to consider when you do presentations or lead discussions on the new idea.

While listening to their objections, help resistors understand that learning a new idea does not mean throwing away their experience. Use Personal Touch(198) to show how the innovation can improve things for them. Sometimes people who are resistant to an innovation can become quite enthusiastic if they are just given the opportunity to try it.

Don't assume that a skeptic's position is fixed. Just because he is initially opposed to your new idea doesn't mean that he can't be open to what you have to say. It's a natural human tendency to shy away from criticism, but it can be a sign of a healthy, vital culture when people care enough to air their concerns. Don't avoid it but engage it and assess its merits with the critic. If the person is an Influential, his ability to sift through information and see benefits as well as problems—as well as revise his assessment when it is merited and to tell others—makes him a valuable complainer. He will change his opinion when he sees cause for change.

Invite resistance so that all concerns are heard. Find something to appreciate in all those who aren't on your wavelength. Appreciation asks for nothing and gives everything. Research shows that it is physiologically impossible to be in a state of appreciation and a state of fear at the same time. Thus, appreciation can be an antidote to fear.

Be humble in your efforts and compassionate toward imperfections, including your own. While you may like some people more than others, keep in mind that a range of personalities lives in each person. The way you operate toward them will elicit the personality you see—the resistor you fear or the best person someone is capable of being.

The skeptics must be willing to talk and to listen—if they are not, put your energy elsewhere. It's sad, but there are also people who will never be happy no matter what, and you probably don't want to encourage them by spending a lot of time with them. Sometimes the resistance is due to a personality clash. If others who have adopted the new idea are willing to help, try Bridge-Builder(110). If some resistors become too difficult, find a Shoulder to Cry On(213)—you might discover other ways to deal with them.

If you know a resistor who is a strong opinion leader, consider giving him the role of Champion Skeptic(116).

= = = = = = = = =

This pattern builds a relationship with a skeptic. It allows you to use resistance to your advantage rather than allowing others to use it against you. Listening to skeptics will bring to light the limitations of the new idea so that issues can be addressed frankly and honestly. Resistors may not welcome the new idea with open arms, but if you have done your best to calm their fears, some will come around or try to be open-minded. Other people who see you dealing respectfully with resistors, and even raising objections in advance, are likely to be impressed with you as the messenger of a new idea.

The risk is that resistors can overwhelm you if you are not prepared to handle criticism. Encourage them to talk with you one-on-one to protect yourself from a verbal attack in public that can end up damaging your cause.

You always know who "they" are—the people who don't show up for your presentations, the people who don't stop by to ask about a new idea, the people who just don't care. So, you slip into denial and focus on the positive responders. You tell yourself that "they" will come around because your idea is so good. That was Roger's strategy until another reorganization and subsequent move put him next to one of "them"—one of those guys who had been with the company forever. Roger was polite and nodded, "Good morning! How's it going, Bill?" One day he heard him over the cubicle wall, "Okay, Roger, tell me about that new idea!" Roger was up like a shot. He spent nearly a half-hour with Bill and got to hear first hand what the skeptical co-worker thought the problems were. It was amazing that the two men were almost always in agreement. Bill brought up some things Roger hadn't considered, so Roger included these points in his next presentation about the new idea. Roger and Bill still have great discussions, even though they've both left the company.

Lynn was giving a talk about a new idea and someone in the audience was angrily disagreeing with everything she said. After hearing a few negative comments, Lynn decided to ask the guy to have lunch, which was scheduled just after the talk. She sat down with him, pulled out her notebook, and said, "I can't promise to do anything about your concerns, but I want to hear all of them. Fire away!" He kept her busy for the entire meal, and after it was over he said sincerely, "Thanks for listening. Everyone is usually too busy to care and they treat me like a crackpot. I appreciate that you took the time. Thanks." Lynn wasn't sure she had won him over, but she was glad she took the time to hear his viewpoint. That's important for new ideas or anything else.

Group Identity

A group of people involved in facilitating project retrospectives gathered in Oregon in 2002 to share their interest in retrospectives and brainstorm ways to increase their use across the software development industry. When the group created a list of action items, the first on the list was: Who are we? What are we trying to accomplish? Do we share a set of common goals? Once these fundamental questions were answered, the group was ready to move forward and make progress. The group is called Retroasis and convenes annually at different locations around the world.

Give the change effort an identity to help people recognize that it exists.

You are an Evangelist(144) or Dedicated Champion(129). You've had a Brown Bag(113) or perhaps just an informal meeting in the cafeteria or hallway.

It's harder to introduce a new idea when people aren't aware that the effort exists.

It's easier to recognize and talk about something if it has an identity. This is why organizations often assign a name to individual projects and sports groups give their teams a name. This is why patterns are given a name! When the name is mentioned, people will think about the new idea and know what you are talking about. If they don't know what it's all about, they are likely to ask.

Assigning an identity to a change initiative helps people become aware that it exists and what it is trying to do. The more people hear and see the name, the more likely they are to become curious about it and get involved.

Therefore:

Give the change effort an identity.

A good way to begin is to give your group a name. It can be one that is created by the group itself—this builds camaraderie. The name can also come from other sources. At one company, a new process was introduced called the Product Input and Planning Process. When the CEO decided to champion this effort, he joked, "So the product owner is Gladys Knight and your team is the PIPs!" It stuck, but it gave the new approach instant visibility. Having support from a Corporate Angel(123) may have had something to do with that!

Use the name often and everywhere you can. Display it when you use your e-Forum(135), In Your Space(167), and when holding an event.

There are other ways to give a group an identity. For example, a regular meeting signals an organized effort. The meetings can be for planning and other business or incorporated with another activity. Ask for Help(104) from those who attend the meeting. The meetings may have few attendees, especially in the beginning, but even a small group begins to build a community. But use the meetings carefully. In some company cultures, holding meetings will give the initiative a negative identity. This is especially true if they are run badly.

A Web page, a URL, or an e-mail address helps make the group look official.

If the group decides to write a mission statement and objectives, display them where everyone can see. Mission statements and/or group objectives help those involved in the effort focus on what they are trying to do.

= = = = = = = = =

This pattern establishes an identity for your efforts with the new idea. An identity makes the initiative more visible in the organization, gives it more credibility, and creates something that others can ask about, talk about, and get involved in. It helps form a vocabulary for the group that supports the new idea; this can be the beginning of a subculture.

But when you label something, people can label you. If they see your group as exclusive, they will develop misconceptions. Be clear about the purpose of the group and Involve Everyone(173).

One organization identifies the internal faculty of practitioners who contribute to the company's internal training program as "University Faculty." They have Web pages that include their biographies and pictures, and each person is given a new shirt every term with the corporate logo and the title of the training program. This creates a sense of identity for the faculty so that there is pride in ownership and participation.

In the German-based xpedition courses (www.xpeditionstraining.de), the first assignment for the teams of participants is to create a name. During the break, one of the trainers arranges for t-shirts to be printed for each team with their name. Since the training only lasts two days, this speeds up the team jelling process.

Guru on Your Side

After I gave the first Brown Bag *on the new idea, one of the attendees said, "This is good stuff but no one knows you. You should talk to Jeff or Randy. If they like it, then others will follow." I immediately went to see these senior programmers and sure enough, at the next* Brown Bag, *attendance doubled and most of the newcomers said, "Jeff (or Randy) said I should hear about this." I was grateful for the help!*

Enlist the support of senior-level people who are esteemed by members of the organization.

You are an Evangelist(144) or Dedicated Champion(129) trying to introduce a new idea into your organization.

People in an organization can be reluctant to show interest in a new idea unless it has the support of colleagues they respect.

Most people are continually bombarded with information and are too busy to keep up with the latest and greatest, so they depend on others to help evaluate new ideas. Usually these trusted advisors are senior-level people who are respected by everyone. When these people get behind an idea, it's one of the strongest kinds of approval you can have.

If managers follow the patterns that Don Olson and Carol Stimmel have written, <u>Shameless Ignoramus</u> and <u>Get a Guru</u>, then they admit they can't keep up with technical matters and have established a trusting relationship with a reliable technical expert. When such an expert is convinced of a new idea, he can help persuade the managers and other people in the organization.

Therefore:

Enlist the support of experienced, senior-level gurus who are respected by both managers and non-managers alike.

Approach gurus with humility. You're there to learn from them, not educate them about every nuance of the innovation. Instead of hitting them over the head with your new idea, use Just Enough(180) to present it gradually, asking for the guru's opinion about it. Instead of saying, "Wow! I was at this cool conference and I found this great new way of doing things. I'm so excited about it! I thought I'd have a meeting and tell the team," try, "I'm sorry you didn't get to go to the great conference last week. You would have enjoyed seeing all the latest stuff. I heard about this new way of doing things and I wanted to see what you thought of it before I run off at the mouth telling everyone."

Another way to approach the guru is by saying something like, "I know you're the local <*topic*> guru but I also know that you're interested in new things, so I thought you'd like to hear about the symposium I attended last week." Research has shown that engineers are fearful of being labeled an expert in an area if it keeps them from learning new things. They don't want past knowledge to limit their potential for future growth.

Take the guru out for coffee. Give an appropriate two-minute "elevator speech" on the innovation and then be prepared to listen. Someone with a great deal of experience has a lot to share. Use Personal Touch(198) to show how the innovation can address some of the problems he mentions, and use Tailor Made(234) to suggest where the innovation would fit in the organization.

If you're new to the organization, ask Connectors(119) who these gurus are. It helps if you know a high-level manager or another guru who can make an introduction.

Give gurus a chance to be involved if they find the innovation worthwhile; encourage them to talk with others or invite them to be part of a Guru Review(161).

= = = = = = = = =

This pattern creates a community of people who can supply technical credibility for the new idea. If you can convince them that the innovation is a good idea, others will at least hear you out. Management, especially upper management, often depends on respected individuals to provide an assessment of potential solutions. So once they are on your side, your battles are half over.

But these veterans can make or break you. If the person thinks the idea sounds like a "pile of garbage," he is likely to share his feelings with others. Encourage him to take on the role of Champion Skeptic(116) so that his resistance can make a constructive contribution.

Alan was the Evangelist for the introduction of Java in our organization. The biggest worries among the skeptics were the fear of the new technology and worries about performance and scalability. The hardest person to convince was the head of the architecture group. He was a very active, vocal skeptic who had the ear of the vice president. Alan knew that because this skeptic's expertise was respected in the organization, he would be more open if his expertise was validated. Therefore, Alan tried to understand his objections and help him feel less threatened. The skeptic was ultimately convinced by: (1) the proof of concept and (2) subsequent discussion of how much more difficult it would be to implement the project in C++. After he said Java was okay, convincing the rest of the team was easy.

When presenting a proposal to the faculty senate, Pamela always glances now and then at the person who is the most respected member of the senate. If she sees anything that indicates approval by this guru, such as a nod or a smile, she winds down her speech because she is quite certain that the hard work is done.

Guru Review

The managers seemed to have that "Oh no, not another silver bullet" look every time I mentioned the new idea. But when one of them asked me what Garrison thought of the idea and another asked me what Carol thought of it, it hit me that that the managers looked to these two individuals for advice. So I asked all the managers if they would help me create a review team for the idea. Each of the managers who agreed appointed one member. When the team met one afternoon, I was there to give a short presentation and to answer their questions. I took notes and wrote a report which the team approved before it was forwarded to management. Not only did this exercise help me convince management that the innovation had merit, but it also uncovered some issues I had not considered. As I recall, there were even skeptics on that review team who were eventually won over to the benefit of all concerned.

Gather anyone who is a Guru on Your Side and other interested colleagues to evaluate the new idea for managers and other developers.

You are an Evangelist(144) or Dedicated Champion(129) working to introduce a new idea into your organization.

Some managers and developers are supportive, but others are reluctant to join in until they have some assurance that this is a worthwhile idea.

Managers and developers are overwhelmed by information. They can't keep up with the latest and greatest. They have probably been disappointed by the promises of the never-ending stream of silver bullets and have become skeptical and reluctant to go along with even the most convincing arguments.

However, they are always interested in something that will help make their jobs easier and improve the quality of their products. They just need solid evidence. Usually, managers and developers will trust the judgment of their local guru, especially if they have a long-term relationship.

Because this guru usually keeps up with the latest trends, he can be referred to as a Maven, a reliable source of knowledge. This perception of reliability allows him to influence a large audience, including managers.

Therefore:

Gather a review team of respected gurus in the organization to evaluate the new idea.

Start looking for potential team members among the individuals you have identified as a Guru on Your Side(158). The team must be respected by management and other influential people and have backgrounds that will allow them to be effective evaluators. Ask for Help(104). Get names from managers or from Connectors(119). Include all the right people. Leaving someone out could hurt your cause. If one of the gurus is a vocal skeptic, you may want to include him as Champion Skeptic(116) in this group.

Personally invite these individuals to be part of an organized review. Do Food(132) and Location, Location, Location(189) if the budget allows. Hold a series of information sessions or a half-day or full-day workshop. Give the team a list of questions or issues to address. Encourage discussion to uncover any areas where there is doubt. Include sources of External Validation(148). Be present when you can to answer questions and address concerns.

Prepare a report for management. Keep the results around to use when a manager wants to know "What's this stuff all about?" Be ready to answer questions generated by the report and have a plan for the Next Steps(195). If this sparks some management support, it may be a sign that it is The Right Time(207) to take advantage of this.

This one-time task force may be willing to continue as an ongoing review committee for the innovation. This committee can include gurus who were appointed to the original task force and others who are interested enough to join in. Remember to Just Say Thanks(183) for any support.

= = = = = = = = =

This pattern produces data about the innovation through a firsthand evaluation from respected colleagues. The report, if positive, can be used to spark more support for the new idea, especially among management.

But use of this pattern can be risky. If the team's report is not positive, or if a few members are vocal about their apprehensions, the efforts to introduce the new idea can be brought to a standstill. Head off this possibility by using Corridor Politics(126) and use Stay in Touch(221) during the evaluation process.

The vice president and his staff requested a review after Brad's initial presentation about the new idea. Each member of the vice president's staff named one person for the evaluation team. Innovators who had been involved from the beginning were also invited. After a positive evaluation, the management became active supporters of the innovation and the word spread throughout the organization.

Before bringing Lotus Notes into one organization, a cross-functional Information Needs Committee was formed to gather information on the feasibility of the software. After conducting a thorough review, they made the recommendation to implement Notes. Some of the members then created a project team to define what applications to attack first.

Hometown Story

My first two presentations about the new idea had generated some interest among the In-novators and the Early Adopters in the organization. But I knew that the Early Majority weren't likely to accept a new idea until they had heard what their co-workers thought. So my next presentation included some time for people who had used the new idea to talk about their experiences.

To help people see the usefulness of the new idea, encourage those who have had success with it to share their stories.

You are a Dedicated Champion(129) trying to introduce a new idea into your organization.

People who haven't used the new idea may not be aware that other people have used it successfully.

Hearing the experiences of respected colleagues is the next best thing to having the experience yourself. People are attracted by the Smell of Success(219) and are curious about what successful individuals are doing. However, we tend to see the same people up front giving presentations. We know others could talk about their experiences, but they don't want to take the time to prepare and deliver a formal presentation. Yet informal, interactive presentations require little preparation and can be very effective. People are more likely to talk about experiences when they can do it in an informal way with little or no preparation.

Therefore:

Encourage individuals to share their experiences with the new idea in an informal, highly interactive session.

Do the legwork to prepare and promote the event. Advertise In Your Space(167) and on e-Forum(135). Do Food(132) or a Brown Bag(113). You do not need a large audience. Small group settings can create the atmosphere you want. Be there to help in any way you can, especially if the presenter is not good at leading a discussion.

Although you may wish to ask anyone who has had a positive experience with the innovation to do a Hometown Story, any Guru on Your Side(158) or Early Adopter(138) is likely to have the biggest impact because they are generally seen as opinion leaders.

Use this pattern as often as you can. Make sure a variety of experiences are heard, not just the ones from a few elite groups. Innovators(170) are the only ones likely to get excited about the new idea after hearing only one success story. Others will need many experience reports from many different people before they become supporters.

Hand out a Token(243) to help people remember the new idea that was discussed during the session.

= = = = = = = = =

This pattern creates an event in which individuals share their experiences. It is likely to increase the appeal of the new idea because most people are intrigued by success stories.

But if you choose the wrong person, this can run the risk of hurting your cause. For example, arrogant presenters who are likely to drone on about all the wonderful things they did could end up turning people off. Try to encourage individuals who are liked and respected. If someone with an unpleasant personality insists on doing a Hometown Story, you can ease his influence by combining his presentation with those from other, more likeable, speakers at the same event.

Sally was a little worried about the presentation she was asked to give about a new technology. But she got a lucky break when her co-worker, Steve, stopped by her cubicle while she was working on the slides. He told her that he had played around with the technology a bit. Sally reacted with such interest and excitement that Steve offered to give the second half of the presentation. Even though his experience with the new idea was limited, his presentation ended up being so natural and believable—he just leaned on the desk in the front of the room and told his story. Sally just sat there and smiled. She had put a lot of work into preparing the formal slide presentation, but the real hit of the event was Steve's story.

At Ken's company, success stories were often on the agenda at regular team meetings. The group prided itself on being innovative, so they were always excited and interested when someone on the team tried something new. They didn't even mind if an occasional failure was the topic instead of a success. It gave them the courage to keep learning.

In Your Space

As the faculty advisor of the student Management Association, I tried to encourage management students to regularly check the association's Web page for new opportunities and upcoming events. Nothing seemed to work until one of the officers made a simple poster with the Web page address and hung it in the computer lab where many of the students work and hang out between classes. The number of hits to the site increased ten-fold!

Keep the new idea visible by placing reminders throughout the organization.

You are an Evangelist(144) or Dedicated Champion(129) trying to introduce a new idea into your organization.

Unless people are reminded, they may forget about the new idea.

People like to be in the know, but many don't have the time to periodically read articles or information on the Web. Yet, they'll notice and are likely to discuss things that are posted in places they see often. E. M. Rogers has shown that keeping a new idea visible throughout an organization has a positive impact on the rate at which people adopt it. A gathering place, where a group can come together and talk amongst themselves, is one means for communicating a new idea and showing progress.

Therefore:

Post information about the new idea around your organization—wherever people are likely to see it and discuss it.

Display information so it will be noticed and not forgotten. Materials placed in high traffic areas may be easy for people to see but also easy to forget as they move on. Malcolm Gladwell, author of *The Tipping Point*, suggests that you make your message "stick" by using bright colors, an usual graphic, or a memorable quote. Provide ways for the viewers to interact in the space by asking for feedback or posing a question that will stimulate discussion. Ask for Help(104). Include announcements about upcoming events. Update the information regularly; otherwise, people will get used to it and not notice it any more.

Consider putting information in a place Paul Taylor explains in the Team Space pattern, a physical space for casual, unplanned interaction, or in Christopher Alexander's Work Community, a pattern that encourages the formation of small clusters in the workplace. Author Alistair Cockburn, in *Agile Software Development*, describes an "Information Radiator," a display of information in a place where passersby can see it. The passersby don't need to ask questions; the information simply hits them as they go by. He suggests that the information change over time because it will make it worthwhile to look at the display.

Be creative in finding the space. Look for the bulletin board that just seems to accumulate junk flyers and make it more appealing. Also, you can simply post a sign near your office that says, "Ask me about *<new idea>*."

= = = = = = = = =

This pattern establishes a space where people can see and discuss the latest information about the new idea. It will stay "in the space" and in the mind of the organization. People who see the space may become intrigued enough to become involved in the change initiative.

But despite your best efforts to make the message noticeable, people can become oblivious to the space if they see it all the time. Try to make it something that people look forward to seeing or consider moving it to a new location once in awhile.

Joe Bergin has applied this pattern to a larger "space." He is one of the educators who formed the Pedagogical Patterns Project (http://www.pedagogicalpatterns.org/). The team is working on documenting successful teaching practices in the form of patterns. To encourage contributions, Joe has created buttons with witty sayings about the project. Team members and other supporters wear these buttons and provoke interest at conferences and other gatherings.

Ralph and Julie read about something they thought was a big problem in their department—one author called it "SpecGen." They made signs with the letters "SG" in a red circle-slash and the slogan, "Thank you for not speculating." The signs were a big hit. Nearly every cubicle had one posted by the end of the day.

Innovator

Roger lived next door, so every time he bought the newest, coolest gadget, I would hear all about it. He would get so excited about his purchases, even when the items were much too overpriced. But if he convinced me that something was really useful, I would wait and buy it months later when the cost came down to less than half of what Roger paid.

When you begin the change initiative, ask for help from colleagues who like new ideas.

You are a new Evangelist(144) or Dedicated Champion(129) just starting to introduce a new idea into your organization.

You need people to jumpstart the new idea in your organization.

You can't interest everyone in a new idea all at once, but you need to start somewhere. A community of even a few people who share your interest and want to work together will make a world of difference in the confusion and inconsistencies that invariably arise. Virtually every significant change initiative starts with a small number of deeply committed individuals, often as few as two or three.

It's easier to begin with those people who will be most receptive to the new idea. Innovators make up a small percentage of the population. They get intrigued and excited about something just because it is new. They don't need much convincing, just a little information. They enjoy trying to figure out how the latest thing works. This puts them in a good position to help launch the new idea into the organization.

Therefore:

Find the people who are quick to adopt new ideas. Talk to them about the innovation and ask for help in sparking an interest for it in the organization.

Look for Innovators among those who attend early Brown Bags(113) and other meetings where new ideas are being introduced. Some of them will come to you once you start talking about the new idea.

Encourage these individuals to take on the role of gatekeepers. Invite them to Test the Waters(237) by using Just Do It(177) and doing an early evaluation. Ask for their feedback about the innovation and listen to their suggestions for appealing to the larger community. Because they are the first to come on board with a new idea, perhaps they could lead one of the first Study Groups(228) for other people who are curious about learning more. Those who are especially enthusiastic may become Evangelists(144) in their own groups.

= = = = = = = = =

This pattern establishes support from a group who can help get a new idea going in the organization. It doesn't take a lot of work to interest them and then you won't feel so alone. Since they are willing to accept some of the uncertainty that comes with a new idea, they ease the risk for later adopters.

However, you may not be able to depend on them in the long term. Their interest in new ideas makes them move from one thing to another. In addition, their willingness to quickly accept new ideas causes others to be suspicious of their claims. Therefore, they generally aren't good opinion leaders. Count on their help as gatekeepers in the short term. If they offer more, consider that a bonus.

Bill's eyebrows seem to rise to his hairline when he hears about something new. So he was one of the first people Julie talked with about the new idea. He tried it, reported the results, and helped Julie plan a few events to pass the word. His enthusiasm was just what she needed to keep her going in the early days of trying to convince other people whose eyebrows did not rise as quickly.

Some people know when you've returned from a conference and drop by to see what new books you've bought or new techniques you've seen. They wanted to be there but couldn't take the time. So Sam always tries to bring something back for them. It is fun to watch how happy these people get about anything because their need to be in on the "latest and greatest" is almost physical. Sam knows what his boss means when he says, "Sure, you can go to the conference, but bring something back for the team!" He is thinking about these guys.

Involve Everyone

Margaret Wheatley, *author of* Leadership and the New Science, *observes that "…great things are possible when we increase participation. I always want more people, from more diverse functions and places, to be there.… I learn a great deal from other people. I expect them to see things differently from me, to surprise me."*

For a new idea to be successful across an organization, everyone should have an opportunity to support the innovation and make his own unique contribution.

You are a Dedicated Champion(129) working to introduce patterns into your organization. There are others in the community who might get involved with a little encouragement.

Even when you ask for help, there's a tendency to take on too much. Others, especially those who don't see the value in the new idea, may think of it as "your show."

---

*Wheatley, M. J., *Leadership and the New Science: Discovering Order in a Chaotic World*, 2nd ed., Berrett-Koehler Publishers, 1999.

You're the person dedicated to spending time on introducing the new idea. You want to do as much as you can to help your organization improve but you don't want the organization to be too dependent on you. Moreover, the corporate picture of the new idea may tend to converge around your own. As a result, there's less definitional discussion because you are setting the stage and the pace.

If you take on too much, you can become the single point of failure. Because people will tend to see the new idea as being about you, your personality and history can color their view. People who might contribute to a discussion of how best to make the innovation work will instead defer to you, seeing themselves as students learning "the right way."

A small group interested in a new idea can become a clique isolated from the needs of the organization. Those who aren't part of the effort may become defensive and withdrawn, afraid of not being able to keep up with the change. Wide involvement is essential for the development of a good implementation strategy. Some things might be less stressful if everyone was alike, but the long-term plan would not be robust enough to stand the test of time.

You can never predict who will be the real enthusiasts for the new technique. In organizations, as with prairies, you can't get far with pristine and hermetically sealed experiments. This is one reason for reaching out to a broad cross-section of support. In addition to contributing skills and strengths, a diverse group of people will bring awareness of the limitations and organizational constraints that any successful change effort must transcend.

Leading change is not a one-person job. Increasing the number of people involved means that the innovation belongs to the entire organization instead of just one person or a small group. Because of the extensive participation, it becomes everyone's product. Shared experiences can keep others interested. When you share the opportunity to lead, you discover that the extent to which people "own" a project is the extent to which they invest their time and energy to make it succeed.

Ownership is important. It is a term that describes not only literal owners, but more importantly, the emotional investment of employees in their work. It describes personal connections to the organization; the powerful emotions of belonging that inspire people to contribute. A tried and true maxim of organizational behavior is that "people support what they create."

Therefore:

Make it known that everyone is welcome to be part of the change effort. Involve people from as many different groups as possible: management, administrative and technical support, marketing, and training.

Do the best you can to involve a variety of people from the start. If the innovation is viewed early on as a clique, it may never be able to lose that image. Even when you're not sure how it will work out, even when you're not sure where things are going, involving everyone creates a stronger community.

Give everyone ownership of some part of the change effort. For example, encourage the Innovators(170) to help test the new idea and the Early Adopters(138) to be responsible for some leadership roles. Find Connectors(119) and get a Guru on Your Side(158) to help spread the word. Don't restrict involvement because of any preconceived ideas. Even skeptics can contribute by becoming a Champion Skeptic(116).

Try to bring together a diverse group of people from different parts of the organization. Seek out a variety of roles and ideas. Invite people who could hold untapped wisdom—not the same voices, but new and different ones. Alistair Cockburn's pattern <u>Holistic Diversity</u> advises creating a team with multiple specialties, and Neil Harrison's pattern <u>Diverse Groups</u> recommends including different kinds of members in determining requirements. Give everyone the freedom to express an individual perspective on the new idea.

Create forums and processes that allow a variety of people to have their voices heard about the new idea. Make sure it is not a passive system in which individuals merely say what's on their mind. Rather, create active discussions where people offer suggestions for any problems they raise.

Put the "spotlight on others." Convince individuals to take on public leadership tasks by running an event or doing a Hometown Story(164). Help each individual become an effective leader. People have different abilities and interests. Some are not comfortable writing, while others don't like public speaking. Sometimes you can just use Ask for Help(104) to hear what they would like to do.

If you're appointing someone as a leader, you have to be ready to follow. Prepare yourself mentally to cede ownership of the new idea to someone else.

= = = = = = = = = =

This pattern builds a community of people committed to the new idea, ready to take on leadership roles in the change effort. Increasing the number of people involved in the process results in an innovation that belongs to the entire organization rather than something produced by one person or a small group. Your attempt to involve everyone ensures that as many individuals as possible will see themselves as active participants in the change process. People who have this perception will view the success of the innovation as their responsibility. This means that they have accepted the change in some small measure, and you have that much less resistance to overcome. Those who become leaders of the change effort will soon become experts in others' eyes, and they will probably do so as your close partners. Your effectiveness will be multiplied because you have people to talk with and fall back upon. They'll tell you which ideas worked out well and which didn't work out so well. They'll tell you which contacts were helpful and which weren't. They'll keep talking to you. And you'll keep learning from them. It's a loop.

But every time you involve another group, you run the risk of getting so many points of view that it becomes overwhelming. Acknowledge the differences with Fear Less(151), but put your focus on the common ground. This will allow you to move forward rather than using your energy on the countless issues that cannot be immediately resolved. Everyone doesn't need to agree on everything before you can start taking action.

Tim has been actively trying to convert others to be leaders of the change effort for the innovation. For example, he was asked to give a keynote talk on the innovation at a software testing conference. Instead of accepting, he said, "You should ask Elisabeth. She's up and coming, working with the innovation, and a good speaker." That's what happened. Similarly, Tim nudged someone else to be the host of the conference. Neither started out that enthusiastic about the innovation, but they gained enthusiasm at the workshops, and Tim thinks they will get more caught up in it as they play a more public role. Tim has also noticed that encouraging others to become involved makes the innovation seem less like one of his weird ideas, which, he thinks, was initially the impression of some.

Karen is the Executive Director of RiverLink, a nonprofit organization spearheading the economic and environmental revitalization of the French Broad River. She was asked to identify the one thing that had the most positive influence on the successful progress River-Link has made over 15 years. Without hesitation, she described the ability to pull together people with a variety of interests including lawyers, accountants, engineers, architects, bike-riders, kayakers, and other athletes. Community outreach was often accomplished through personal visits and more public forums such as focus groups, public hearings, and even a 24-hour brainstorming session. Karen noted that this allowed each person to come away feeling that he or she owned a part of the project.

Just Do It

A letter in the "In My Humble Opinion" column of Fast Company *magazine expressed frustration about a company filled with people who refused to try anything new. The writer claimed that she knew exactly how to save the company, but no one above her would let her do it. Seth Godin, Change Agent, responded:*

> "What you're looking for is an insurance policy that will protect you against retribution if your plan goes awry. What you're waiting for is someone way up the ladder to tell you that you can launch a product or institute a cost-savings plan. You want their approval to free you from risk. That's not going to happen.
>
> Just do it. If you wait for approval, it means that you want someone to cover your backside if you fail. People higher up on the corporate ladder are well aware of the risk that comes with trusting you. If you screw up after receiving their approval, then they'll be the ones who get into hot water, not you."*

To prepare to spread the word about the new idea, use it in your own work to discover its benefits and limitations.

*Godin, S., "In My Humble Opinion," Fast Company, November 2001, 80.

You are an Evangelist-wanna-be, motivated to adopt a new idea. You are interested in spreading the word to others in the organization, but you don't have enough understanding of what the new idea can offer. When you talk about the possibilities, people ask questions that you can't answer.

You don't have any experience with the innovation yourself, just good ideas that might work. You believe that the innovation can help the organization, but you're not sure.

People will be wary if you only have a good idea but no experience to back it up. They are likely to ask questions you can't answer. Sometimes it's better to labor in secret until demonstrable success is in hand.

If you wait until you're comfortable, if you wait until you know what you're doing, you will have wasted precious time. Many of us who could be doing something do nothing because we think we don't know enough. But when we aren't willing to explore a new idea, we miss the opportunity to learn.

Do your research. Lack of experience is easy for opponents to attack while positive experience is more difficult to refute. In addition, an understanding of the innovation's limitations helps you avoid overselling and provides insight into approaches that will work.

Therefore:

Gather first-hand information on the benefits and limitations of the innovation by integrating it into your current work.

Learn as you go. Record the strengths and pitfalls you encounter along the way. If possible, quantify the benefits (although this can be difficult). Gather enough information so that you can show others how the innovation will be useful for them.

Be realistic about what you can and cannot do. Make sure that your work with the innovation does not distract from your official duties. Rather, it should relate to and improve the quality or speed of your official work; otherwise, your story will not be credible.

Before you begin, you may want to check around for others in the organization who may also be working with the new idea. It is more effective, and will avoid jealous feelings, to "just do it" together rather than in separate projects.

If you find a few Innovators(170) who are also interested in exploring the new idea, ask for help. But keep this group small in number. Make sure they are willing to take it slow, set realistic goals, and follow your lead.

While you are experimenting with the innovation in your own work, search for every bit of information to help you. Read articles, look at Web sites, and talk with anyone you can find outside the organization who has experience using the innovation. This will provide some External Validation(148).

To spread the word about your findings, present a Hometown Story(164). Help your colleagues understand that the innovation is not beyond their grasp with Personal Touch(198). Take a low-key approach when you report your experiences. Don't be overly optimistic or insistent that the new approach is a silver bullet. You may want to simply demonstrate it to a few people and tell them how you benefited from it. When you have enough information, try to convince the organization to Trial Run(245) the innovation.

= = = = = = = = = =

This pattern generates the knowledge you need to take on the role of Evangelist(144). You will increase your understanding of the innovation and, in turn, be more prepared to talk intelligently about it and address other people's questions.

But you are using this pattern because you know so little. Therefore, others are likely to see you struggle and this can turn them off to the new idea. Don't discount your struggles, but make sure others see an overall positive attitude in you.

One organization had a software application project that was stalled for a long time. Everyone mentioned it but no one was able to get it moving. Because the project was technically "adjacent" to what Daniel's team was working on, they decided to just do it. The team built a limited version of the application and called it a "test program." It allowed the team to try their preferred design, a low-risk exercise that would speak for itself if it turned out viable. When they started receiving some positive feedback for their efforts, they felt some hope that their work would eventually be recognized as the "first version" of the larger application.

Frances hoped to encourage her fellow team members to write their software documentation in pattern format. So she started writing her own documentation in this form. It allowed her to better understand the difficulties and the advantages so that she could explain these things to her team. The team members started becoming accustomed to seeing her documentation written in the new format and eventually it didn't even seem like an unusual way of writing—it just began to make sense.

Just Enough

Most of us have had the kind of teacher who knows so much about a certain topic that he feels compelled to tell his students all about it as fast as he can. He doesn't seem to notice the blank stares—he just keeps talking and his students just keep staring.

To ease learners into the more difficult concepts of a new idea, give a brief introduction and then make more information available when they are ready.

You are an Evangelist(144) or Dedicated Champion(129) working to spread the word about a new idea in your organization.

Difficult, complex concepts can overwhelm novices.

All new ideas involve a learning curve. Some of the new things people will have to face are complex and cannot be understood in a short time. Although learners should understand the challenging concepts at some point so they can use the innovation effectively, giving a thorough explanation of such concepts while you are covering the basics can be confusing. This may cause them to think the innovation is too complicated. It may discourage busy people from taking the time to learn more.

A slow but sure introduction to a new idea can be compared to Christopher Alexander's <u>Gradual Stiffening</u> pattern. He recommends that, when creating a complex building structure, one should "…build a building in such a way that it starts out loose and flimsy while final adaptations in plan are made, and then gets stiffened gradually during the process of construction, so that each additional act of construction makes the structure sounder."*

Each new concept that is taught to learners should allow their comprehension to become sounder. If you introduce too much of a good thing too fast you may overwhelm your learners and, at the same time, reduce your flexibility and increase your costs.

Therefore:

When introducing the new idea, concentrate on the fundamentals and give learners a brief description of the more difficult concepts. Provide more information when they are ready.

If you are doing a presentation to introduce the new idea, include more advanced concepts in a slide or two. If you are having an informal discussion, give learners the information they can comfortably handle and let them know that there is more to learn. Provide enough information to start interested individuals on an investigation of their own.

When giving a presentation to high-level management, give the conclusions first. Paint the big picture and save the details to present only if you're asked. Stress the gains rather than the losses. Emphasize the wins without stretching the truth or ignoring the risks.

Even though you shouldn't overwhelm learners with too many details, you want to offer the encouragement and resources they need to consider advanced concepts when they have more experience. Give URLs or a list of references to help. Make yourself available to answer questions. Use Personal Touch(198) to show how the innovation can be useful in their jobs.

After learners have had time to understand the basics, find opportunities to revisit the advanced concepts for a more in-depth discussion. This will allow

---

*Alexander, C. A. et al., *A Pattern Language*, Oxford University Press, 1977.

them to develop confidence about what they've learned, which is likely to spark their interest in learning more.

= = = = = = = = =

This pattern initiates a slow but sure understanding of complex topics. This approach also keeps change leaders from hyping the innovation as a perfect and complete solution from the beginning.

But what works for some people will not necessarily work for others. At one extreme, there may be people who won't comprehend the basics and worry that there are even more difficult concepts to come. At the other extreme, there will be people who want to know more and may feel that you don't think they're smart enough to handle the advanced concepts. Keep open lines of communication with everyone so they are comfortable asking questions to get the amount of information they desire.

When Janet introduces patterns during her tutorials, the difficult concepts such as QWAN and generativity are mentioned as important but are not covered in detail. Instead, attendees are pointed to Christopher Alexander's book, The Timeless Way of Building, *if they wish to read more. Janet always reminds students that she is available to answer questions when they are ready to learn about these and other advanced concepts.*

When moving from CMM (Capability Maturity Model) Level 1 to Levels 2 and 3, the process introductions were synched with the development cycle. Rather than try to give the team all the process changes at the beginning, they introduced "just enough" of the process changes to get through the next stage.

Just Say Thanks

A friend of mine was laid off from a large company where he had worked for nearly 30 years. I saw him after his last day and he said that the worst thing about the experience was that no one, not even his boss, had come by to say they would miss him or that they appreciated his work. I thought about my last day when I was laid off. I recall a constant stream of people coming by to share a brief story— how something I had done or said had influenced their lives for the better and how I had made a difference for them and the company. I don't remember sadness on that day but an overwhelming gladness at having had the chance to work in that company with those people— and all they did was just say "Thanks!"

To show your appreciation, say "Thanks" in the most sincere way you can to everyone who helps you.

You are an Evangelist(144) or a Dedicated Champion(129). Others are helping you introduce your new idea into the organization.

People feel unappreciated when they work hard and no one notices or cares.

It's easy to take for granted the work that people do—after all, they're getting paid! But people are happier and feel their contribution is appreciated with a simple acknowledgement and encouragement. Even when you don't have resources to reward supporters with anything tangible, an expression of your gratitude costs nothing and means so much to the receiver.

A recent survey of 1,400 chief financial officers showed that a simple thank you can go a long way in motivating employees. When asked what, other than monetary reward, is the most effective means of motivating employees, 38% chose frequent recognition of accomplishments as the best way to encourage staff members.

However, in today's fast-paced business world, there often isn't enough time or resources to acknowledge these efforts in large ways. There may not be enough money to buy gifts for everyone or time in busy schedules to celebrate accomplishments with a meal.

Usually, everyone on a team performs a heroic act during any project. We seem to have lost the ability to give someone a "high five" or say "great job," so heroes often remain unappreciated. Yet, when many different company presidents and CEOs were asked the following question, "What do you know now that you wish you'd been told 25 years ago?" Their advice was to occasionally stop for a few moments and think about the people to whom you owe thanks, and then take the time to express your gratitude to them.*

Therefore:

Find everyone who has helped you and say thanks in the most sincere way you can.

Even an informal recognition will make an impression—a private discussion, a phone call, or even an e-mail message. Spending a small amount of money can generate a huge return—a card, a morning pastry, a piece of fruit, or a small gift. Any of these shows that you took extra effort and time to think about what the receiver might like. When you can, give supporters something they will value. It does not have to be anything expensive; recipients just have to attach value to it and associate it with their efforts in the change initiative. An invitation to a Royal Audience(210) is another way to acknowledge people whose work made a difference.

Take a few minutes to write a thank-you note. Nancy Austin, author of the management classic *A Passion for Excellence*, reminds us that a personal note is a quick, responsive, cheap, and surprisingly effective way to win friends and influence people. It is "shoestring marketing…. People remember thank-you notes (and the people who write them) because good ones are so rare."

*Edler, R., *If I Knew Then What I Know Now: CEOs and other smart executives share wisdom they wish they'd been told 25 years ago*, G. P. Putnam's Sons, 1995.

When appropriate, acknowledge achievements publicly. Recognize special effort and the people who helped achieve even small successes.

Don't thank only the individuals who have lent a hand. Also consider the people who attended an event you organized, such as a Brown Bag(113) or Hometown Story(164). Let them know how much you appreciate their time. A follow-up gesture of thanks will go a long way to help people remember what you had to say.

Tailor the thanks to each individual. Let people know they are appreciated by interacting with them frequently. Be generous with the acknowledgement and always make people feel important. Even if a considerable amount of time has passed, don't let this stop you from telling people you are still thankful for what they have done.

= = = = = = = = = =

This pattern builds stronger relationships with people who have contributed to the initiative. A sincere expression of gratitude is likely to make such an impression on people that it will be easier to ask for help and receive their assistance again in the future. The spirit that it creates is incredible. More importantly, it will remind you that you didn't do it all alone. It will keep you humble and be a real boon for those who have made a difference in your efforts.

But once you start thanking people, you run the risk of offending others who feel they were left out or did not receive the same level of appreciation as another person did. Try to reward equally. Thank everyone who helps you, not just the people who do the high-profile tasks. Continually apologize in case you forget a contribution to anticipate a sin of omission.

The inspiration for this pattern came from a co-worker who expressed extreme frustration because her manager did not say thanks after a long, difficult project was completed. Although she didn't mind working the long hours, she was very upset that her manager didn't show appreciation with even a simple "thank you" to the team.

Adam was a team leader at a large satellite telecommunications company. As each phase of the project was completed, he wrote personal, printed hardcopy letters to the supervisors of everyone who contributed (they were all contractors), expressing his appreciation for their effort. The trickle down benefit was amazing. The contractors were surprised and delighted to be treated well and even complimented, and so the barriers between the company and the contractors came down, at least in this area. Such expressions have a big pay off over the long term.

Local Sponsor

One day I asked a manager what he did to make his branch such a successful one. "Well," he replied, "I believe my primary job is to support my employees by finding resources and taking care of all the roadblocks that get in the way of them doing their jobs well."

Ask for help from first-line management. When your boss supports the tasks you are doing to introduce the new idea, you can be even more effective.

You are an Evangelist(144) trying to introduce a new idea into your organization.

You need attention and resources for the new idea.

Management support legitimizes things in the workplace. It's hard to get some people involved in a new idea unless they think management is behind it.

One of the most important things is sponsorship. There must be a manager who believes that the change needs to happen, who understands the decisions that need to be made, and has the power to allocate the resources that will be needed during the transition. Site leadership is critical. Experience suggests that an innovation will have broad impact in those settings where local management takes responsibility for it.

We have seen no examples where significant progress has been made without first-line management and many examples where sincerely committed Corporate Angels(123) alone have failed to generate any significant momentum. Managers have significant business responsibility and bottom-line focus. They head organizational units that are large enough to be meaningful microcosms of the larger organization, and yet they have enough autonomy to undertake meaningful change independent of the larger organization.

Therefore:

Find a first-line manager to support your new idea, ideally, your boss.

Use Tailor Made(234) to help managers understand how the new idea can help the organization. Offer to organize a Guru Review(161). Personally invite managers to attend events such as a Brown Bag(113) or Hometown Story(164). If a Big Jolt(107) visit is planned, offer the opportunity for a Royal Audience(210). Address any concerns with Whisper in the General's Ear(248). Stay in Touch(221)—keep interested managers informed on a periodic basis.

Keep any manager's part in the change initiative one of support. Similar to Jim Coplien's <u>Patron Role</u> pattern, the manager should be encouraged to help find resources and remove barriers that hinder progress.

If you can enlist the backing of your boss, begin to think how you can ask for help to become a Dedicated Champion(129). A first-line manager may be your best hope for capturing the attention of a Corporate Angel(123).

Sponsorship should not come from just one person. Try to build sponsorship among all the managers who have the power to influence project adoption of the innovation.

= = = = = = = = =

This pattern establishes first-line managerial support for your work in introducing a new idea. With this, you can get resources for the change initiative and capture the interest of those who look to management for guidance. You may even be able to become a Dedicated Champion(129).

But the wrong kind of sponsor can cause you to lose focus and direction. When you bring in management, you run the risk that they will push things in a direction that is different from yours. An overpowering one can even steal your ideas and take the credit. A manager who is overzealous can give the damaging impression that the new idea is being mandated. Look for respected sponsors who will help, not hurt, your good intentions.

Alex had three managers who were the backbone of all the activity surrounding the new idea at his company. Yes, he did the legwork. Yes, he wrote the articles. Yes, he devoted his time. But it was the encouragement, the unflagging support of these managers and their belief in him that made it happen.

In Amanda's organization, the change initiative would not have started without the support of her manager. He gave her the budget line to support her time and fund the activities surrounding her efforts. Without these things, Amanda would not have been able to get things off the ground as quickly as she did.

Location, Location, Location

In his book on project retrospectives, Norm Kerth has observed that onsite locations "*may be seen by participants as cheap and therefore unimportant, the site is 'the same old place,' the [event] is easily interrupted, and participants may not prepare as well since they can duck out to look for whatever materials they need at the last minute.*"*

To avoid interruptions that disrupt the flow of an event, try to hold significant events off site.

You are planning a half- or whole-day seminar or other event.

When you hold an event onsite at the organization, attendees can be easily distracted with their nearby work obligations.

As any real estate agent will tell you, the three most important qualities of any property are: location, location, location. The same can be said of special events in your company.

---

*Kerth, N., *Project Retrospectives: A Handbook for Team Reviews*, Dorset House, 2001.

It is natural to assume that company events will be held onsite. This is normally seen as a good use of resources, and it presents attendees with a comfortable and familiar environment. However, an event that is a half-day or longer inevitably leads to breaks, and people will wander off to look at their e-mail or may be grabbed by their managers or co-workers to just look at "a small problem." People always seem to spend longer than planned, and "a small problem" is rarely that—so people are late, distracted, or even pulled out of the event for a few hours or the duration of the event.

Such disruptions reduce the impact of the event and, as a result, people tend to believe they must get back to some task that suddenly seems more important (to someone else, if not the attendee in question). Even without actual disruption, there is often the feeling that "real work" is just a knock-on-the-door away.

Training costs money, so don't squander your investment. That means paying attention to things that may seem trivial but that actually make a big difference. Location is one of these. You could say that the worst place for workplace training is at work!

Therefore:

Hold significant events of a half-day or longer offsite but nearby.

The best place to conduct training is often in your company's own offsite facility. If this is not available, try a nearby hotel, training center, or retreat facility. The alternative location should not be inconvenient. People still have children to pick up from school, car pools to organize, and so on. A nearby location means that the usual beginning and end of day rituals can continue and that if there is an interruption during the day, it is not a big effort to get back to the office.

Make sure the event is a beneficial one. It will probably take extra effort for people to come to the offsite location, so this puts added responsibility on you to make it worthwhile. A unique, comfortable location can't overcome a bad agenda.

Remind attendees to turn off mobile phones and pagers. Nothing brings back the daily work pressure more urgently, even if you're offsite.

= = = = = = = = =

This pattern creates a better environment for an event. It allows participants to be more focused because they are insulated from the worries of work minutiae, as the sources of work minutiae are from them. A new context often makes the event more special, creating a freer environment, less constrained by the expectations back at the office. It allows the opportunity for constructive discussion about the event during the breaks and for more personal contact and bonding. The sense of a company outing makes the event more fun. Some people are more open because the perception is that "this isn't work."

Inevitably, offsite venues will cost more than onsite ones. But if you're going to do it, do it right. However, despite your best efforts, some people will not be able to get their minds off what needs to be done back at the office. Assure them that the genuinely high-priority interrupts will get through. Minor queries and problems will resolve themselves or wait, as will e-mail. Try a variation of the "I'm Too Busy" exercise, as suggested by Norm Kerth, to help people understand that the things they want to do back at the office are not as important as what will transpire during the event.

My company is located in Campinas in Brazil. A partnering organization is located in Curitiba. Meetings were held in one city or the other, which provided an offsite experience for the visiting group. The onsite group suffered all the disadvantages mentioned in this pattern, while the offsite group gained all the benefits. The two organizations decided to have future meetings in a third city, to allow both groups to go offsite.

Kevlin ran a workshop onsite for a company just outside Oslo. Over the three days of the workshop people disappeared and reappeared mysteriously, but it was the interruption and call of work rather than alien abductions that were to blame. Whether it was the lure of e-mail or "just a quick word" from a colleague or boss, it led to an unsettled atmosphere. The next time the workshop was run, the company rented a room offsite less than a five-minute walk away. In spite of the physical proximity, there was just enough separation to reduce interruptions. It turns out that almost everything that was normally "urgent" could wait until the end of the day or after the workshop. The atmosphere was relaxed and less transient, and all the delegates were more focused.

Mentor

We held a three-day pilot patterns training. Everyone in the class thought there was too much material. One suggestion in the evaluations was the need for some help in the actual use of the patterns. So we expanded the three days to a full week. Monday had all-day training while Tuesday through Friday had both a half-day of training and a half-day of mentoring. During the half-days of mentoring, we provided consulting on real projects. The new schedule made a tremendous difference in the effectiveness of the training.

When a project wants to get started with the new idea, have someone around who understands it and can help the team.

You are a Dedicated Champion(129) trying to introduce a new idea into your organization. A project is interested in the innovation but some/all of the team members are unfamiliar with it.

People want to use the new idea on their project but don't know how to begin.

If team members are willing to introduce the new idea into their project, they can study it on their own to some extent. However, they probably need help to apply it effectively. The team is likely to make more progress if it has access to an expert who can guide them through their problems. Mentors can prevent small mistakes from growing into huge delays.

Beginners need to understand what experts do. Apprenticeship learning is ideal because it gives beginners access to an expert's "cognitive library." This is better than any help system or documentation.

Therefore:

Find an outside or internal consultant or trainer to provide mentoring and feedback while project members are getting started with the innovation.

Encourage the Mentor to use a hands-on approach, work side-by-side with the team members, and let them know that he has struggled with the same problems. This will help open learners' minds to the innovation. The Mentor should use Just Enough(180) to introduce complicated topics and use Personal Touch(198) to help each team member understand how the innovation can be useful.

Carefully check the credentials of a potential Mentor. Don't simply trust what anyone claims to be able to do. Ideally, the Mentor should have experience in using the innovation and should know something about the team's problem domain. In addition, look for a Mentor whose personality will mesh with the team culture, although it may be impossible to find one person who everyone will like and relate to. If the Mentor alienates some team members and turns them off from using the innovation, you may need to bring in Mentors with different personality types for these people.

Make certain you are clear about what the Mentor should do. Clearly state why you are hiring him and define the deliverables. Ask the Mentor to help outline specific goals for the educational experience the team members will have.

Don't allow a team to become dependent on the Mentor. Otherwise, they may not want to let him go or will call on him for every little thing. Ask the Mentor when and how he plans to leave his role. The best Mentors strive to work themselves out of a job. You may need to set a time when the Mentor will be available and then, at some point, encourage team members to move forward on their own.

The organization may wish to use a Mentor to train an entire team to prepare for a project, as described in Don Olson's pattern <u>Train Hard, Fight Easy</u>. The benefit lies in the shared experience of training together, which not only enables the team to communicate effectively about the innovation but also serves as a team-building exercise.

= = = = = = = = =

This pattern produces a better understanding of the innovation while people are starting to use it. Users will have an easier time because they will have an experienced person to get them over the hurdles. This helps to create a good impression of the innovation and increases the likelihood that people will be willing to continue to use it.

A Mentor is not always easy to find. The number of experts is usually small compared with the number of projects, especially in the early days of an innovation's appearance. Look for Mentors among the Innovators(170) and help teams grow their own expertise so that this mentoring activity continues with internal support.

Pattern guru Jim Coplien says that "the use of pattern mentors in an organization can speed the acceptance of patterns and can help provide a balance between encouraging good design practices based on patterns and discouraging overly high expectations of designs based on patterns. Initially mentors can help developers recognize the patterns that they already use in their application domain and show how they could be reused in subsequent projects. Mentors should also ensure that the wrong patterns are not applied to a problem (i.e., people tend to reuse things that they know and the same temptation will apply to patterns, regardless of whether the pattern actually fits the problem)."*

Cathryn worked for a large defense subcontractor back in the early 1980s. They were learning Ada and object-based design from a small consulting group. The owner of the consulting firm had hired people who used very different approaches. She thought it was just a curiosity at the time, but now she sees that this consultant-owner was very wise. He knew that different people learn differently and what would work with one person might not work with another. His team included Gary the Nice (everyone liked Gary, but as she looks back on it, she thinks if he had been the only mentor he wouldn't have been as effective; as it was he balanced out the others); Ed the Barbarian (Ed was the owner and knew a lot but he could be a little over-the-top for some); Johan the Master (he also knew a lot but he was more subtle and more laid back, a "slow reveal"); and Brad (just Brad, a plain spoken, good guy to work with). This way, everyone could find someone they felt comfortable with and the mix provided the best way to learn the new approaches. They each brought their own take on the material to the table.

---

*Anderson, B., "Toward an Architecture Handbook," OOPSLA *Addendum to the Proceedings*, Washington, D.C., January 1994, ACM Press.

Next Steps

At the end of a training class, one of the attendees stopped by and said, "I enjoyed the class today. That's one of the perks of working here. We have the chance to learn the latest and greatest, but the problem is, I go back to my project and I don't know what to do next. Any ideas?" I realized then that I was saturating students with knowledge but not helping them to apply it.

Take time near the end of an event about the new idea to identify what participants can do next.

You are giving a presentation or having a meeting to explain a new idea to an organization.

A presentation in a training class or another event can leave attendees uncertain about what to do with what they have learned.

Hearing or learning about a new idea is different from applying it. Training classes are useful for sharing a variety of information in a short, intensive time. However, the experience can leave participants exhausted, overwhelmed, and unsure about being able to apply what they learned to their real work. A successful event can stimulate attendees to do more. Build on this excitement before the attendees leave the room.

Even when people are motivated with a clear vision of the desired future, if they don't know what to do next, little or no progress will be made.

Therefore:

Take time near the end of a presentation to brainstorm and discuss how the participants can apply the new information.

Lead the participants in creating a loose plan. Topics for discussion include: How can participants use the information? Where can it be put to use in the organization? How can participants learn more? What can be done to spread the word? Should we begin an e-Forum(135)? Start a Study Group(228)? Invite a Big Jolt(107) speaker?

If you're an outsider and have had experience in introducing the idea into other organizations, you may be tempted to tell the attendees what they should do next. Try to avoid this, since the participants know their needs better than you do and should create and own their own plan. Make suggestions only when appropriate; however, to maintain credibility, have some recommendations if you are asked to contribute.

Create a list of ideas and action items. Prioritize them. Decide what can be done now and what can wait until later. Add some time frames. Ask for Help(104). Encourage those who attended the event to be responsible for each action item. E-mail the list to everyone as a reminder. Hand out a Token(243) to help people remember the new idea that was discussed during the session.

Charles Weir and James Noble's <u>Brainstorming</u> pattern contains some ideas for leading a brainstorming session.

= = = = = = = = =

This pattern initiates the opportunity for people to expand their knowledge of the innovation and get involved in introducing it into their organization. It leaves attendees at a presentation or meeting with more than just a good idea; rather, they are left with things to do in order to begin applying the innovation.

The risk is that the brainstorming may be so enthusiastic that people become overwhelmed with all the things that need to be done. Help them to keep the action items realistic and centered on what the people in the organization can truly do. Encourage them to take things Step by Step(224).

Janice and Kim end their training courses with a discussion of how the attendees can apply what they learned. Attendees brainstorm a rough plan for sharing their knowledge with co-workers and for introducing the new ideas into their organization.

Norm Kerth, author of **Project Retrospectives**, *has observed that team members will get so excited about what is uncovered during a project retrospective session that they will be anxious to lead improvements in their organization. His "Make It a Mission" exercise at the end of the retrospective teaches participants how they can create and follow a mission that will actively deliver a message of change.*

Personal Touch

A manager was struggling with one of his staff. He had tried his standard approaches for bringing him on board and failed. He asked me how he should handle the problem. Should he fire the recalcitrant? After all, his usual techniques had not worked. I asked the manager to show me his key ring. I selected a key and queried, "What does this open?"

"The door to my car."

"Will it also unlock your wife's car?"

"No, of course not."

"Well, it's a perfectly good key. We know it works. Why don't you just junk her car and get another one that will open with this key?"

People are different, so we can't expect everyone to fit with the way we see things. Instead, find out what will unlock each person's resistance to the new idea.*

To convince people of the value in a new idea, show how it can be *personally* useful and valuable to them.

---

*Brown, W.S., *13 Fatal Errors Managers Make and How You Can Avoid Them*, Berkley Books, NY, 1985.

You are an Evangelist(144) or Dedicated Champion(129) who is introducing a new idea into an organization.

Presentations and training will arouse curiosity and some interest in the new idea, but you must do more—the old habits of most individuals will not die without effort.

We tend to focus on the change we want to see in a team, a department, or an organization, when in reality, change happens one individual at a time. Changing a paradigm in an organization means convincing the individuals in the organization. People take change personally. They want to understand how the new idea can personally benefit them.

David Baum reminds us that your employees do not work for you, the department, the organization, the board of directors, or even the company's clients. They work for themselves. This mean that, in a time of organizational change, what matters most is the individual benefit each employee sees for his own life. It's not that humans are inherently selfish, but rather that all change is essentially local.

One of the biggest mistakes change agents make is to just talk about the technical benefits. But people need to first see a personal need for an innovation before they will listen to a discussion of the benefits. Successful change agents will determine what individuals need and ensure that the innovation addresses those needs.

Therefore:

Talk with individuals about the ways in which the new idea can be *personally* useful and valuable to them.

Take time to learn a person's needs before you talk to him or her. Consider "eavesdropping" on problem discussions to discover how the innovation can solve an immediate problem. Ask questions and do a lot of listening. Practice "active listening" by acknowledging, restating, and summarizing ideas and discussion points.

Explain to the individual the ways in which the new idea will help with a work-related problem and how it is an improvement over what is already in place. You may want to concentrate on the ways it can help the individual meet deadlines, because this is usually more convincing than showing how it may improve the quality of work. Keep in mind that your goal is not to change people, but rather to help them become more of who they already are.

Take advantage of the fact that people who learn about a promising innovation and see even small successes will seek additional information. When you see that someone is interested, find a comfortable, informal environment for discussion. Use Just Enough(180) to introduce them to the concepts.

Don't wear yourself out by trying to talk with everyone. Recognize that you do not have the power or the personality to convince everyone. When an individual doesn't want to listen, try to find a Bridge-Builder(110).

= = = = = = = = =

This pattern builds a relationship with individuals, enabling them to discuss their personal needs that the innovation might address. People who hear about something that is personally useful are more likely to move past curiosity and become more interested and enthusiastic.

But some people may see you as their personal guide to the innovation and will run to you with every problem. This can take time away from your primary responsibilities. Create an e-Forum(135) and use In Your Space(167) to communicate general solutions and uses for the innovation.

At one site in a global Fortune 500 company, the new technology group worked hard to become a part of each development team. They attended team meetings and listened for developers' pain and tried to understand team dynamics. This helped formulate a strategy they could use when negotiating changes later. They looked for opportunities to add value and provide impromptu explanations of the new technology.

Budget cutting and layoffs often create an organization full of overworked, busy people. This is true in Jerry's organization. So when he wanted to introduce a new idea, his colleagues responded with questions about the amount of work the idea would save them and create for them. Because everyone's job is different, Jerry had to respond with different answers for each person.

Piggyback

I *was convinced that red meat was bad. No doubt about it, my family was going to eat tofu. They, on the other hand, were preparing for battle. "No way! That tofu stuff is slimy and yucky!" I could see the ordinary arguments about healthy eating were doomed. Then I found a recipe for tofu cheesecake. My friend Susan was the first to experiment. A group from our co-op had lunch one afternoon and, you know what, it was great!*

I slyly presented it the next weekend and the family lapped it up. "Hey! This is great cheesecake! Is it a new recipe?"

I debated—yes, no, yes, no. Finally, I decided. "Yup, it's a new recipe. If you like it, I can do a chocolate version next time!"

"Yeah, chocolate! Thanks, Mom!"

When faced with several obstacles in your strategy to introduce something new, look for a way to piggyback on a practice in your organization.

You are an Evangelist(144) or Dedicated Champion(129). There are some practices in place in your organization that relate to the new idea.

Several procedures or hurdles are required for the introduction of your new idea but you're looking for an easier way.

We're all being asked to do more with less these days. So when you have a new idea, it can be hard to find the time and energy to do all the things you know will help get the idea accepted by the organization.

All organizations have policies and procedures that are important for creating order and decreasing misunderstanding. It's often necessary to follow some of these procedures to some degree in order to create a place for a new idea. This can take a lot of time and become frustrating because the idea can get caught in inertia.

But organizations also have established practices that, over time, have become well accepted and could be used to help bring in the new idea. If you can market a new idea as an add-on to one of these practices, you are likely to bypass some of the rules and procedures it would take to introduce the idea as something completely new and different.

After all, in many cases the new idea is just another way to help people do their current work. Promoting it as an entirely new initiative can generate a lot of hoopla and apprehension. It is likely to be introduced in a much calmer manner and be met with less resistance when it is viewed as an extension or small improvement to an established practice.

Therefore:

Piggyback the new idea on a well-accepted practice in the organization.

Introduce the new idea as an improvement on an existing practice rather than as an entirely new initiative. Take advantage of what is already in place. Leverage the environment, resources, and opportunities.

Ask for Help(104) from others who might be able to develop ways to take advantage of what's already in place. Capture the support of those who know the ins and outs of the practice upon which you are attempting to Piggyback.

When looking for opportunities to talk about your plan, Piggyback on events in the organization. Try to get on the agenda of a team meeting or on the program of an internal conference. Make a brief announcement when it is appropriate in any gathering.

= = = = = = = = =

Using this pattern gets the new idea going in the organization with a minimal amount of red tape. By being associated with something that is well established in your organization, you show that the new idea is not some hair-brained scheme. It can also ease some of the effects on the organization that will concern the people who are fearful of the new idea.

But your effort to help people see the new idea as an add-on to an existing practice can cause them to think it isn't really anything special. This can limit the resources you need for continuing and building it. Stay in Touch(221) with your supporters even after the idea has been established.

Members of a university department wanted to introduce a new program—an MFA in software design, using fine arts teaching methods for software design. Creating a degree program is a complicated committee approval process, so they started with a certificate program, which would require only department approval. After a year of success with the certificate program, it will become an alternative for an MS in Computer Science, again requiring only department approval. By that time, the plan for a Master of Software Engineering (MSE) degree program would be underway. They would have enough success to propose the two-year MFA-style program as an alternative to the second year of the MSE degree work. Finally, they would propose that the two-year MFA-style program stand on its own, perhaps as a Master of Software Arts or Master of Software Engineering (Design).

Anne-Marie had been talking about the new idea in the organization, but didn't seem to be sparking a great amount of interest. She needed to give a presentation. Her boss suggested getting on the agenda for the monthly Tech Talk series. All she had to do was sign up. The people responsible for the Tech Talk series did all the publicity and other work. That presentation turned out to be her first big break. It was well attended and allowed her to identify Innovators and a guru who were interested enough to help her spread the word about the new idea.

Plant the Seeds

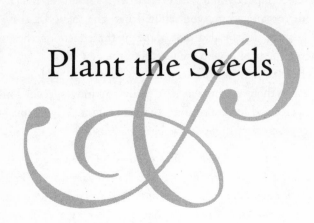

When I give a presentation, I always have a stack of books available on the topic, both for reference during the talk and for perusing at breaks and after the presentation. People like looking at books. One participant said, "Some of my happiest times have been spent with books."

To spark interest, carry materials (seeds) and display (plant) them when the opportunity arises.

You are an Evangelist(144) or Dedicated Champion(129) working to introduce a new idea into your organization. You have some printed materials about the idea.

You want to spark some interest in the new idea.

People like to keep up on the latest buzzword and will be drawn to sources of information, especially if the sources are easily accessible. When they are in the early stages of making a decision about a new idea, they are persuaded by mass media materials, such as articles and books.

The rule of reciprocity holds across cultures. We feel an obligation to repay others when they have given us a gift. Charities rely on reciprocity to help them raise funds. For years, the Disabled American Veterans organization, using only a well-crafted fundraising letter, reported an 18% response rate to its appeals, but when they started enclosing a small gift, the response rate doubled to 35%. The gift, personalized address labels, was modest, but it wasn't what the donors received that made the difference. It was that they had received anything at all. The articles and books you bring to a meeting may not seem like much, but those who take a copy of an article or borrow a book will be positively influenced toward you and your idea.

Therefore:

Carry materials about the new idea to events where people gather. Put them in places where people are likely to pick them up and look at them.

When you give a presentation or attend a meeting, provide sources of External Validation(148), such as books, journal articles, and online articles. Make copies of online materials rather than simply providing the URL, so that it is more likely people will see the information you think is important. If you want to point out some interesting things on the Web, make the URLs available electronically to save the recipient the trouble of typing them. Prominently display anything that has your name as author, or acknowledged contributor, to increase your credibility.

If possible, don't just place the materials on a table and walk away. Make yourself available to answer questions. This will also help ensure that valuable things, like your books, won't disappear!

If you are scheduled to give a presentation during the event, refer to the materials to spark even more interest. The books or articles will attract attention and get conversation going during breaks.

When people ask to take or borrow the materials, stop by your office later, or send an e-mail asking for more information, use Personal Touch(198) and Just Enough(180) to show how the new idea may be useful to them. Don't be discouraged if most people simply stack any handouts you provide in their office and never look at them. People like to pick up free material; however, only some will read them and become interested in the new idea. But don't underestimate the power of this pattern. Although the "seeds" usually spark interest in only a few, they may be key individuals, such as Connectors(119), Early Adopters(138), or a Guru on Your Side(158) who can help you spread the word to others.

$$= = = = = = = = =$$

This pattern creates awareness of a new idea and sparks some interest in it. People will be drawn to the materials, pick them up, and ask about them.

Carrying a lot of books or articles can be a problem on a plane. Even in a car, you might have to make several trips to the parking lot or get help unloading material. If books are displayed, you run the risk that someone could borrow one and not return it. Make sure your name clearly appears on all your valuable materials.

Alan takes patterns books to every object technology or Unified Modeling Language (UML) training course he delivers. The books always generate a lot of interest. In fact, he's learned only to bring them out on the last day, or he risks losing the attention of the participants for the topic at hand. Most often, if consultancy follows, it's on patterns, not object technology or UML.

Karl reports good experiences when he brings drafts of unpublished books to training sessions. It shows his audience that the topic is still evolving and interesting and ensures that he is a source of information about what's going on, so they are getting the latest information.

The Right Time

It's good to request the last or second-to-last interview slot of the day, since these are the time slots that are the most memorable for the interviewer. If you want to be remembered, make your appointment as late in the day as possible.

Consider the timing when you schedule events or when you ask others for help.

You are an Evangelist(144) or Dedicated Champion(129) trying to introduce a new idea into an organization.

When people face deadlines and have too much to do, they tend to focus on things that move them toward completing necessary tasks and making the deadlines.

People are busy. However, there are less busy times.

When you're really excited about a new idea, you want to tell everyone immediately. But you should temper your enthusiasm with the realization that by springing your news at an inconvenient time, you risk irritating members of your target audience and losing converts to your cause.

Timing is also crucial when approaching someone to Ask for Help(104). If people are busy, they could react as if you're trying to add one more thing to their busy schedules. But if your request comes when they're less busy, they are likely to be more responsive.

Therefore:

Be aware of those times when people are likely to be the busiest. Schedule events and requests for help outside those times.

Some suggestions for less busy times: immediately after a project has been delivered, at the beginning of a new year, or possibly during the summer. The best timing will vary from organization to organization, group to group, and person to person. What is good for one will not be good for another. Avoid planning events when almost everyone is too busy to attend.

If you're able, personally ask as many individuals as you can about their time preferences for an upcoming event. This will make them feel that you would really like them to be present.

Don't worry about finding the perfect time. You can spend a lot of effort trying to find the best time when there really isn't one. One approach is to schedule the event more than once. Choose different days or times so more people can attend.

Announce dates as early as possible and send out reminders on the e-Forum(135) and In Your Space(167). Busy people need lead time and reminders. Personally remind individuals when you have the opportunity.

Elicit feedback. Ask attendees at any event what could have been done to improve the event—and this includes timing. You might learn that some people, for example, would like an early morning event, while others prefer a noontime Brown Bag(113) or a late afternoon meeting at the end of the day.

You don't have to consider the timing in planning every event. For example, Study Groups(228) are usually held on a regular basis and it is expected that people will come when they can. Big Jolt(107) presentations have to be held at the convenience of the speaker.

Be sensitive of timing during meetings or conversations. "When the student is ready, the teacher appears" is a big part of this pattern. Keep your ears open for a problem that the new idea can help to address. The receptiveness of your group will increase considerably at a time when they have an immediate application.

= = = = = = = = = =

This pattern creates more appropriate timing for introducing the new idea. If you can find a good time, you are likely to increase participation.

But, despite your efforts, some people will claim to be too busy to do or attend anything that doesn't directly relate to their immediate job. Use Personal Touch(198) to reach them. Encourage them to hear a one-time Big Jolt(107) speaker.

Ian tried to be aware of the needs of many different people while he waited for the opportunity to help someone with a problem. It doesn't help a team to talk about testing patterns during design or to talk about configuration management patterns during analysis. When the solution fits the needs, the timing is right and people will be ready to listen.

Nilesh held the first workshop about a new idea during the start of a semester. The second one was held at the end of the semester, just after grades were due. Both events were well attended. Attendees were excited about continuing the workshops. But when the third event was scheduled during the fourth week of the semester, just as the workload was heating up, it had to be cancelled due to lack of positive responses.

Royal Audience

The first time my company invited a big-name speaker, I tried to make sure the day was full of activities. I wanted as many people as possible to take advantage of the opportunity. When he said, "I'll be here the night before; if anyone is interested, we could do dinner." Aha! Dinner! Lunch! Good times for interaction! I learned from this experience to always invite people to meals with any famous visitor because the relaxed atmosphere can be more fun and even more interesting than the visitor's formal presentation.

Arrange for management and members of the organization to spend time with a Big Jolt visitor.

You are an Evangelist(144) or Dedicated Champion(129). A Big Jolt(107) visitor has a few spare hours during the day or during the evening before and/or after the day of the visit.

You want to get the most out of a visit from a famous person.

It's better if a visit from a well-known individual is more than just a presentation to a large group. Famous people are usually charismatic and can give your cause a boost. If management and other influential people in the organization will take time for a short, one-on-one meeting with the Big Jolt, this can lead to more interest and support for the new idea.

Therefore:

Use spare hours or lunchtime during the day or evenings, before and/or after the featured presentation, to make the visitor available for teams, individuals, or managers.

Arrange lunch, dinner, or time for informal discussion with the speaker during the day. Personally invite people to attend, especially those who have helped with the change effort. The visitor may also be willing to take some one-on-one time with managers who still need to be convinced of the value in the new idea. This can lead to support from a Local Sponsor(186) or Corporate Angel(123). It is also a good way to Stay in Touch(221).

If you can, try to schedule several audiences, enough opportunities so that no one minds not being invited to all of them. For example, dinner may need to be a small group, but lunch in the cafeteria could be open to everyone. You might schedule "consulting time" when the visitor could meet with teams to discuss particular problems.

Don't wear out the visitor. Make certain he agrees to do more than a presentation. Give him a chance to turn down any opportunities that he wishes. Sometimes we assume that someone who comes in for a presentation will want to spend lunch and dinner with us, but we should be sensitive to the fact that everyone needs time to relax away from others. Remember to Just Say Thanks(183) for any extra time he spends with the organization.

Don't expect everyone to accept the invitation to meet with the speaker. It is important that you offer them the opportunity. For those who can't come, it may be enough for them to know that they were invited.

= = = = = = = = = =

This pattern creates an opportunity for people to meet with a Big Jolt speaker. Participants will enjoy the time spent getting to know a famous person. This can be a reward for those who have helped with the effort, and can be a public relations opportunity for management who have not yet bought into your new idea.

But be careful that this doesn't backfire. If you need to keep the audience small, people can be upset at not being invited. But if you always Involve Everyone(173) as much as you can and are a fair person, then people will accept that they weren't invited to a particular occasion but will be included in the next one or will be involved in some other way.

Dorothy sent invitations to everyone to join famous visitors for lunch or an open discussion forum. Free consulting time was also announced on the e-Forum. Even if people couldn't attend, they always felt that the opportunity was open to them.

Deloy always invited everyone to meet with well-known visitors for lunch or a coffee break after the presentations. Because the meetings were held in the cafeteria, there was room for everyone at the presentation to attend. Even those who couldn't talk one-on-one with the visitor still enjoyed listening to him chat with others in an informal setting.

Shoulder to Cry On

When I was trying to introduce a new idea into the organization, I would often make mistakes and become discouraged. Then I would see one of my favorite movie lines displayed on my office bulletin board: "One of the best things you have going for yourself is your willingness to humiliate yourself." (Simon to Melvin in the movie As Good As It Gets*). That was just like me, and because of this, I was willing to continue trying to introduce the new idea despite the embarrassing mistakes. So instead of giving up, I'd usually find a shoulder to cry on—someone who would help me recognize that things weren't as bad as I thought they were.*

To avoid becoming too discouraged when the going gets tough, find opportunities to talk with others who are also struggling to introduce a new idea.

You are an Evangelist(144) or Dedicated Champion(129) working to introduce a new idea into your organization.

When you're struggling to introduce a new idea, it's easy to become discouraged.

Misery loves company, but if it's the right kind of company, commiserating can lead to rejuvenation. Getting together with others who share the same or similar problems can lead to surprising solutions. The group dynamic helps everyone become more creative in tackling tough situations. Research has shown that for certain issues, group support can be very helpful. Even if you are enthusiastic about the new idea, you will need and deserve a boost now and then. You'll want to feel like you're not the only one dealing with an issue. This by itself is useful.

Those who are first to adopt an innovation are often frustrated when they can't understand complicated material. A common solution is to form a user group. Together they can "group think" and can solve problems that individuals in isolation can't.

Therefore:

Get together regularly with others who are also working to introduce the new idea or are interested in the process.

Meet informally for lunch, dinner, or coffee. Try to find a place away from home or the office. Look for a "third place"—a local, public establishment that is a friendly, neutral spot where people gather together to relax and talk and take a break from everyday life.

If funding permits, attend a conference where you can learn more about the innovation and meet with others to talk about your mutual struggles.

There should be give and take among the participants. Give everyone a chance to "cry" and to "provide a shoulder to cry on." Remember to Just Say Thanks(183) for any support.

When you can't find a group of people, consider the <u>Cardboard Consultant</u> pattern written by Charles Weir and James Noble. It recommends that when you can't find a solution to your problem, you explain it, in detail, out loud to someone or something. This will help you understand your basic assumptions, the chain of logic that led to your being stuck and your conclusions. They claim this works even with your dog.

= = = = = = = = =

This pattern creates opportunities for you to discuss the challenges and successes you are having with your change effort. A community begins to form wherever people gather with a shared purpose and start talking among themselves. This community provides a confidence boost when you're discouraged and a source of helpful suggestions and strategies. This is also a good way to meet Innovators(170) and Connectors(119) in your larger community.

But if you are not careful, a meeting can degenerate into a whining session. This will only make people drown in the negative and feel sorry for themselves. While some complaining is appropriate, focus on solutions to the problems that people raise. Once people have the chance to unload, you can use the larger intelligence to move forward.

When the Houston Independent School District made a major commitment to purchasing technology for the classrooms, teachers found that they had to confront the technology alone, using ideas from scattered sources with only modest results. The Electronic Community of Teachers was created to help teachers across the district learn from each other about computing in the classroom. This virtual community of practice allows teachers who find themselves isolated in their classrooms to build relationships with other teachers as they share experiences and document their best practices.

In the Greenville, South Carolina area, businesspeople gather monthly at the Wall Street Capitol Breakfast Club America meeting. During a recent event, the guest speaker, Rich DeVos, the co-founder of Amway Corporation, reminded them, "You are never alone. There are people all around you at this meeting to help and support you."

Small Successes

As David Baum, author of Lightning in a Bottle, recommends, "If you talk about what you want rather than what you don't want, your subconscious can rarely tell the difference. Focus on the positive and you will move toward it with deliberate speed."*

To avoid becoming overwhelmed by the challenges and all the things you have to do when you're involved in an organizational change effort, celebrate even small successes.

You are an Evangelist(144). You've applied some patterns from this language, and some worked but others didn't.

Every organizational change effort has its ups and downs. It's a difficult process.

We are so often caught up in our destination that we forget to appreciate the journey. After successfully completing a task, we often don't acknowledge our achievement and may even underestimate what we have done. Our memory can be so focused on the struggle it took to get the job done that we don't take the

---

*Baum, D., *Lightning in a Bottle: Proven Lessons for Leading Change*, Dearborn, 2000.

time to appreciate what we have accomplished. We often concentrate on everything that still needs to be done instead of on the Small Successes that have come our way. Usually we're too busy. Our "To Do" list is infinite, so when we finish any task, we're already thinking about the next one. We can become discouraged and burned out.

All too often, our focus is on that "big win"—some dramatic event that defines success. We care more about some magic silver bullet than the continuous improvements that will eventually lead to our desired goal. As a result, most jobs provide few opportunities to be recognized as a winner. Celebrations are usually reserved for the big events and only a few are singled out.

But author and software guru Luke Hohmann urges that "achieving any goal should be an opportunity for enjoying the fruits of your labor. You've earned it! More importantly, achieving one goal gives you the confidence to do it again, producing a positive feedback loop of goal-setting and goal-achieving success!"*

Large-scale change can be a long, formidable undertaking, so create short-term wins. A number of early victories, even if they are small, create self-confidence and the belief that bigger successes are possible. This belief builds a psychological momentum that sustains the effort needed for large-scale, long-term change.

Therefore:

As you carry on Step by Step, take the time to recognize and celebrate successes, especially the small ones.

These don't have to be big celebrations. You can buy a cake for everyone to share, or just give a "high five" all around. Involve everyone who has helped to achieve the small success. Even when you can't include others, it is still important to give yourself a pat on the back.

Success can come in many forms. Look for it. For example, at the end of the week, ask yourself what you and your team have learned or done differently. This simple question can go a long way in promoting continual, but focused, change.

Focus on the gains rather than the losses. Even when you don't get all the things you wanted, you can still celebrate the things you *didn't* get that you didn't want!

---

*Hohmann, L., *Journey of the Software Professional*, Prentice-Hall, 1997.

Take Time for Reflection(240) and view each success as an opportunity to work toward larger undertakings. Your present success, no matter how small, is something to be proud of because it allows you to do bigger and even more successful things. Build on what you have accomplished.

Use e-Forum(135) and In Your Space(167) to inform others about the progress. The Smell of Success(219) will attract others.

= = = = = = = = =

This pattern creates the realization that each small success puts you one step closer to the goal. Even though there is still work to be done, recognizing and celebrating small accomplishments encourages a focus on the positive. It makes you feel productive and energized to do even more.

But your success can turn off people who are jealous and resentful of what you are trying to do. Others may see the celebration as a sign that the effort is at an end. Stay in Touch(221) with your supporters and nonsupporters alike to be sure that everyone is on the same page. Help them understand that the Small Successes are cornerstones for tackling the bigger problems and their support is still needed to reach the final goals.

Since 1961, Peace Corps volunteers have embarked on ambitious projects but are often overpowered by feelings of frustration. Successful change agents persist despite setbacks and celebrate even small successes. A small success is worth a lot because it empowers the volunteer and the community members to try another new project. After a small victory, a volunteer could make more suggestions because the locals will no longer think that the outsider is quite so crazy. Some volunteers finish their stint with Peace Corps thinking they didn't accomplish much. Taking time to recognize the small successes is the key.

John was leading the development of a new center in his organization. There was a lot of work to be done. The task could have become overwhelming if not for the "action items" that the team created during each weekly meeting. At the following meeting, team members looked forward to going over that list and would often cheer "All right!" when one of the larger items was finally completed or all of the smaller items on the list could be removed.

Smell of Success

It is both invisible and intangible, and yet it invokes such powerful human reactions that people are swayed to affection or revulsion because of it. It is that most subtle and subjective of senses—the sense of smell.

When your efforts result in some visible positive result, people will come out of the woodwork to talk to you. Treat this opportunity as a teaching moment.

You are an Evangelist(144) or Dedicated Champion(129) trying to introduce a new idea. You've had at least limited success.

When you start to have some success, newcomers will ask you about the innovation.

Some people, especially the Early Majority(141) and the skeptics, are drawn to a new idea when there is visible success. Unlike the Innovators(170), who love the excitement of being part of the latest and greatest, most others wait until the early bugs are worked out and there is some evidence that a new idea is useful. This evidence can be provided by the successes others are having. When people who have not yet adopted a new idea smell success, they are likely to become interested enough to ask you about it.

Therefore:

When people comment on the success they see with the innovation, treat their inquiry as a teaching moment.

Use Just Enough(180) to spark some interest and Personal Touch(198) to match the innovation to the inquirer's needs. If you think it is appropriate, Ask for Help(104)—identify a small task and ask the inquirer to complete it. This is the "Yes, that's a difficult problem; would you volunteer to tackle it?" ploy!

Manage the expectations of people who smell success and then look forward to a silver bullet. Give them a realistic view of what has been accomplished and what still needs to be done.

Learn what you can from these inquiries. Even as you experience success and become convinced of the value in the new idea, remain open and listen to comments from everyone.

= = = = = = = = =

This pattern creates the opportunity for you to use your success to create more successes. It draws people to the new idea, giving you the opportunity to answer their questions and encourage them to be active supporters.

But a smell of success can also draw people who have been negatively impacted by the new idea. If they are looking for a way to neutralize that effect, listen to their story and use Fear Less(151) to find a win-win solution.

After a project was completed on schedule and received high acclaim from the users, someone from another team dropped by to talk about some issues that concerned her in our project's technology. She seemed interested in knowing how our techniques, which were quite different from the "standard" practices, allowed us to be productive and successful—despite our having an inexperienced team. It was the perfect opportunity to enlighten her about our new approaches.

My work with patterns attracted the interest of someone who was well known and well respected in the patterns community. When he offered to come to my organization to give a presentation, people were impressed. As a result, inquiries about patterns increased. I made sure I addressed each one, often by suggesting that we take a coffee break or have lunch to discuss their questions.

Stay in Touch

Everyone is busy and overworked. Yet I've discovered that if I don't take a moment to stop by my co-workers' offices to have a chat now and then and occasionally spend lunchtime with them, I lose touch with the most important part of my organization—the people.

Once you've enlisted the support of key persons, don't forget about them and make sure they don't forget about you.

You are an Evangelist(144) or Dedicated Champion(129) working to introduce a new idea into an organization. You've captured the interest of a handful of key persons.

Your key supporters have too many things to think about and can forget about the new idea.

Support for any new idea depends on the continuing awareness of management and other key people, but their support can lapse. Since there's always something important going on and critical decisions to be made, your message will be lost if you don't call attention to it.

Finding proactive ways to keep the information flowing is essential. You do not want your key supporters to feel embarrassed or frustrated because they lack information about the change initiative. Any effort to keep a communication link will pay off handsomely in the end.

Just because people decide to adopt an innovation doesn't mean they can't change their minds. They're always seeking reinforcement for their decisions. They always have new questions. If they don't get answers, they may revert to their old ways.

Therefore:

Stay in touch with your key supporters.

Make an effort to talk regularly with people such as Early Adopters(138), Local Sponsors(186), a Guru on Your Side(158), and the Corporate Angel(123). You're busy too, so put the "stay in touch" reminder on your calendar. It can be a short meeting, lunch, or coffee break, or just an informal stop by an office. Present information in a helpful manner. Keep messages timely and interesting. Use External Validation(148) to make them aware of what is happening outside the organization. If a Big Jolt(107) visitor is of special interest to your supporters, offer them a Royal Audience(210).

Strive to build a relationship with key individuals so you can casually but continually make them aware of progress in small ways. On the other hand, you don't want to make a pest of yourself. Be sensitive to individual tolerances for new information. Don't overwhelm supporters or they will become annoyed when they see you coming. It can be hard to determine the happy medium for information, so you may want to ask how often each person would like to receive a formal report, and at the same time provide informal reports when you get a good opportunity.

Talk to management even when you don't need anything. A lot of people make the mistake of reporting to management only when they need support. As a result, managers will think that any time you come to talk, you must want something.

If you need a more formal approach for staying close, submit a regular status report that contains a concise record of your activities. Record your accomplishments, even small successes, so people know you are making progress. Also note your concerns so that your manager, or your Local Sponsor(186), has the information he needs to help you.

= = = = = = = = =

This pattern establishes more solid connections with key supporters. Over time, it turns support into an expanding community of relationships.

But this takes work. A personal interaction is best, but an e-Forum(135) or In Your Space(167) can help. If it is difficult to reach some upper-level managers, ask Connectors(119) or your Local Sponsor(186) to help.

*It was easy for Amy. The company brought in 8' x 8' cubicles and the vice president was nearby. Okay, he had **two** cubicles, one with a little conference table, **and** his secretary's cubicle was also part of his area, but still, he was just around the corner from Amy's team. When she walked in each morning, he was often there, and if he looked up, she could sometimes catch his eye and say, "Good morning!" If he asked, and usually he did, she could tell him about the latest activity surrounding the introduction of the innovation. She wouldn't let him forget about it!*

Bradley was the chair of a large international conference. His committee consisted of 12 people located in various countries. In between the meetings, Bradley made random calls to each individual just to ask how things were going. One day he connected to a frantic committee member on the other end of the phone. She was amazed at the timing of his phone call because she had just discovered a major error in her duties. He calmed her and then explained what he could do to "fix" things. They both appreciated the value of staying in touch that day.

Step by Step

E. L. Doctorow once said that *"writing a novel is like driving a car at night. You can see only as far as your headlights, but you can make the whole trip that way."* You don't have to see your destination or everything you will pass along the away. You just have to see two or three feet ahead of you. This is right up there with the best advice about writing, or life, I have ever heard.*

Relieve your frustration at the enormous task of changing an organization by taking one small step at a time toward your goal.

You are an Evangelist(144). After applying Test the Waters(237) and Time for Reflection(240), you realize that there is interest in the new idea in your organization.

You wonder what your plan should be for introducing the new idea into your organization.

---

*Lamott, A., *Bird by Bird: Some Instructions on Writing and Life*, Anchor Books, 1995.

"If we can see the path ahead laid out for us, there is a good chance it is not our path; it is probably someone else's we have substituted for our own. Our own path must be deciphered every step of the way."* There are no shortcuts to anyplace worth going.

It is impossible to instantly convert everyone to your way of thinking. An attempt to create a master plan for the change initiative is probably setting yourself up for failure because there are too many unknowns in any organization. The very nature of a complex problem can bring you to your knees and cause you to make no progress at all. Yet, to climb a ladder, you don't leap from the ground to the top. Rather, you climb slowly and surely, one step at a time. Similarly, organizational change happens, not with a giant leap, but in small, sometimes hardly noticeable steps. People are less resistant to small changes than large ones, but lots of small changes will ultimately create major shifts.

We can become discouraged and find it difficult to maintain enthusiasm for a single goal that is so far out it's hard to imagine you can ever reach it. There's an advantage to setting short-term goals and seeing clear progress. It's definitely more exciting to identify small steps and celebrate when you reach each one than it is to outline an overpowering vision that will take months or years to achieve.

The most common mistake change agents make is to take on too much, too soon. They are often like anxious gardeners standing over their plants, imploring them: "Grow! Try harder! You can do it!" But good gardeners don't try to convince a plant to grow.** Instead, they realize that significant change starts slowly and evolves steadily over time. In organizational change, as in nature, new developments should spread quietly at first, so that the leaders can learn from the failures and build on the successes.

Therefore:

Use an incremental approach in the change initiative, with short-term goals, while keeping your long-term vision.

Focus on a few meaningful organizational problems. Create a compelling vision, but keep it broad enough to increase your chance of success. You may wish to

---

*Whyte, D., *The Heart Aroused: Poetry and the Preservation of the Soul in Corporate America*, Currency Doubleday, 1994.
**Senge, P. et al., *The Dance of Change: The Challenges to Sustaining Momentum in Learning Organizations*, Doubleday, 1999.

list the things that need to happen in order to achieve your vision, but you don't need an exact plan for *how* you will make these things happen. Rather, set a few short-term goals and be prepared to adjust your expectations as you learn what works and what doesn't.

Identify things you can achieve quickly, then implement some small portion of the initiative. Work toward early wins that bring about any change. Use your initial successes as stepping-stones to increasingly ambitious gains. Remind yourself each time you achieve a short-term goal to celebrate the Small Successes(216).

Encourage people to experiment using a Trial Run(245) even for a small part of the new idea. Make small changes that don't disrupt the system and trust that the collection of small changes will result in big change. Before you go tearing in to change something, step way back, calm down, and think about the least perturbation you can introduce and still get the result you want. Over time, with enough little efforts, a new order emerges—one you could not have planned no matter how many flip charts you hauled out. Help what wants to happen, happen. Rather than attempting a complete system overhaul, remove just one little obstacle or add one little ingredient. Launch your first step and then take Time for Reflection(240) to decide what to do next.

As new Evangelists(144) come on board, let them plan their own part of the journey. They'll have more success by doing what's appropriate for their part of the world and you won't have to know everything there is to know about every part of the organizational change. The change is bigger than you and it's not important that you travel each path to the goal. The important outcome is that the goal is reached, and that will happen as a result of a coalition, not one person's efforts.

Be wary of promising specific times in which goals can be achieved. Cultural change tends to be organic and hard to predict. Be suspicious of people who promise big changes on a cultural level in some specific time frame—they're blowing smoke.

Remain optimistic even if you take one step forward and two steps back. Find a Shoulder to Cry On(213). As pointed out in Brian Foote and Joe Yoder's <u>Piecemeal Growth</u> pattern, mistakes are inevitable and growth is a slow and continuous process that cannot be achieved in a single leap.

= = = = = = = = =

This pattern builds an incremental approach to your change initiative. Because you can't possibly know everything that could happen, this approach gives you the chance to learn as you go. You can take advantage of what you learn along the way to adjust your plans accordingly.

But people might think you don't know where you're going. Help them understand that the goal and the path to get there are not the same thing. Even though you don't know the exact path, devise a clear goal and continually communicate it with your current plans. This pattern doesn't suggest you shouldn't plan ahead at all. After all, Noah didn't wait until it started raining to build the ark.

From 1992 to 2001, the University Hospital of North Norway gradually introduced a digitized radiology system. This was successful because the system "grew" into place. First it was a small, customer-built image managing system, then a patient flow handling system, and, finally, an upgraded common version in all 11 hospitals in northern Norway. The gradual approach let developers alter the system based on user feedback without spending large sums and involving too many users. A more robust and well-tested system could then be introduced to a wider user group.

The leaders of RiverLink started with a 10-year plan to revive the French Broad River into a place where people can live, work, and play. But after many unexpected challenges, such as a fire in one of their central buildings and the loss of some land, their plan had to be altered many times. So they began constructing strategies with shorter time frames. They have found that the short-term plans make "people more believable that this can happen." In addition, the Executive Director noticed that the ability to readjust "has, I think, ended in a better place than our original plan."

Study Group

Joshua Kerievsky, well-known agile software development coach, writes about learning: "While attendees of a lecture may seek information, attendees of a study group seek transformation; they want to make what they study not only something they understand, but something they may use in their everyday lives or work. The study group thus acts as a bridge, helping people move from passive to active learning."*

Form a small group of colleagues who are interested in exploring or continuing to learn about a specific topic.

You and others in the organization would like to learn more about a new idea. There are some resources on the topic, such as books or other written materials.

There may be little or no money for formal training on the specific topic.

Software guru Gerald Weinberg describes the lecture method as "getting material from the teacher's notes into the student's notes without passing through the

---

*Kerievsky, J., "A Learning Guide To Design Patterns," http://www.industriallogic
.com/papers/learning.html

brain of either one." The intense training experience can be compared to drinking from a fire hose. It isn't the best learning environment, especially for adults, who want to think about useful information and contemplate how it could be applied to their daily work.

When you read a book by yourself, what you get out of it is limited by your own perspective and experience. When you read a book in a group setting, you can take advantage of a variety of backgrounds and expertise. More formal independent study has its own difficulties. The learner relies on a technical interface, videotapes, or broadcast classes but little social interaction. As a result, the learner goes through material in isolation with no chance for discussion or timely questions.

Research shows that simply explaining or lecturing to a group does little to change their way of thinking, while discussion groups, role-playing, or visualization techniques are powerful persuaders. In one study, two groups were introduced to a new approach. One group was given a presentation on the advantages of the approach. The other was led through a discussion and a group decision-making process. There was little or no change in behavior resulting from the training presentation, while the number of people adopting the new approach varied from over 60% to 100% in the group that had used facilitated decision making.

Institutional learning depends on developing the ability to "flock"—moving people around and fostering an effective mechanism of social transmission. Teams of disparate people must undergo some kind of training experience where they are expected to both teach and learn.

Therefore:

Form a group of no more than eight colleagues who are interested in exploring and studying an interesting topic.

Cover a chapter in a book or a well-defined topic at each regularly scheduled meeting. Make certain participants understand that they must be prepared. Assign one participant as the facilitator who guides everyone through the material. Rotate the facilitation role to spread this responsibility throughout the group.

If resources are available, ask your company to buy the material you will study, such as books or copies of articles. Consider meeting over lunch if this is the time when most people are free. Have a Brown Bag(113) if no resources are available for food.

Linda has co-authored an article about one company's success with study groups. It was published in the *Bell Labs Technical Journal* and can be downloaded from her Web site, http://www.lindarising.org. Joshua Kerievsky has another useful source of information for this effective learning activity. See *Knowledge Hydrant: A Pattern Language for Study Groups* at http://www.industriallogic.com/papers/khdraft.pdf.

= = = = = = = = =

This pattern provides an opportunity for individuals to explore an interesting topic at a reasonable pace. The group members get a genuine educational experience and focus on topics they have chosen. It allows timely, convenient scheduling and a sense of ownership of the learning path. The result is maximum learning with minimal money invested. Even when companies buy lunch for eight participants and individual copies of a book, the cost per learner for a 12-week study group is less than $200.00. Other more formal training costs can run from $800.00 to $2,000.00 per learner.

However, the discovery process in study groups isn't appropriate for all types of learning. Technical topics, such as a programming language, may need an expert to be present when learners get stuck on problems. In addition, this type of exploration may not work for everyone, especially those who are not energized by interaction with others or are "sponges" rather than contributors. Study groups are only one way of learning; they should be considered as a part of the total teaching and learning strategy in an organization.

A couple of years ago, Todd recognized a real gap in the company's knowledge of XML. Since they are a systems integrator, this could have been a fatal hole. They didn't have any homegrown experts, so they formed a study group to make themselves knowledgeable about the subject. They turned what they learned in the study groups into a course that they originally described as "The Myopic Leading the Blind." They now have key work done with XML, and a broad curriculum of XML classes that they teach internally and one that they are teaching externally.

A four-year university and a nearby community college wanted to incorporate more "service learning" in their institutions, but they needed to understand how to make these types of experiences more meaningful for their students. So faculty from each institution banned together to form one study group of 12 members. The university purchased books on the topic and members partnered into teams of two to lead a biweekly group discussion on one of the sections. The participants learned techniques for making service learning successful as a pedagogical technique in their classes and they are preparing to spread the word to other faculty.

Sustained Momentum

We can think of introducing ideas as planting a sapling: without water, sun, and a source of nourishment, the young tree will die. It will need attention to keep it alive and growing. Sometimes we forget how important this ongoing support is—for all living things.

Take a pro-active approach to the ongoing work of sustaining the interest in the new idea in your organization.

You are a Dedicated Champion(129). You have made some progress introducing the new idea into your organization.

The many other things that need to be done will tempt you to put the task of introducing the new idea on the back burner for a while. But this can cause you and other people to lose interest in it.

It takes work to maintain interest. Even though it may be easy to start the change effort with a lot of enthusiasm, the never-ending list of things to do can make you feel tired of the investment it takes to introduce the new idea. But without continuing, pro-active efforts, any new idea can wither and die on the vine. If you don't reinforce the benefits of your new idea, you run the risk that excitement and interest will fade, especially when everyone gets busy with other things. You can't become complacent. You may have told your story countless times, but you have to keep on giving your sales pitch and providing support. It never really ends. There are always new people to bring in and new management to sell.

There's a danger that when success is evident in the change initiative, it's easy to just rest on your laurels and not do anything for a while. But even when the new idea has been accepted and is being used, people still require periodic confirmation that their decision to adopt it was a good one or they may discontinue their use. They need continuous invitations to become involved and continuous reassurances that they will get their wins.

During any change initiative, you must keep yourself inspired. Newton's Third Law was never so true: An object at rest tends to stay at rest until acted upon by external forces. You need to keep the new idea in a motion that it is difficult to stop because momentum is hard to get back once you lose it.

Therefore:

Take a pro-active approach in the organization to the ongoing work of sustaining the interest in the new idea. Take some small action each day, no matter how insignificant it may seem, to move you closer to your goal.

The following are some suggestions for ongoing activities that will keep the information flowing.

- Keep an e-Forum(135) and In Your Space(167) alive and interesting.
- Use Personal Touch(198) and talk about the new idea every chance you get.
- Plan frequent events, such as a Brown Bag(113) and Hometown Story(164).
- Bring in a Big Jolt(107) speaker to stir up more curiosity and interest.
- Start a Study Group(228) to keep people learning.
- Piggyback(201) on already scheduled events.
- Be aware of outside events and call them to the attention of the organization.
- Attend conferences to learn new things and network with others. Share this information with others using External Validation(148) and Stay in Touch(221).
- Keep your knowledge up to date. Your continuous learning is an important part of this effort. Read and make information available—Plant the Seeds(204).
- Take Time for Reflection(240) to learn what is working well and what should be done differently.
- Just Say Thanks(183) so that people feel their continuing support is appreciated.

Keep the momentum going even when you encounter a setback. Those who get back on the horse and do something constructive will probably make it while others who have trouble weathering the storms are likely to fail. Find a Shoulder to Cry On(213) for help in handling your difficult problems.

= = = = = = = = =

This pattern builds a sustained change initiative. It keeps the idea alive in you and in others and helps to reinforce individuals' decisions to adopt it. When the change effort is living and growing, members of the organization will see the new idea as an active and evolving initiative, even when they are too busy to take advantage of everything that is offered.

But keeping a steady momentum on any one project goes against the grain. Our natural tendency is to work in cycles. After completing a big task, we like to do something else for a while. But the longer we wait, the harder it is to return to the project because we lose some of our passion for it. In the long run, we usually find that periodic bursts are more stressful and less effective than simply doing something, even something small, on a regular basis.

It never occurred to Carl that introducing patterns is like growing a garden. You can't just throw the seeds in the ground and say that's that! No, you have to water, feed, and weed. Carl discovered this after he had given a few brown bags. As more and more people came by to ask about one design pattern or another, he realized that he was now the official encourager of pattern use and that once the mantle had been placed on his shoulders, it was up to him to make sure he thought about it all the time. After a while it became second nature. He would say, "I 'do' patterns!"

Poet David Whyte writes, "I decided on two things: firstly I was going to do at least one thing every day toward my future life as a poet. I calculated that no matter how small a step I took each day, over a year that would come to a grand total of 365 actions toward the life I wanted. One thing a day adds up to a great deal over time. One thing a day is a powerful multiplier. Sometimes that one thing was writing poetry itself or memorizing lines of a newly read poem that caught my eye, or just writing a letter to an organization to say I was available for readings or talks. Sometimes it was a phone call to someone in a position of influence, letting them know what I could do. Sometimes it was preparing the ground in my mind before the conversation. Soon I felt as if I was being prepared by the conversations themselves. Over the ensuing weeks it was beginning to add up. I began to overhear a background buzz in the ethers that added to my dedication."*

---

*Whyte, D., *The Heart Aroused: Poetry and the Preservation of the Soul in Corporate America*, Currency Doubleday, 1994.

Tailor Made

I was having trouble convincing Tom, a fellow manager, of the usefulness of my new idea until I mentioned that it could be used as a tool in the organization's knowledge management efforts. This was something Tom could understand and it was enough to convince him that the new idea could be of value in our organization.

To convince people in an organization of the value they can gain from the new idea, tailor your message to the needs of the organization.

You are a Dedicated Champion(129) using Personal Touch(198) to show how your new idea can be personally useful.

Individuals can be intrigued by interesting ideas, but to have impact on an organization, the idea has to be more than just interesting.

An innovation is good not because it is cool or trendy, but because it is *useful*. The value a new idea can provide an organization is not always apparent because results do not appear overnight. Yet, when management and Early Adopters(138) consider a new idea, they want to see the benefits to the organization.

Organizational decision makers are more willing and able to adopt innovations that offer clear advantages, do not drastically interfere with existing practices, and are easy to understand. They want to see how a new idea can fit into and improve what the organization already does. When it comes to new ideas, packaging matters. Even the best ideas will have no impact if they are not sold in a way that gets through people's filters. A commonly heard piece of advice is "Don't sell the technology, sell the business solution."

Therefore:

Tailor your message about the innovation to the needs of the organization.

Study the organization's processes and goals to identify a need or a problem that the innovation can solve. You must first help the organization realize that what they have now is not working in order to convince them that your idea is worth considering. Then, rather than presenting the general benefits of the new idea, explain the specific advantages it can offer the organization. Use buzzwords and information from specific projects in the organization that people will relate to. Persuade them from their point of view. Focus on what people are trying to do and show how the innovation can create change for the better.

Frame your new idea in a way that speaks to the manager who will be funding the initiative. Listen carefully when you meet with him and then include his needs in your proposal. Describe the steps you can take to solve the organizational problems he has discussed with you.

Don't hype the innovation as a perfect solution because no matter how beneficial it may be for the organization, implementation is usually riddled with glitches.

Be clear about the motivations for the change. While these can appear obvious to you, this understanding may not be shared by everyone.

If there is an organization similar to yours that is having success with the innovation, use External Validation(148). Management likes to hear what other companies are doing, especially if the organization is in the same business, a partner, or even a competitor.

Make no mistake about it, this is a sales job, and you will need to give a different sales pitch to different groups. But make certain that each pitch contains the same basic facts and philosophy.

= = = = = = = = =

This pattern produces an understanding of how the innovation can help the organization. It helps to spark confidence in the decision makers that the innovation is not simply a good idea but rather is something to allow the organization to improve its current practices.

It takes a special effort to use this pattern. Instead of using a canned presentation, you have to do some research. You must take the time to examine the needs of the organization so that you can match the new idea to these needs.

Sybil works for a large organization and sent us this advice: "Particularly in today's market when everybody is tightening belts, the things that will sell to upper managers are those that can be executed fairly quickly and will lead to faster time to market, reduction of cost or a proven practice that leads quickly to higher quality. I frame any new idea as an outcome that speaks to the manager who will be funding the effort. I listen a lot the first couple of times I meet with him and then include the needs that I have heard in the proposal that I make. Then I describe the steps that we can take that will lead to solving the problems that have been articulated."

Nationally syndicated business columnist Dale Dauten writes, "I remember reading that the one reason people say "no" to a salesperson is the fear of making a mistake. This changed the way I sold my ideas to the company. I realized that while I was going on about the wonderful things we might accomplish, executives were sitting there thinking only one thing: What can go wrong? I've learned to explain how we can minimize risk, especially the risk of management looking bad."*

---

*Dauten, D., *The Gifted Boss*, William Morrow & Company, 1999.

Test the Waters

David Baum in his book Lightning in a Bottle *notes, "The change process for most people is to slowly dip their toes into the water and ease into the shallow end, splashing a little water around and complaining about how cold it is."** *

When a new opportunity presents itself, see if there is any interest by using some of the patterns in this language and then evaluating the result.

You are excited about a new idea and you would like to be an Evangelist(144) for it in your organization.

When you learn about something new, you wonder if the organization is ready for it.

It isn't always obvious where to start introducing a new idea into an organization. You don't want to put much effort into introducing it if there really isn't any interest. There's a natural tendency for an enthusiastic change agent to try

---

*Baum, D., *Lightning in a Bottle: Proven Lessons for Leading Change*, Dearborn, 2000.

to make an impact much too quickly. Yet, you need to get your bearings. A "listen and learn" approach shows that you are willing to consider the opinions of others as you explain your new ideas.

You can't fix everything at once, so the trick is to find the minimum number of leverage points to create a dramatic impact. Once you find the hot buttons, you can get things going.

Therefore:

Choose a pattern or two from this collection, use them, and then evaluate the result.

Begin with a few things that don't take much effort, such as:

+ Use Personal Touch(198) during a coffee break to informally talk with one of your colleagues, who might be an Innovator(170) or become a Guru on Your Side(158).
+ Just Do It(177) and then give a simple demo or a Hometown Story(164) to a few colleagues.
+ Schedule a Brown Bag(113) to present the idea to the rest of your team.
+ Piggyback(201) on a regularly scheduled event.
+ Plant the Seeds(204) around your organization.

These initial steps can help you decide what to do next. Evaluate what went well and what didn't. Use Time for Reflection(240) to determine if it is The Right Time(207) for the new idea in your organization. If you encounter resistance, you may need to modify how you are presenting the proposed change. If you see some spark of interest, try some other patterns that will take more effort, such as Big Jolt(107) or Study Group(228).

Don't just use this pattern when you begin to introduce an innovation. Test the Waters along the way and every time you see a new opportunity.

= = = = = = = = =

This pattern builds a foundation upon which you can use other patterns. It is the first step in trying to become an Evangelist(144). It helps you to see if you should proceed and, if so, what you should do next.

But be prepared for possible disappointment. Sometimes an idea is too new or radical for ready acceptance by an organization, or it may run counter to other constraints, such as a preference for a vendor or product. Rather than pushing harder, it may be better to wait a bit until the organization can support the change. Save your energy for when you can get payback. The time you took to investigate and learn about the innovation will still work to your own personal advantage.

When Peace Corps volunteers arrive at their destination, they are brimming with energy and enthusiasm. But volunteers must fight the impulse to hit the ground running because a slow crawl works much better. Volunteers are advised, "During your first two weeks on site, don't start calling meetings and making pronouncements. Spend time observing your village and listening to people talk about their lives. Slowly, you will identify some natural places where you can intervene and share some ideas. To earn trust, you must demonstrate a presence and show that you're genuinely interested in learning as well as teaching."*

In their best selling book, Built to Last, *Jim Collins and Jerry Porras noted that "3M did not select innovations based strictly on market size. With mottos like 'Make a little, sell a little' and 'Take small steps,' 3M understood that big things often evolve from little things; but since you can't tell ahead of time which little things will turn into big things, you have to try* **lots** *of little things, keep the ones that work, and discard the ones that don't."***

---

*Layne, A. "Training Manual for Change Agents," *Fast Company,* November 2000.
**Collins, J. C. and J. I. Porras, *Built to Last: Successful Habits of Visionary Companies,* HarperBusiness, 1994.

Time for Reflection

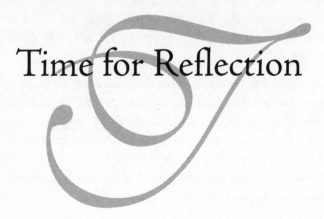

How noble and good everyone could be if, every evening before falling asleep, they were to recall to their minds the events of the whole day and consider exactly what has been good and bad. Then, without realizing it, you try to improve yourself at the start of each new day; of course, you achieve quite a lot in the course of time. Anyone can do this, it costs nothing and is certainly very helpful.*

—Anne Frank at age 15

To learn from the past, take time at regular intervals to evaluate what is working well and what should be done differently.

You are an Evangelist(144) or Dedicated Champion(129) using Test the Waters(237) to try to introduce a new idea into your organization.

We make the same assumptions and the same mistakes based on those assumptions over and over again.

---

*Frank, A., *The Diary of a Young Girl*, Bantam Books, 1967.

It is much easier to keep doing what we've always done than it is to stop and think about whether it is the best thing to do. In our attempts to use every moment, we rush to do this, to do that. Keeping this continual pace makes it difficult to step back and reflect, to take a broader view. It can be uncomfortable to do this because we may discover that what we are doing is no longer working. Yet, Betty Sue Flowers, author of *The Power of Myth*, explains that most of us create the future by extrapolating from the past.

In the movie *Dances with Wolves*, a tribe of Native Americans takes time to examine the success of a buffalo hunt by telling and retelling the story of the hunt around a campfire. This is an important ritual because it provides lessons for all the hunts to come. It is the way wisdom is passed on. A retrospective works in much the same way. Its purpose is to help review a recent project to understand what worked well and what can be done differently next time.

In 1988, Joseph M. Juran wrote about deriving lessons learned from retrospective analysis and named this process after philosopher George Santayana, who once observed, "Those who cannot remember the past are condemned to repeat it." Many large organizations have some form of the Santayana review and call it a retrospective, postmortem, postpartum, or project review. The idea is simple—examine what happened on the last project and learn from it.

Even failed projects can identify valuable accomplishments for which a team can be proud. At the same time, even in the most successful project, things can be improved. To create learning organizations, we must make it a practice to discuss what went on in our projects. Similarly, to learn as an individual, we must take the time to reflect. President Lincoln stated that we may learn more from what has *not* been done right than what has been done right. But learning doesn't happen unless we allow time for it.

Therefore:

Pause in any activity to reflect on what is working well and what should be done differently.

Take time out at regular intervals. Reflection is more likely to occur if it is made part of the process rather than something that may happen when you have time. Build reflection time into the process as you apply Step by Step(224) and evaluate the adjustments to make in your strategy. When you celebrate Small Successes(216), talk with others about what is going well and what should be done differently. Even when things aren't going as well, you don't need to feel bad about making mistakes as long as you take the trouble to learn from them. For you often learn more by being wrong for the right reasons than you do by being right for the wrong reasons.

To reflect as a group, run a project retrospective, a series of fun and highly effective activities that help a team review the past so that the members can become more productive in the future. Use Location, Location, Location(189) if possible. For more information on leading a retrospective, see Norm Kerth's excellent book *Project Retrospectives*.

= = = = = = = = = =

This pattern helps you understand what happened in the past and what can be improved in the future. You'll see things that hadn't occurred to you. You can plan your next step, note the things that are going well, and think about how you can improve. You can even document your successful practices so that they can be shared with others.

But you have to carve out time to reflect, and this isn't easy in our fast-paced world. Yet, it can be argued that failing to think about the past and plan your next step can cause you to lose even more time in the long run because of the mistakes you may be making over and over again.

*"Every day, I have to make difficult decisions, and I base them primarily on what has happened in the past," says Nathan Myhrvold, Chief Technology Officer of Microsoft Corporation. "History can lead you to see important abstractions, and it also offers great lessons....If you want to make good decisions about what's to come, look behind you."**

Blockbuster Inc. wanted to increase the amount of time their employees spent with customers by decreasing some of their administrative duties. They made observations and brainstormed suggestions from the people doing the work. Their reflection created some improvement. For example, employees changed their reshelving process by putting videos/DVDs on a cart so that customers taking movies off the cart would reduce the effort of putting them back. As a result of some process changes, employees have gone from spending 36% of their time with customers to 50% and climbing. They learned that a company can conceive of new ideas for improvement when they stand back and reflect on what they already do.

---

*Lucas, J. R. *The Passionate Organization: Igniting the Fire of Employee Commitment*, American Management Association, 1999.

Token

I collect name badges from the conferences I attend and hang them on the walls of my cubicle. They remind me of the conferences I have attended, the many friends I have met, and the things I have learned.

To keep a new idea alive in a person's memory, hand out tokens that can be identified with the topic being introduced.

You are a Dedicated Champion(129) trying to get people interested in a new idea. You have limited resources.

People may be enthusiastic about a topic when they first hear about it, but the enthusiasm quickly wanes as they forget tomorrow what excited them today.

Our brains can only hold so much; today's information will be quickly replaced by tomorrow's information. Individuals need reminders. A physical object associated with a particular topic can nudge their memories. It can help people reconnect with a new idea even after their thoughts have moved on to something else or with an event long after it has taken place.

Sociologists have observed that in all cultures, the receipt of even a small gift obligates the receiver, even if the gift was not highly valued. Free samples are given away in supermarkets and by salespeople in a variety of settings because the value of the return has been shown to be more than the cost.

Therefore:

Hand out small tokens that will remind people of the new idea.

Examples of tokens are magnets, buttons, coasters, cups, pencils, or a set of bound notes, a "quick reference" printed on special paper, or copies of articles. Be creative in finding or constructing items that will form a link with the event. The monetary value need not be high.

Don't get carried away and distribute too many tokens—it reduces the effect. There is no need to be disappointed if some people dispose of them; not everyone will appreciate them. Those who don't "get" the topic will be less inclined to keep them around. We know what it's like to have another thing around that just takes up space. Most will get cleaned out over time, and this is all right.

= = = = = = = = =

This pattern creates a reminder of the new idea. People who identify with the topic will keep their token, often prominently displayed, as a memento. Initially, this identifies the group of people to each other, helping to create a critical mass and establish a Group Identity(155). Over time, the token serves as a reminder to the individual to revisit the topic.

But it might be difficult to convince your organization to fund tokens. In this case, think about spending some of your own money. It doesn't have to take a lot of cash, but your colleagues and your management will be impressed that you believe in the new idea enough to support it.

At our poster session at a conference, we gave "Good Job!" stickers for participants' badges if they drew a picture of any pattern we had displayed on our poster. The sticker was just a token but it got their attention. Many who said they couldn't draw were convinced by the ridiculously small sticker, even though it meant they had to read every pattern, looking for one that spoke to them.

Craig Tidal, President and CEO of Net Solve Inc., teaches customer interaction to new employees, from receptionists to senior managers. He rewards correct answers with a crisp two-dollar bill. "It's just a token, but if somebody puts one in their wallet, it will remind them of the event," he says of the gimmick.

Trial Run

To me a bicycle was balloon tires and baskets. You rode it to your friend's house or maybe to school. I loved my bicycle; it was blue, a three-speed from Wards. When I met Karl, he had more than one bicycle and he raced. He wore funny clothes and a helmet. When I found out how much the equipment cost, I was horrified. I bought my bike for about $100.00 and I thought that was a lot of money. "Just try it," he coaxed. "You can see for yourself what a racing bike is like. Even if you ride in jeans, you can tell the difference." I wasn't convinced, but I thought I would be nice and, what the heck, it was just a ride around the block. I hopped on. The seat needed some adjustment. The handlebar was down and it seemed a little strange, but then I began to pedal. The bike took off. It almost had a life of its own. It seemed to be pedaling for me. "Wow!" I shouted! "This thing really goes!" I was hooked after that run!

When the organization is not willing to commit to the new idea, suggest that they experiment with it for a short period and study the results.

You are an Evangelist(144). You're getting worn out as you attempt to address the concerns people have about the new idea because it doesn't look like the questions and objections are going to end anytime soon.

There are people in the organization who are expressing an endless supply of objections to the new idea. It would be a daunting, or even impossible, task to try to ease everyone's worries before the new idea is adopted.

Fear is often what keeps us talking and questioning but stops us from doing anything. However, even though people may be fearful of change, they usually love to experiment. Change means risk. An experiment is something you can undo and walk away from when you are all the wiser.

Ideas that can be tested on an installment plan are generally adopted more rapidly than those that are not. If people are offered a trial period, they will have the opportunity to experiment with the innovation under their own conditions. This is likely to ease their uncertainties and give meaning to something that was previously seen as only an abstract idea.

It's more effective to let people convince themselves through sight and touch than to try to convince them with words and logic. For "test purposes" is a convenient label for temporarily transferring "unacceptable" ideas into an "acceptable" category, until such time that the idea can gain the persuasive power to become part of the established way of doing things.

Therefore:

Suggest that the organization, or a segment of the organization, try the new idea for a limited period as an experiment.

Be specific about the time and what you and others in the organization will do during this period. Suggest how you and the organization will evaluate the success of the new idea at the end of this period. People must feel that there is limited risk and no obligation to go on after the trial period.

Make certain people understand that their concerns will not be discounted during the trial period; keep a record of all points of view. Use Fear Less(151) and Champion Skeptic(116) for people who are not willing to temporarily put their skepticism aside during the experiment.

Adopt the attitude that any failure during this trial run is not a mistake, but rather a lesson. If you take Time for Reflection(240), you will find that growth is a process of experimentation, a series of trials, errors, and occasional victories. Things that don't work out as you had hoped are as much a part of the process as the things that do work.

If you see some Small Successes(216), spread the word with Hometown Story(164). Start a Study Group(228) to explore the future possibilities.

Don't expect to get everyone on board after this limited experiment. This is one way to Test the Waters(237). It is likely to be most effective for reaching

Innovators(170) and Early Adopters(138), but even the die-hard skeptics may appreciate a new idea if you can show that it will make their jobs easier.

= = = = = = = = =

This approach builds validation for the new idea as it moves through the test period. The trial will help potential users understand how the innovation can fit into their organization. This puts you in a better position to capture the attention of a Local Sponsor(186) and to justify continuing work with the new idea. If it is truly a good idea, it will sell itself. If it's not, it remains a "test" and fades away.

This trial period can place a lot of extra work on your shoulders. People will probably see you as the leader of the experiment even though you are still learning about the innovation yourself. Prepare for this task by first taking the time to Just Do It(177) before you suggest a trial run in the organization.

Ellen devised a new process for assigning individuals to committees in the organization. Because it was quite different from what was already in place, it was met with controversy. Ellen patiently addressed as many concerns as she could, but when the proposal came to the decision makers for approval, the questions continued during the meeting for almost 30 minutes. Finally, one of the few supporters said, "Look, what we have isn't working now. We need something better. This document is what we're proposing . . . if you don't like it, propose something else, but for heaven's sake, propose something because our present system needs to be improved." After a few moments of silence, Ellen suggested that the organization just try the new process, evaluate it, and make any needed modifications after it had been in place for a year. She also promised to take an active role in carrying out the details. The document passed with an 8 to 3 vote in favor.

The Office of the Vice Chancellor was overworked. The university had grown and, as a result, the number of issues and problems was increasing at a rate that could no longer be handled by the office with any efficiency. So the Vice Chancellor proposed adding three associates to the office. The faculty responded with fear since they were not accustomed to dealing with an additional level of administrators. The Vice Chancellor arranged a few forums in which he explained the serious problems that existed in the office. He responded to many questions but, at the final forum, he realized that there was still a great amount of trepidation. So he asked the faculty to accept the new structure for a few years and assured them that he would readjust if it didn't work well. The faculty finally agreed. Throughout the following months, when someone would voice his apprehension about the new structure, someone else would usually remind him that it wasn't a permanent arrangement if things didn't work out well.

Whisper in the General's Ear

I noticed that a particular manager was always absent from my presentations about the new idea. He had good excuses, but I think he was avoiding the subject. His staff never came to any of my training classes. I stopped by his office and said, "I know you're too busy to come to my presentations. I understand that, but I'm willing to get together one-on-one, any time, to answer any questions you have."

He was caught. He fumbled with his calendar. "Hmm, not much time. I do have an open slot but it's at 7:00 a.m. next Friday. That's probably too early for you" (he was hoping).

I jotted down the date and said, "Great! Thanks for your time." I stopped by the day before our meeting and said, "See you tomorrow!" On Friday, we spent a good half hour talking and he seemed relieved that my idea wasn't just some new technology thing but really did apply to his area. He never became an enthusiastic supporter, but he never spoke up against it and his people started coming to my training classes.

Managers are sometimes hard to convince in a group setting, so meet privately to address any concerns.

◆◆◆

You are a Dedicated Champion(129) working to get management support for your new idea. There are troublesome managers who have not been convinced by any presentations you have made.

Managers who are against your new idea have the power to block your progress.

Many managers aren't that interested in technical details. In a group situation their attention span is much less than it is one-on-one. Managers are overwhelmed by new ideas and are reluctant to head blindly down new paths without some justification. You can't publicly push a manager in a new direction, but in private you can gently show the benefits of a new way of doing business that will reflect well on those who are successful with the new approach. Many managers need a little extra time to think about a new idea before they're willing to support it publicly.

Because accountability is always centralized and flows to the top of organizations, executives feel an increasing need to know what is going on, while recognizing that it is harder to get reliable information. That need for information and control drives them to develop elaborate information systems alongside the control systems and to feel increasingly alone in their position atop the hierarchy.

Some high-level executives are "productive narcissists" and are extremely sensitive to criticism or slights. They cannot tolerate dissent. In fact, they can be extremely abrasive with employees who doubt them—with subordinates who are tough enough to fight back. Some are so defensive that they make a virtue of the fact that they don't listen. As one CEO bluntly put it, "I didn't get here by listening to people!"

Therefore:

Set up a short one-on-one meeting with a manager to address any concerns with the innovation and the effort to introduce it.

Say exactly what you know and what you can do to help. Don't exaggerate what your new idea can do. Nothing can hurt your cause more than overselling something. Play the Evangelist(144) role—let your natural enthusiasm show. Encourage the manager to ask questions to understand technical details. This may be embarrassing for him to do in front of others, because it's human nature to want to save face in front of a group.

Make sure the information is Tailor Made(234) appropriately for the management audience. Be ready to address the costs and benefits of your idea but don't overwhelm him with data. Tell him Just Enough(180), that is, educate, but don't talk down or overburden him with too many technical details. When first hearing of a new idea, managers usually want to know the big picture and how it will impact them.

Give the manager ideas, but consider letting him take the credit for them. Find out what he thinks before presenting your views. If you believe he is wrong, show how a different approach would be in his best interest. Take his views seriously. Analyze them, don't brush them aside—they often reveal sharp intuitions. Disagree only when you can demonstrate how he will benefit from a different point of view.

Always empathize with the manager's feelings, but don't expect any empathy back. Understand that behind any display of infallibility, there hides a deep vulnerability. Praise his achievements and reinforce his best impulses, but don't be shamelessly sympathetic. An intelligent narcissist can see through flatterers and prefers independent people who truly appreciate him. Show that you will protect his image, inside and outside the company.

Persuade, don't alienate. Stay calm. Back off when he starts to glaze over or push back. Great salespeople will tell you the way to influence others is to understand their needs and communicate on their level, not on yours. The idea is that in the process of talking to him, he will have an "aha" moment; he's come to this realization on his own, he'll own the idea and feel comfortable about asking for help with the next steps.

If you are persistent and patient but still have not succeeded in scheduling a meeting with the manager, there is one other tactic you can use in extreme cases. Next time you see the manager heading from his office to the cafeteria, walk along and causally mention some arresting piece of news. Keep a two-minute "elevator speech" in your head at all times. A good salesperson must take advantage of unscheduled opportunities as well as rehearsed and organized ones.

Remember that your goal is to build trust with the manager. This will take time. The manager who needs this kind of special attention may be insecure or may have been burned by false promises. It will take patience and great strength of character on your part to face these obstacles.

Once you have the manager's support, Stay in Touch(221) so he won't forget about you.

======== =

This pattern builds management support for the new idea. It maintains the manager's dignity while giving you the chance to get your story heard and achieve your objectives.

Your private meetings with a manager can look like back room dealing to outsiders. Be open and straightforward with others. Let them know you have talked with the manager, but don't break any confidences by revealing details of the discussion, especially if they might show the manager in a bad light.

David Pottruck, the number-two executive for Charles Schwab Corp., frequently clashed with his boss, Larry Stupski, at top-management meetings. Pottruck made two big mistakes: He failed to recruit others to his cause, and he disagreed in an unpleasant way. Then Pottruck met with his boss and proposed a solution. He would never publicly argue with him again. He might disagree, but he would do so only in private. By questioning his boss only behind closed doors, he got his ideas into the room and kept the power struggle out of it.

Anna had a boss who was hard to convince in a group meeting (darn near impossible!). The boss would move forward on an issue during a meeting only if he had all the information and all his doubts removed beforehand. Anna learned that when an upcoming meeting would have an issue that was important, she would meet with her boss before the meeting and address his questions and concerns one-on-one.

External Pattern References

Throughout this part we have referenced patterns outside our pattern language. This is good for several reasons. It shows that we didn't write our patterns in a vacuum; we were aware of others' contributions and pointed to their work. It also means that we didn't struggle to capture good ideas that have already been documented. Finally, it points out that patterns are grown by a community. We need to show connections to that community by showing how our work relates to the contributions of other pattern writers. Here's a little information on the external patterns and where you can read more about them.

Brainstorming. Get the team members together for a brainstorming session.
http://www.charlesweir.com/Publications.html

Cardboard Consultant. Explain the problem out loud to someone or something. http://www.charlesweir.com/Publications.html

Communal Eating. Give every institution and social group a place where people can eat together. Alexander, C.A. et al., *A Pattern Language*, Oxford University Press, 1977.

Diverse Groups. Include different kinds of members in a team to create requirements. Coplien, J.O. and N.B. Harrison, *Organizational Patterns of Agile Software Development*, Prentice-Hall, 2004.

Get a Guru. Managers should establish a trusting relationship with a guru and defer to him on technical matters. Olson, D.S. and C. L. Stimmel, *The Manager Pool*, Addison-Wesley, 2002.

Gradual Stiffening. A flimsy structure can gradually be made sturdier by building on prior work. Alexander, C.A. et al., *A Pattern Language*, Oxford University Press, 1977.

Holistic Diversity. Create teams from members with multiple specialties. Coplien, J.O. and N.B. Harrison, *Organizational Patterns of Agile Software Development*, Prentice-Hall, 2004.

Introvert – Extrovert. Teach yourself to play a role so that observers believe you are extroverted, bold, and outgoing. Teach yourself to recognize the situations in which this role is appropriate and to gather your resources and play the role. http://csis.pace.edu/~bergin/patterns/introvertExtrovert.html

No Surprises. Adjust schedule or feature commitments without losing the confidence of groups that depend on your components by announcing changes early and negotiating solutions. Dikel, D.M., D. Kane, and J.R. Wilson, *Software Architecture: Organizational Principles and Patterns*, Prentice-Hall, 2001.

Patron Role. Give the project access to a visible, high-level manager who champions the cause of the project. Coplien, J.O. and N.B. Harrison, *Organizational Patterns of Agile Software Development*, Prentice-Hall, 2004.

Piecemeal Growth. Incrementally address forces that encourage change and growth and allow opportunities for growth to be exploited locally as they occur. Foote, B. and J. Yoder, "Big Ball of Mud," *Pattern Languages of Program Design 4*, N. Harrison, B. Foote, and H. Rohnert, eds., Addison-Wesley, 2000.

Shameless Ignoramus. Managers should give up the attempt to know it all and become a shameless ignoramus when it comes to technical matters. Olson, D.S. and C. L. Stimmel, *The Manager Pool*, Addison-Wesley, 2002.

Team Space. To maximize people's productive time at work, allow team members to own their space for everything from decision making to social events. Taylor, P., "Capable, Productive, and Satisfied: Some Organizational Patterns for Protecting Productive People" *Pattern Languages of Program Design 4*, N. Harrison, B. Foote, and H. Rohnert, eds., Addison-Wesley, 2000.

Train Hard, Fight Easy. To establish a team mentality and shared skills, train the team together in the innovation. Olson, D.S. and C. L. Stimmel, *The Manager Pool*, Addison-Wesley, 2002.

Work Community. To create a feeling of community in the workplace, build small clusters of workplaces that have their own common area. Alexander, C.A. et al., *A Pattern Language*, Oxford University Press, 1977.

Appendix

Theme	Pattern Name	Summary
Throughout	Evangelist	To begin to introduce the new idea into your organization, do everything you can to share your passion for it.
Throughout	Small Successes	To avoid becoming overwhelmed by the challenges and all the things you have to do when you're involved in an organizational change effort, celebrate even small successes.
Throughout	Step by Step	Relieve your frustration at the enormous task of changing an organization by taking one small step at a time toward your goal.
Throughout	Test the Waters	When a new opportunity presents itself, see if there is any interest by using some of the patterns in this language and then evaluating the result.
Throughout	Time for Reflection	To learn from the past, take time at regular intervals to evaluate what is working well and what should be done differently.
Early	Ask for Help	Since the task of introducing a new idea into an organization is a big job, look for people and resources to help your efforts.

Theme	Pattern Name	Summary
Early	Brown Bag	Use the time when people normally eat lunch to provide a convenient and relaxed setting for hearing about the new idea.
Early	Connector	To help you spread the word about the innovation, ask for help from people who have connections with many others in the organization.
Early	Do Food	Make an ordinary gathering a special event by including food.
Early	e-Forum	Set up an electronic bulletin board, distribution list, listserve, or writeable Web site for those who want to hear more.
Early	Early Adopter	Win the support of the people who can be opinion leaders for the new idea.
Early	External Validation	To increase the credibility of the new idea, bring in information from sources external to the organization.
Early	Group Identity	Give the change effort an identity to help people recognize that it exists.
Early	Guru on Your Side	Enlist the support of senior-level people who are esteemed by members of the organization.
Early	In Your Space	Keep the new idea visible by placing reminders throughout the organization.
Early	Innovator	When you begin the change initiative, ask for help from colleagues who like new ideas.
Early	Just Do It	To prepare to spread the word about the new idea, use it in your own work to discover its benefits and limitations.
Early	Just Say Thanks	To show your appreciation, say "Thanks" in the most sincere way you can to everyone who helps you.
Early	Next Steps	Take time near the end of an event about the new idea to identify what participants can do next.

Theme	Pattern Name	Summary
Early	Personal Touch	To convince people of the value in a new idea, show how it can be *personally* useful and valuable to them.
Early	Piggyback	When faced with several obstacles in your strategy to introduce something new, look for a way to piggyback on a practice in your organization.
Early	Plant the Seeds	To spark interest, carry materials (seeds) and display (plant) them when the opportunity arises.
Early	The Right Time	Consider the timing when you schedule events or when you ask others for help.
Early	Stay in Touch	Once you've enlisted the support of key persons, don't forget about them and make sure they don't forget about you.
Early	Study Group	Form a small group of colleagues who are interested in exploring or continuing to learn about a specific topic.
Early	Tailor Made	To convince people in the organization of the value they can gain from the new idea, tailor your message to the needs of the organization.
Later	Big Jolt	To provide more visibility for the change effort, invite a high profile person into your organization to talk about the new idea.
Later	Corporate Angel	To help align the innovation with the goals of the organization, get support from a high-level executive.
Later	Dedicated Champion	To increase your effectiveness in introducing your new idea, make a case for having the work part of your job description.
Later	Early Majority	To create commitment to the new idea in the organization, you must convince the majority.
Later	Guru Review	Gather anyone who is a Guru on Your Side and other interested colleagues to evaluate

Theme	Pattern Name	Summary
		the new idea for managers and other developers.
Later	Hometown Story	To help people see the usefulness of the new idea, encourage those who have had success with it to share their stories.
Later	Involve Everyone	For a new idea to be successful across an organization, everyone should have an opportunity to support the innovation and make his own unique contribution.
Later	Just Enough	To ease learners into the more difficult concepts of a new idea, give a brief introduction and then make more information available when they are ready.
Later	Local Sponsor	Ask for help from first-line management. When your boss supports the tasks you are doing to introduce the new idea, you can be even more effective.
Later	Location, Location, Location	To avoid interruptions that disrupt the flow of an event, try to hold significant events offsite.
Later	Mentor	When a project wants to get started with the new idea, have someone around who understands it and can help the team.
Later	Royal Audience	Arrange for management and members of the organization to spend time with a Big Jolt visitor.
Later	Shoulder to Cry On	To avoid becoming too discouraged when the going gets tough, find opportunities to talk with others who are also struggling to introduce a new idea.
Later	Smell of Success	When your efforts result in some visible positive result, people will come out of the woodwork to talk to you. Treat this opportunity as a teaching moment.

Theme	Pattern Name	Summary
Later	Sustained Momentum	Take a pro-active approach to the ongoing work of sustaining the interest in the new idea in your organization.
Later	Token	To keep a new idea alive in a person's memory, hand out tokens that can be identified with the topic being introduced.
Resistance	Bridge-Builder	Pair those who have accepted the new idea with those who have not.
Resistance	Champion Skeptic	Ask for help from strong opinion leaders, who are skeptical of your new idea, to play the role of "official skeptic." Use their comments to improve your effort, even if you don't change their minds.
Resistance	Corridor Politics	Informally work on decision makers and key influencers before an important vote to make sure they fully understand the consequences of the decision.
Resistance	Fear Less	Turn resistance to the new idea to your advantage.
Resistance	Trial Run	When the organization is not willing to commit to the new idea, suggest that they experiment with it for a short period and study the results.
Resistance	Whisper in the General's Ear	Managers are sometimes hard to convince in a group setting, so meet privately to address any concerns.

References

Accountemps, press release, "Just Say Thanks," http://www.recognition.org/articles/article_just_say_thanks.asp.

Agile Software Development Manifesto, http://agilemanifesto.org.

Alexander, C.A. et al., *The Oregon Experiment*, Oxford University Press, NY, 1975.

Alexander, C.A. et al., *A Pattern Language*, Oxford University Press, NY, 1977.

Alexander, C.A., *The Timeless Way of Building*, Oxford University Press, NY, 1979.

Alexander, S., "The politics of value," *Infoworld*, May 11, 2001.

Alur, D., J. Crupi, and D. Malks, *Core J2EE Patterns: Best Practices and Design Strategies*, Prentice-Hall, NJ, 2001.

Alur, D., J. Crupi, and D. Malks, *Core J2EE Patterns 2nd Edition: Best Practices and Design Strategies*, Prentice-Hall, NJ, 2003.

Anders, G., "The Carly Chronicles: An Inside Look at her Campaign to Reinvent HP," *Fast Company*, Gruner & Jhar, NY, February 2003, 66–73.

Anderson, B., "Toward an Architecture Handbook," *OOPSLA Addendum to the Proceedings*, Washington, D.C., ACM Press, NY, January 1994.

Austin, N.K., "Just Say Thanks," *1099*, February 16, 2000, http://www.creativepro.com/story/feature/4046.html.

Bacal, R., "Organizational Conflict—The Good, the Bad and the Ugly," April 2003, http://www.work911.com/conflict/carticles/orgcon.htm.

Baum, D., *Lightning in a Bottle: Proven Lessons for Leading Change*, Dearborn, Chicago, IL, 2000.

Beck, K., J. O. Coplien, R. Crocker, L. Dominick, G. Meszaros, F. Paulisch, and J. Vlissides, "Industrial Experience with Design Patterns," *Proc. 18th International Conference on Software Engineering*, Technische Universität, Berlin, Germany, 25–30 March 1996, 103–114.

Beck, K., *Extreme Programming Explained*, Addison-Wesley, Boston, MA, 2000.

Belasco, J.A., *Teaching the Elephant to Dance: Empowering Change in Your Organization*, Crown Publishers, NY, 1990.

Bergin, J., "The Introvert-Extrovert Pattern," http://csis.pace.edu/~bergin/patterns/introvertExtrovert.html.

Biro, B. D., *The Joyful Spirit*, Pygmalion Press, San Diego, CA, 1998.

Bouldin, B. M., *Agents of Change*, Yourdon Press, NY, 1989.

Brazelton, J. and A. G. Gorry, "Creating a Knowledge-Sharing Community: If You Build It, Will They Come?," *CACM*, ACM Press, NY, February 2003, 23–25.

Brooks, F. P., *The Mythical Man-Month*, Addison-Wesley, Reading, MA, 1995.

Brown, W. S., *13 Fatal Errors Managers Make and How You Can Avoid Them*, Berkley Books, 1985.

Buschmann, F., R. Meunier, H. Rohnert, P. Sommerlad, and M. Stal, *Pattern-Oriented Software Architecture: A System of Patterns*, Wiley, Chichester, 1996.

Carnegie, D., *How to Win Friends and Influence People*, Simon & Schuster, Inc., NJ, 1981.

Carroll, J. M., R. L. Mack, S. P. Robertson, and M. B. Rosson, "Binding Objects to Scenarios of Use," *Int. J. of Human-Computer Studies*, 41, 1994, 243–276.

Carter-Scott, C., *If Life is a Game, These are the Rules*, Broadway Books, NY, 1998.

Chew, W.B. and D. Leonard-Barton, "Beating Murphy's Law," *Sloan Management Review*, MIT, Cambridge, MA, 32, Spring 1991, 5–16.

Cialdini, R.B., *Influence: Science and Practice*, Allyn and Bacon, Boston, MA, 2001.

Cockburn, A., *Surviving Object-Oriented Projects: A Manager's Guide*, Addison-Wesley, Reading, MA, 1998.

Cockburn, A., *Agile Software Development*, Addison-Wesley, Boston, MA, 2002.

Collins, J. C. and J. I. Porras, *Built to Last: Successful Habits of Visionary Companies*, HarperBusiness, NY, 1994.

Coplien, J. O., "A Generative Development-Process Pattern Language," *Pattern Languages of Program Design*, J. O. Coplien and D. C. Schmidt, eds., Addison-Wesley, Reading, MA, 1995, 183–237.

Coplien, J. O., *Software Patterns*, SIGS Books, NY, 1996.

Covey, S. R., *The 7 Habits of Highly Effective People*, Simon & Schuster, NJ, 1989.

Dauten, D., *The Gifted Boss*, William Morrow & Company, 1999.

Dauten, D., "Wake up your brain, and ask it what it learned in past year," *The Arizona Republic*, December 25, 2003, D3.

deGeus, A., *The Living Company*, Harvard Business School Press, 1997.

DeMarco, T., *Slack: Getting Past Burnout, Busywork, and the Myth of Total Efficiency*, Broadway Books, NY, 2001.

Desouza, K. C., "Barriers to Effective Use of Knowledge Management Systems in Software Engineering," *CACM*, ACM Press, NY, January 2003, 99–101.

Dikel, D. M., D. Kane, and J. R. Wilson, *Software Architecture: Organizational Principles and Patterns*, Prentice-Hall, NJ, 2001.

Dossey, L., *Reinventing Medicine*, Harper, San Francisco, 1999.

Edler, R., *If I Knew Then What I Know Now: CEOs and other smart executives share wisdom they wish they'd been told 25 years ago*, G. P. Putnam's Sons, 1995.

Edralin, J., "Letters" in *IEEE Software*, Mary/June 2002, 11.

Fichman, R. G. and C. Kemerer, "Adoption of software engineering innovations: The case of object orientation," *Sloan Management Review*, Winter 1993, 7–22.

Fishman, C., "One Man's Drive—One Company's Courage," *Fast Company*, June 2003, 114–123.

Foote, B. and J. Yoder, "Big Ball of Mud," *Pattern Languages of Program Design 4*, N. Harrison, B. Foote, and H. Rohnert, eds., Addison-Wesley, Boston, MA, 2000.

Frank, A., *The Diary of a Young Girl*, Bantam Books, 1967.

Gabriel, R. P., *Patterns of Software*, Oxford University Press, NY, 1996.

Gamma, E., R. Helm, R. Johnson, and J. Vlissides, *Design Patterns: Elements of Object-Oriented Software*, Addison-Wesley, Reading, MA, 1995.

Gilbreath, R. D., *Escape from Management Hell*, Berrett-Koehler Publishers, 1993.

Gladwell, M., *The Tipping Point*, Little, Brown and Company, NY, 2000.

Godfrey, A., "The Santayana Review," *Quality Digest*, February 1999, 20.

Godin, S., "In My Humble Opinion," *Fast Company*, November 2001, 80.

Goldfedder, B., *The Joy of Patterns*, Addison-Wesley, Boston, MA, 2001.

Grand, M., *Patterns in Java, Vol. 1, A Catalog of Reusable Design Patterns Illustrated with UML*, Wiley, NY, 1998.

Grenning, J., "Launching Extreme Programming at a Process-Intensive Company," *IEEE Software*, November/December 2001, 27–33.

Guzdial, M., *Emile: Software-Realized Scaffolding for Science Learners Programming in Mixed Media*, Ph.D. Thesis, Ann Arbor, MI: University of Michigan, 1993.

Hackworth, D.H. and E. England, *Steel My Soldiers' Hearts: The hopeless to hardcore transformation of U. S. Army, 4th Battalion, 39th Infantry, Vietnam*, Rugged Land, LLC, NY, 2002.

Hadden, R. and B. Catlette, "Training—Your Place or Mine?," February 19, 2002, http://www.contentedcows.com/20020219.html.

Harrison, N. B., "Organizational Patterns for Teams," *Pattern Languages of Program Design*, J. Vlissides, J. O. Coplien, and N. L. Kerth, eds., Addison-Wesley, Reading, MA, 1996, 345–352.

"Case Study: What to do when the boss won't budge," *Harvard Business Review*, Harvard Business School Publishing, Cambridge, MA, Jan/Feb 2000, 25–35.

Helgesen, M. and S. Brown, *Active Listening: Building Skills for Understanding*, Press Syndicate of the University of Cambridge, England.

Hildebrand, C. "Our Own Worst Enemy," *CIO Magazine*, Nov. 1, 1996, http://www.cio.com/archive/110196/chan_content.html.

Hill, C., interview at OOPSLA'02, November 2002.

Hohmann, L., *Journey of the Software Professional*, Prentice-Hall, Upper Saddle River, NJ, 1997.

Hutton, D. *The Change Agents' Handbook: A Survival Guide for Quality Improvement Champions*, ASQ Quality Press, Milwaukee, WI, 1994.

Jaslow, H., personal conversation, September 2002.

Jones, G. R. and J. M. George, *Contemporary Management*, McGraw Hill, NY, 2003.

Juster, N., *The Phantom Tollbooth*, Knopf, NY, 1961.

Keller, E. and J. Berry, *The Influentials*, The Free Press, NY, 2003.

Kelley, T., *The Art of Innovation: Lessons in Creativity from Ideo, America's Leading Design Firm*, Doubleday, 2001.

Kerievsky, J., *A Learning Guide To Design Patterns*, http://www.industriallogic.com/papers/learning.html

Kerievsky, J., *Knowledge Hydrant: A Pattern Language for Study Groups*, http://www.industriallogic.com/papers/khdraft.pdf, July 1, 2001.

Kerth, N., *Project Retrospectives: A Handbook for Team Reviews*, Dorset House, NY, 2001.

Kim, A.. J., *Community Building on the Web*, Peachpit Press, Berkley, 2000.

Korson, T. D. and V. K. Vaishnavi, *Object Technology Centers of Excellence*, Manning Publications Co., 1996.

LaBarre, P., "Marcus Buckingham Thinks Your Boss Has an Attitude Problem," *Fast Company*, August 2001, 88–98.

Lamott, A., *Bird by Bird: Some Instructions on Writing and Life*, Anchor Books, NY, 1995.

Larsen, D., "Embracing Change: A Retrospective," *Cutter IT Journal*, Cutter Consortium, Arlington, MA, February 2003.

Layne, A., "Training Manual for Change Agents," *Fast Company*, November 2000.

Letourneau, J., workshop contribution, ChiliPLoP'2000.

Leuf, B. and W. Cunningham, *The Wiki Way*, Addison-Wesley, Boston, MA, 2001.

Lindstrom, L., personal communication, 2002.

Loeschen, S., *The Magic of Satir: Collected Sayings of Virginia Satir*, Event Horizon Press, Palms Springs, CA, 1991, 7–15.

Lowe, D. E., "A Rapid Design and Deployment Method for CMM Level 3," *1996 SEPG Conference*.

Lucas, J. R., *The Passionate Organization: Igniting the Fire of Employee Commitment*, American Management Association, 1999.

Lundin, S. C., H. Paul, and J. Christensen, *Fish! A Remarkable Way to Boost Morale and Improve Results*, Hyperion, NY, 2000.

Maccoby, M., "Narcissistic Leaders: The Incredible Pros, the Inevitable Cons," *The Harvard Business Review*, January–February 2000, 69–77.

Mackie, R. R. and C. D. Wylie, "Factors influencing acceptance of computer-based innovations," *Handbook of Human-Computer Interaction*, M. Helander, ed., Elsevier Science Publishers B.U., 1988.

McCarthy, J. and M. McCarthy, *Software for Your Head*, Addison-Wesley, Boston, MA, 2001.

McClelland, W. A., "The Process of Effecting Change," Presidential address to the Division of Military Psychology, American Psychological Association (Unpublished).

Messmer, M., *Managing Your Career for Dummies*, Hungry Minds, Inc., 2000.

Mills, H., *Artful Persuasion*, Amacom, NY, 2000.

Moore, G. A., *Crossing the Chasm*, HarperCollins Publishers, Inc., 1999.

Norman, D. A., *The Invisible Computer*, The MIT Press, Cambridge, MA, 1999.

O'Keefe, B., *Teamwork Module: Problem Solving*, http://www.vta.spcomm.uiuc.edu/PSG/psgl3-ov.html.

Oldenburg, R., *The Great Good Place*, Paragon House, NY, 1989.

Olson, D., personal communication, 2002.

Olson, D. S. and C. L. Stimmel, *The Manager Pool*, Addison-Wesley, Boston, MA, 2002.

Olson, D., "HandsInView," *The Patterns Handbook*, L. Rising, ed., Cambridge University Press, NY, 1998, 139–140.

Olson, D., "TrainHardFightEasy,", *The Patterns Handbook*, L. Rising, ed. Cambridge University Press, MA, 1998, 145–147.

Pascale, R. T., M. Millemann, and L. Gioja, *Surfing the Edge of Chaos*, Crown Business, 2000.

Paulk, M. C., "The Rational Planning of (Software) Projects," *Proceedings of the First World Congress for Software Quality*, San Francisco, CA, June 1995, 20–22.

Petroski, H., *To Engineer is Human*, St. Martin's Press, NY, 1985.

Pietersen, W., "The Mark Twain dilemma: The theory and practice of change leadership," *The Journal of Business Strategy*, September/October 2002, 32–37.

Pink, D. H., "Are you on the bus?", *Fast Company*, February 2002, 48.

"Caught in the Happiness Trap," *Prevention*, Rodale, Emmaus, PA, February 2003, 132–139.

Price Waterhouse, *Better Change: Best Practices for Transforming Your Organization*, Price Waterhouse, 1995.

Radle, K. and S. Young, "Partnering Usability with Development: How Three Organizations Succeeded," *IEEE Software*, IEEE Computer Society, Los Alamitos, CA, January–February 2001, 38–45.

Reingold, J., "Teacher in Chief," *Fast Company*, September 2001, 66–68.

Rischler, L., "Seven Secrets to Good Brainstorming," *Fast Company*, March 2001.

Rising, L. and J. Watson, "Improving Quality and Productivity in Training: A New Model for the High-Tech Learning Environment," *Bell Labs Technical Journal*, Lucent Technologies, Murray Hill, NJ, January–March 1998, 134–143, http://members.cox.net/risingl1/articles/studygroups.pdf.

Rising, L., "Agile Meetings," *STQE*, Software Quality Engineering, Orange Park, FL, May/June 2002, 42–46, http://members.cox.net/risingl1/articles/STQE.pdf.

Roberts, L. J., "Join the Revolution," *Software Development*, November 2000, 68–70, http://www.sdmagazine.com/articles/2000.

Rogers, E. M., *Diffusion of Innovations*, 4th Edition, The Free Press, NJ, 1995.

Rybczynski, W., *The Most Beautiful House in the World*, Viking Penguin, 1989.

Sagan, C., "The Burden of Skepticism," in Shermer, M., *Why People Believe Weird Things*, W.H. Freeman & Company, NY, 1997.

Salter, C., "(Not) the Same Old Story," *Fast Company*, February 2002.

Sanders, T., "Love Is the Killer App," *Fast Company*, February 2002, 64–70.

Schaffer, R. H., *The Breakthrough Strategy*, Harper Business, NY, 1988.

Schank, R. C., *Tell Me A Story*, Charles Scribner's Sons, New York, NY, 1990.

Schein, E. H., "Three Cultures of Management: The Key to Organizational Learning," *Sloan Management Review*, Fall 1996, 9–20.

Schmidt, D., M. Stal, H. Rohnert, and F. Buschmann, *Pattern-Oriented Software Architecture*, Vol. 2, Wiley NY,, 2000.

Senge, P., *The Fifth Discipline*, Doubleday/Currency, NY, 1990.

Senge, P., *The Leader of the Future*, Jossey-Bass, San Francisco, CA, 1996.

Senge, P. et al., *The Fifth Discipline Fieldbook: Strategies and Tools for Building a Learning Organization*, Doubleday, NY, 1994.

Senge, P., A. Kleiner, C. Roberts, R. Ross, G. Roth, and B. Smith, *The Dance of Change: The Challenges to Sustaining Momentum in Learning Organizations*, Doubleday, NY, 1999.

Souder, W. E., A. S. Nashar, and V. Padmanabban, "A Guide to the Best Technology-Transfer Practices," *Technology Transfer*, Winter–Spring, 1990.

Swap, W., D. Leonard, M. Shields, and L. Abrams, "Using Mentoring and Storytelling to Transfer Knowledge in the Workplace," *Journal of Management Information Systems*, Summer 2001, 95–114.

Taylor, P., "Capable, Productive, and Satisfied: Some Organizational Patterns for Protecting Productive People" *Pattern Languages of Program Design* 4, N. Harrison, B. Foote, and H. Rohnert, eds., Addison-Wesley, Boston, MA, 2000.

Trubo, R., *Courage*, Ivan R. Dee, Chicago, IL, 2001.

Tveito, A. and P. Hasvole, "Requirements in the Medical Domain: Experiences and Prescriptions," *IEEE Software*, IEEE Computer Society, Los Alamitos, CA, November/December 2002, 66–69.

Vaughen, S. J., "The Sweet Smell of Success," http://japanupdate.com/previous/00/12/21/story14.shtml.

Waugh, B. and M. S. Forrest, *Soul in the Computer*, Inner Ocean, Makawao, Maui, HI, 2001.

Weeks, J. and C. Galunic, "A Cultural Evolution in Business Thinking," *Financial Times*, London, October 29, 2001, 2–3.

Weinberg, G. M., *The Secrets of Consulting*, Dorset House, NY, 1985.

Weinberg, D. and G. M. Weinberg, "Learning by Design: Constructing Experiential Learning Programs," *Readings for Problem Solving Leadership*, Weinberg and Weinberg, 1999.

Wheatley, M. J., *Leadership and the New Science: Discovering Order in a Chaotic World*, 2nd ed., Berrett-Koehler Publishers, San Francisco, CA, 1999.

Whyte, D., *The Heart Aroused: Poetry and the Preservation of the Soul in Corporate America*, Currency Doubleday, NY, 1994.

Williams, L. and R. Kessler, *Pair Programming Illuminated*, Addison-Wesley, Boston, MA, 2003.

Index